THE IRISH LANDSCAPE

About the Author

Peadar McArdle is a professional geologist who has spent much of his career exploring Ireland's landscape. He was formerly Director of the Geological Survey of Ireland, the national agency for geological services. His latest book, *Gold Frenzy*, traces the history and impact of Wicklow's 1795 gold rush.

The Irish Landscape

An All-Ireland Exploration through Science and Literature

Peadar McArdle

The Liffey Press

≋the
liffey
press

Published by
The Liffey Press Ltd
Raheny Shopping Centre, Second Floor
Raheny, Dublin 5, Ireland
www.theliffeypress.com

A catalogue record of this book is
available from the British Library.

ISBN 978-1-908308-69-6

Front cover image of the Boyne Valley courtesy of Anthony Murphy,
author of *Newgrange: Monument to Immortality*

Back cover image of The Cliffs of Moher courtesy of Eugene
O'Loughlin, author of *Exploring Ireland's Wild Atlantic Way*

Printed in Spain by GraphyCems

CONTENTS

v

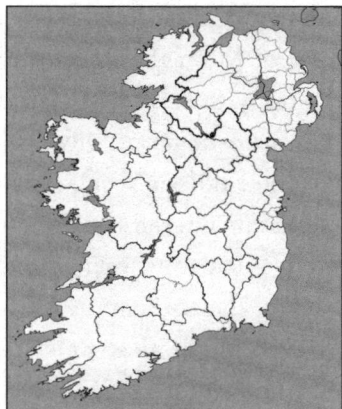

1

INTRODUCTION

[My purpose is to] make every lake or mountain
a man can see from his own door an excitement
in his imagination.
W.B. Yeats[1]

L andscape is easy! It's a mountain, a coastline, a river bank, or perhaps some combination of these and other physical ele-ments. It is simply a jumble of rock and soil and water! And yet instinctively we know it is more than that. Is a mountainside en-joying the warm glow of a summer's lingering evening the same as that same locality as it smarts from a dark wintry storm? Surely our perceptions of landscape are shaped just as much by our expe-riences there, be they emotional, atmospheric, historical or even mythical! The scientist may have mastery of the physical mountain but to really appreciate landscape we need a more inclusive ap-proach and poets have a strong role in this. It is they who guide our mental response and so they have a key role in this book.

1

Perhaps landscape can project its perceived qualities onto its poets. The steep slopes of Monaghan's drumlins may be responsible for a harsh parsimony that we associate with Patrick Kavanagh's people. The warm nostalgia of Oliver Goldsmith's Auburn may find its origins in the Midland's rich farmland. On the other hand, bogs were for long considered the domain of the backward, but now their image has been transformed to that of a cherished habitat and this is partly due to Seamus Heaney's enriching insights. Louis MacNeice thought that Belfast's dour basalt, that callous lava, reflected the character of that city's Protestants and, further south, W.B. Yeats considered that his childhood limestone influenced the simple charms of its inhabitants.

Poets commonly appreciate their landscape as places of solitude, inspiration and renewal. They delight in its scenic beauty and biodiversity, especially its flowers and birds, and observe the rhythm of their lives through seasonal patterns and environmental change. Poets as early as Goldsmith saw each generation as merely custodians of our Earthly abode, responsible for handing it over in good shape to the next. In similar spirit, many avoid portraying a landscape that is exclusively human-centred despite an evident empathy between the two. But they find inspiration in their home landscape, be it bogland, river, mountain, drumlin, lake or coastline. Such landscapes are additionally seen as places of work by farmers and engineers; of leisure by city dwellers eager to walk, climb or fish; and of pilgrimage by the spiritual. Many mining districts and places of pilgrimage have strong traditions of poetry. Poets are not restricted to their local landscape and many, fortified by their home experience, write confidently of foreign landscapes. The backward glance of emigrants causes them to notice not only the scenery and personalities they have left behind but also abandoned sweethearts and a variety of patriotic sentiments.

But poets are not shy of specifically geological topics: Richard Murphy in praise of granite, Seamus Heaney's bogland, W.B. Yeats the lyricist of limestone and Louis Macneice the bard of basalt.

There is also a strong theme in Irish poetry based on landscape layers. While best known from Heaney's bogs, where bodies ranging from the Disappeared to ancient Bog Bodies have marked various layers, this is a robust concept that has found expression in every landscape type. Those layers may be geological, archaeological, historical, mythological or even mental. Landscape can acquire a memory so thoroughgoing that it becomes synonymous with its inhabitants, causing potent divisions in the case of Northern Ireland's planter and native communities. But then Heaney's bog layers can extend back perhaps some hundreds of million years, if we embrace lignite and coal layers, and this offers the prospect that both communities might share in this long-lived heritage.[2]

The fertile shades of green in Ireland's landscape are established on the widespread deposits left by melting ice sheets of another day and enriched by our currently temperate climate. This landscape is founded upon a great variety of bedrock, be it the sandstone of Kerry or the granite of Donegal, the quartzite of Mayo or the limestone of the Burren uplands. The last-mentioned is the bedrock that lies hidden beneath so much of our Midlands. These rocks carry an extensive narrative of Earth's history that includes the story of two separate oceans. The current Atlantic Ocean is still expanding and yet already is responsible for the basalt lavas of Antrim and the relatively young gas-bearing sediments offshore. But there was an earlier ocean, Iapetus Ocean, Iapetus in Greek mythology being the father of Atlantis. Our rocks retain a full record of the cycle of this ocean as it opened and then closed. Indeed it was the welding closed of its opposing margins, or tectonic plates, now largely hidden by younger sediments along a junction from Shannon Estuary to the coast of Louth, that has determined Ireland's present environment. In the interim between the two oceans, some of our most widespread rocks formed – Old Red Sandstones from weathering of the Caledonian mountains that arose as part of Iapetus closure and Carboniferous limestones in the marine inundation that followed. Our geological history is exhilarating and contains a common thread in the enduring importance of earthquakes and volcanoes around the country. The geology of every part of Ireland is interesting, indeed there is a volcanic and seismic element to every single county. Yes, we had a shaky past – and it was also fiery![3]

This is a celebration of Irish landscape, its evolution and character. By combining scientific and literary perspectives, this book seeks to enrich readers' understanding of our diverse landscapes and to encourage them to physically explore Ireland's landscape and the literary richness associated with it. Perhaps you will experience something differently in your surroundings as a result and, if so, I do hope you find it rewarding.

The chapters in this book are arranged so that, broadly speaking, the most recent landscape events such as bogland development are treated initially. Then older events are described in order of increasing age, so that the oldest geological events are dealt with in the final chapters

Acknowledgements

I wish to thank the staff of the National Library of Ireland and Dublin City Public Libraries at Pearse Street and Raheny for their unfailing help, courtesy and friendship while I researched this book. Tom Hanahoe and Tom Reeves both provided me with pertinent feedback and encouragement at several stages of this work. I really appreciate their unstinting, timely (and candid!) wisdom. I readily acknowledge the varied assistance provided by John Darcy, Dermot Hicks, Barry Long, Peter Lynch, Eddie McArdle, CFC, Tom Molyneux and Greg Wall, CFC. Frances and Simon McArdle, Darran and Ruth O'Connor, encouraged and nurtured me at every step of this project. It would not have seen the light of day without them.

It has been a privilege for me to experience Irish landscapes through the eyes and words of a great variety of writers, to all of whom I am deeply in debt. I wish to gratefully acknowledge the following for their kind permission to reprint here copyright material from various works as noted (specific extracts are detailed in the notes to individual chapters): Anvil Press Poetry, London, for *New and Selected Poems* by Dennis O'Driscoll; Blackstaff Press, Belfast, on behalf of the Estate of John Hewitt, for *John Hewitt: Selected Poems* edited by Michael Longley and Frank Ormsby; the author for "Tread-Polished Layers" by Mark Cooper, Belfast; Dónal De Barra, County Clare, for *By Bride and Blackwater* by Patrick Barry; Faber and Faber, London, and the authors' estates for *Opened Ground* by Seamus Heaney and *Four Quartets* by T. S. Eliot; the Estate of the Late Louis MacNeice and Faber and Faber, London, through David Higham Associates, for *Collected Poems* by Louis MacNeice; the author and Occasional Press for *Ballynahinch Postcards* by Peter Fallon; the author and the Gallery Press for *New Collected Poems* by John Montague; Irish Academic Press for *Selected Poems of James Clarence Mangan* edited by J. Chuto and others; Trustees of the Estate of the Late Katherine B. Kavanagh, through the Jonathan Williams Literary Agency, for *Collected Poems* by Patrick Kavanagh, edited by Antoinette Quinn; The Lilliput Press, Dublin, for *Poems 1952-2012* by Richard Murphy; Moyola Books, County Londonderry, for *Geordie Barnett's Gortin: Poetic Tributes to Tyrone* compiled by Graham Mawhinney; the National Library of Ireland, Dublin, for *Letters by George Bernard Shaw* (MS 8381); the Random House Group, London, for *The Complete Poems of C. Day Lewis* by C. Day Lewis, published by Sinclair Stevenson; Salmon Poetry Press, County Clare, for *Merman* by Jean O'Brien; the author and Summer Palace Press, County Donegal, for *New Grass under Snow* by Mary Turley-McGrath; and the University Press of Kentucky, Lexington, for *The Collected Poems and Journals of Mary Tighe*, edited by Harriet Kramer Linkin. While every effort has been made to contact copyright holders in advance of publication, I wish to apologise sincerely for any inadvertent omissions. Where any omissions or errors come to light they will be rectified at the earliest opportunity.

Notes

1 From the "Preface" by W.B. Yeats to Lady Gregory (1902) *Cúchulainn of Muirthemne*. London: John Murray.

2. There are many anthologies of Irish literature and poetry, including these two recent examples: Patrick Crotty (Ed.) (2010) *The Penguin Book of Irish Poetry*. London: Penguin Classics. Julia M. Wright (Ed.) (2008) *Irish Literature 1750-1900: An Anthology*. Oxford: Blackwell Publishing.

3. The authoritative academic text on Ireland's geology is Holland, C.H. and Sanders, I.S. (Eds.) (2009) *The Geology of Ireland*. Second edition. Edinburgh: Dunedin Academic Press. The student will find the following very helpful: Andrew Sleeman, Brian McConnell and Sarah Gatley (2004) *Understanding Earth Processes, Rocks and the Geological History of Ireland*. Dublin: Geological Survey of Ireland. For an introduction to Ireland's geology see Peadar McArdle (2008) *Rock around Ireland: A Guide to Irish Geology*. Dublin: Albertine Kennedy Publishing.

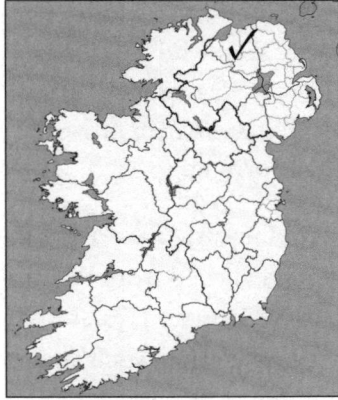

2

FAREWELL TO DERRY!
(Derry)

What we call the beginning is often the end
And to make an end is to make a beginning.
The end is where we start from.
– T. S. Eliot[1]

Walking the Derry quayside that day, my thoughts were on the young emigrant Michael MacGowan (1865–1948) who, in May 1885, boarded ship for America. He would later describe the hardships of his transatlantic passage, the poor rations, uncomfortable accommodation and seasickness. But once he passed between Staten Island and Brooklyn towards Manhattan, the prospect of Michael's new life must have excited him. As he gazed on New York city that first morning, it was a poem by William Wordsworth (1770–1850) which came to his mind, one he had learned during his limited schooling back in Cloghaneely, County Donegal:[2]

Earth has not anything to show more fair:
Dull would he be of soul who could pass by
A sight so touching in its majesty:
This City now doth like a garment wear
The beauty of the morning.[3]

This romantic poet of nature may surprise us with his enthusiasm for an urban scene as viewed from Westminster (alas, not the newly-opened Brooklyn!) Bridge. Equally, MacGowan's capacity for such poetic reflection – even at such an apprehensive moment – is a touching reminder of the resilience of the human spirit. That spirit would sustain him throughout the next two decades in North America, including spells mining copper in Montana and gold in Klondyke, before he retraced his oceanic steps back to Derry.

Michael's youthful migration was no more dramatic than that which separated New York from Derry in the first place. For long, the locations of these two cities were part of the same supercontinent, Pangaea, and it was only the birth and growth of the Atlantic Ocean that meant Michael's passage was necessarily by sea. In Pangaean times Ireland and Newfoundland had little or no seawater between them and Michael might even have crossed without getting his feet wet! But fractures and faults developed in the continental crust and it stretched and subsided. New ocean crust, in the form of basalt lava, began to well up in the gap between the separating continental blocks. The nascent Atlantic had formed and would now widen inexorably. By 10 million years ago the North Atlantic would have had a fairly familiar shape.

Seamus Heaney (1939–2013), Derry's Nobel Prize winner, was raised on the shores of Lough Neagh, the largest freshwater lake of any in Britain or Ireland. He started writing just as the Troubles erupted and this would overshadow his work as he struggled to understand sectarian hatred and "neighbourly murder", before hope and history would in time mercifully begin to rhyme. Although his native place is remote from the extensive raised bogs of central Ireland, the area surrounding Lough Neagh does have bogland. Bogs were places of work, traditional sources of domestic fuel before they became recognised as unique eco-systems that required protection. Heaney was quick to appreciate the idea of digging turf as a metaphor for discovering the past, whether it be violent or geological. Bogland proved to be a fertile landscape for his poetic imagination and digging through layers of meaning is a metaphor that became powerfully associated with him.[4]

Bogs were for long a symbol for the uncultivated nature of Irish people and Heaney sought to positively re-invent that image:

> I wanted to counter the negative associations that clung round the word "bog", and to reverse its cultural charge, go against the grain of terms like "bogman" and "bog-trotter" and "bog-ignorant".[5]

He achieved his purpose through exploring the varied levels of meaning in bogs ("Bogland"):[6]

> The ground itself is kind, black butter

> Melting and opening underfoot,
> Missing its last definition
> By millions of years.
> They'll never dig coal here,

> Only the waterlogged trunks.

This peat is something unique, created from decaying vegetation over millennia, and there is a hint that even coal might follow. It is a landscape where valuables are stored – and not just butter. Delve deeper and you may find gold and other prehistoric artefacts, representing a bountiful past which predates the bog's negative image. No wonder that Heaney began to think of multiple historical layers containing a great diversity and richness of heritage. Bogland was also the repository of Bog Bodies, the remains of ritually sacrificed and buried people. These occur not just in Ireland, but in other parts of northwestern Europe. But when Heaney encountered them, it was with the victims of Ireland's recent violence that Heaney immediately made a connection. These are the bodies of the Disappeared, still a most distressing issue twenty years after the ceasefire.

I experienced Lough Neagh's chilly pastures one Advent morning when its fields were largely devoid of stock. Local advertisements warned residents that worse was to come but white winter salt was available while supplies lasted. As I peered out across the Lough from Ardmore, a dense cloudy curtain swept across the sky, reducing my northerly horizons to grey lake water. It had been merely a fleecy lace curtain of cloud that blurred the full moon earlier that day. The lakeshore is mostly flat-lying and prone to flooding, with widespread areas of bog and marsh. Where the fields touch the Lough they ease themselves into its gentle waters.

When peat is buried beneath sediment it is gradually compressed and heated so that some of its volatiles are driven off and it becomes enriched in carbon. When fully indurated it is called lignite, which is midway between peat and coal, and this is present in the blue-grey clays surrounding Lough Neagh. These clays formed in a lake that was substantially larger than the present one and it would have taken more than just digging to fully explore them. A borehole drilled nearby at Washing Bay intersected a surprising thickness of 350 metres of these sediments, dating back to 25 million years ago. The swamp that gave rise to the associated lignite no longer exists but it had luxurious vegetation and a warm moist climate quite unlike today's. Some of its trees were related to modern California's giant redwoods and in the poem "Relic of Memory" Heaney would recall an oatmeal-coloured stone in his old classroom which was in fact a fossilised fragment of such a tree:

Derry

The lough waters
Can petrify wood:
Old oars and posts
Over the years
Harden their grain,
Incarcerate ghosts

Of sap and season.

The poet fancifully imagines that modern gate posts or farm implements might be rapidly fossilised on Lough Neagh's floor, ignoring the millions of years that have elapsed since those giant redwoods crashed into the ancient lake clays. But what is poetic licence for if not for such circumstances!

The digging metaphor does not terminate when we reach those Lough Neagh clays with their lignite seams. When vegetation is buried to greater depths and temperatures, there is further loss of volatiles and further increase in carbon content, and its colour blackens to eventually form coal. In the eighteenth and nineteenth centuries, coal was mined in the nearby Coalisland Coalfield, which has no surface exposure, and during World War I the suspicion grew that similar – and maybe more attractive – coal seams might extend eastwards at depth under the Lough Neagh area. We would need a very deep borehole to confirm or disprove that such coal is actually present beneath the lough. If confirmed then Heaney might have comprehended the full sequence of layers from peat to coal in his own home place.

Communities have long memories and those of landscapes are even longer. Heaney's poetry explores just how long. Bog burial places are no older than a few thousand years, while the bog itself may date back to around 10,000 years. Heaney's fossilised wood lengthens that timescale very considerably, its memory going back 25 million years. Should the Earth beneath Lough Neagh in time yield up coal seams then their fossilised plants – and we may be sure that such will be present – will push the limits back to about ten times the age of that fossil. And yet, even with that astounding age, Heaney would only be scraping the surface of Earth's memory: the age of those hypothetical coal seams would represent no more than 5 per cent of our planet's life!

Heaney's geologically-oldest specimen was probably the sandstone pebble he collected as a keepsake on a Lough Foyle beach ("Sandstone Keepsake"). He might have been distracted by the ominous presence across the Lough of Magilligan internment camp, nevertheless he saw a complex and even conflicting set of forces as having shaped his pebble. Its sedimentary origin was evident in that it was chalky and sea-worn, yet Heaney colourfully hints at a volcanic past that invokes the "hot river" of hell. It was likely derived from the Dalradian rocks that underlie Inishowen Peninsula, rocks more than half a billion years old, and as he gazed across the Lough's waters he may well have pondered what additional geological secrets they harboured.

I think that I am basically a ground person, you know, if it came to which element … I am sedimentary. That comes out earlier on, I think with poems like "Bogland", which is about going down and down and finding origin there.

Thus Heaney, shortly before his death, confirmed his geological affinity.[7] Heaney had long been conscious of a fascinating relationship between poetry and geology and admired the visionary perspective and detachment of each, seeing them both as distilling and communicating wisdom concerning our wonderful world. And when he deliberated on such universal issues, he could be speaking exclusively of his native Lough Neagh shores, for two of his key concerns were bogland and basalt. Consider "Relic of Memory", which hints at bogland connections with coal and also refers to basalt lava:

Dead lava,
The cooling star,
Coal and diamond
Or sudden birth
Of burnt meteor

Are too simple.
Without the lure
That relic stored.

One geological image after another comes tumbling out in this fascinating stream of consciousness which wonderfully captures the geological history of Heaney's world.

Northern Ireland's troubled past also becomes strangely inter-mixed with basalt in its poetic landscape. This is the same basalt, intersected at depth in the nearby Washing Bay borehole, that formed the foundations of Lough Neagh. Seamus Heaney asks himself whether geology might provide an unconscious answer to another basalt landscape, "the basalt-based and battlemented northeast of Ulster, Fortress Fair Head, as we might call it."[5] He notes that the poet Louis MacNeice (who we will soon meet) as-sociates the basalt landscape of Antrim with Ulster Protestant culture and wonders why something as geologically neutral as the Giant's Causeway could be identified with the Unionist rather than Nationalist tradition. For him, the towering impact of those basalt columns overrides any one-sided claim and, even when exhausted by the violence and recriminations of Northern Ireland, he could still find solace by sitting in the Wishing Chair of that splendid locality. But sadly, many landscapes of Northern Ireland were abandoned in fear for thirty years and subsequently communities still looked to certain ones as representing victory or defeat for themselves. Heaney's poetry suggests how we might relate famil-iar landscapes not to the usual divisive cultures but potentially to a deeper geological understanding. He records approvingly that geologists in the Geological Surveys of Ireland and Northern Ire-land have worked together to help people share ownership of their landscape through new values and interpretation.[8]

While this approach is both appealing and re-assuring, some consider that historical divisions cannot be so easily eliminated by a focus on the subsurface.[9] After all, it is argued, language is as much part of landscape as soil or buildings and, for example, our image of any part of Ireland is shaped as much by its folklore as by any geographical reality. A place constructed through words is a palimpsest of all previous notions, boundaries between fiction and reality become blurred and it is the simulation that becomes reality. In Ireland, a locality itself may become derelict or even inaccessible – but it will still be as vibrant and important as the narrative woven around it.

It is unlikely that Alfred Lothar Wegener (1880–1930) realised that basalt would feature prominently in the posthumous development of his ideas, but he was a man who left a remarkable scientific inheritance.[10] He was regarded as very successful among meteorologists but he managed to upset some geologists. Raised in Germany, he received his doctorate in astronomy in 1905 before embarking on an innovative career in meteorology. Clearly a man of some intellectual agility, but he did manage to upset a lot of geologists. He increasingly focused his research on Polar regions and it was while crossing the Greenland ice sheet for the fourth time that he died at a comparatively young age. But not before he managed to upset the vast majority of geologists of his day!

Alfred's crime was to cross the disciplinary divide and propose, against the collective wisdom of contemporary geologists, that the continents of the Earth once formed a single supercontinent, Pangaea, which subsequently split into component parts and gradually moved apart from each other. He was proposing the idea of continental drift. With hindsight, even a quick glance at a globe suggests that Brazil might be joined back with the coast of Africa, just like pieces of a jigsaw. Madagascar Island looks like it could have floated away from the southeastern corner of Africa, the Saudi Arabian peninsula from the northeastern African coastline. If we examine geological maps of such regions, there are certainly geological similarities between continents which would lend scientific support to such intuitive observations. But Wegener had an additional argument. He realised that the sedimentary rock sequences on the various continents represented climates that were inconsistent with their present latitudes. However, once he could move continents, just like chess pieces on a spherical surface, Wegener as a climatologist found it easy to explain the sequences of climates implicit in their rock sequences.

Wegener could provide no effective mechanism in 1912 to get the continents moving and geologists were in no mood to come to his assistance on this. However, just 17 years later the respected geologist Arthur Holmes (1890–1965) would helpfully suggest that convection currents in the Earth's interior could provide the necessary energy. Nevertheless, most geologists remained in a prolonged sulk because someone unqualified in their science had proposed such an audacious idea as horizontally moving continents. More than half a century later, in my final year degree exam, I was faced with discussing the "hypothesis" of continental drift and I intuitively knew I would not be generously rewarded for plumbing unquestioningly for this still-suspect concept!

It was the renewed interest in seabed geology after World War II that ultimately produced arguments that were utterly compelling. One of the key seabed surveying techniques measures subtle variations in the Earth's magnetic field, the product of circulating molten iron within the Earth's core. Effectively, our world is a giant dynamo and so, for example, magnetic minerals in lava record the orientation of its magnetic field at the time the lava solidified. Detailed mapping has indicated that the positions of the North and South Poles have periodically switched with each other, a process called polarity reversal. The maps reveal that a pattern of normal and reversed polarity in basalt lavas is arranged symmetrically around mid-oceanic ridges, with the lavas becoming older with increasing distance from the ridge. This supported the view that oceans had formed by gradual seafloor spreading and, as a result, plate tectonics became widely accepted by the end of the 1970s. Basalt had come to Wegener's aid at last and his reputation was restored in the process, even if he was never canonised!

Notes

1. T. S. Eliot (1944) *Four Quartets*. London: Faber and Faber. The quotation is from "Little Gidding", section V, page 42.

2. MacGowan, M. (1962) *The Hard Road to Klondyke*. Translated from the Irish by Valentin Iremonger. London: Routledge and Kegan Paul.

3. From "Upon Westminster Bridge Sept. 3, 1802", by William Wordsworth. In Palgrave, F.T. (Ed.) (1970) *The Golden Treasury*. London and Glasgow: Collins, page 272.

4. There are many critical studies of Heaney's poetry, including Corcoran, N. (1998) *The Poetry of Seamus Heaney: A Critical Study*. London: Faber & Faber.

5. Heaney, S. (2004) "Bog bank, rock face and the far fetch of poetry". In Parkes, M. (Ed.) *Natural and Cultural Landscapes: The Geological Foundation*. Dublin: Royal Irish Academy, pages 11-17.

6. Seamus Heaney (1998) *Opened Ground: Poems 1966-1996*. London: Faber and Faber Ltd. The specific poems are: "Relic of Memory" (page 27) and "Bogland" (pages 41-42). I referred to "Sandstone Keepsake" (page 217).

7. Article by Lara Marlowe, page 5 of *The Irish Times*, 3 September 2013.

8. McKeever, P. J. (1999) *A Story through Time*: *Landscapes from Stone*. Dublin: Geological Survey of Ireland

9. See, for example, Cusick, Christine (Ed.) (2010) *Out of the Earth: Ecocritical Readings of Irish texts*. Cork: Cork University Press.

10. Yount, L. (2009) *Alfred Wegener: Creator of the Continental Drift Theory*. New York: Chelsea House.

3

CALLOUS LAVA COOLED TO STONE

(Antrim)

And why should the sea maintain its turbulence,
its elegance,
And draw a film of muslin down the sand
With each receding wave?
— Louis MacNeice.[1]

Thingvellir is probably the most popular tourist destination in Iceland and the poets W. H. Auden (1907–1973) and Louis MacNeice (1907–1963) had this to say about it:

> Thingvellir is where they used to have the Thing, which was the Icelandic name for parliament and a very good name too, don't you think. It is *the* historic showplace. Not that there is anything to see except geology but it is amusing geology — rifts and such.[2]

17

It is wonderful that geology takes pride of place. Thingvellir is situated along a narrow fault-bounded zone of seismic and volcanic activity whose course swirls its way across the Icelandic countryside and marks the landward expression of the Mid Atlantic Ridge, one of the few places it can be inspected on dry land. This is a diverging plate boundary between the American and Eurasian Plates where basalt lava wells up from underground periodically, creating new crust according as the two plates move apart.

The two poets also recommended a visit to Langjokull, "the long glacier", and MacNeice would reflect on how awe-inspiring such ice masses can be in his poem, "Iceland", maintaining they had little respect for human ambitions. The power of nature here is both palpable and overpowering, the poem concluding that Iceland would soon relapse to rock under a cover of ice caps. However that poem recognises that the real threat for most Icelanders emanates from volcanoes rather than glaciers:

> Ignore the brooding
> Fear, the sphinx,
> And the radio
> With tags of tune
> Defies their pillared
> Basalt crags.[3]

Louis MacNeice is the Bard of Basalt and I wonder if those Icelandic basalt crags reminded him of the hills surrounding Belfast. When he gazed at those hills did he see basalt lavas that were among the first to form in that early Atlantic or was his awareness really limited to dreary farmland and the wails of ships' sirens? Of planter stock, he would describe his own community as devout, profane and hard, going on to observe ("Valediction"):

> This was my mother-city, these my paps.
> Country of callous lava cooled to stone.

In "Belfast", a hard, cold fire is frozen into the poet's blood and it comes from his basalt lava which is now a dour solidified rock.

Geysir is a major area of hot springs in Iceland which was another favourite of the visiting poets, with its regular spouting of impressive columns of steam and hot water. Each event is due to the periodic boiling of underground water, the frequency of eruption being determined by how long it takes for freshly introduced cool water to once more reach boiling point. The visitor centre credits James Craig (1871–1940), later Lord Craigavon and first Prime Minister of Northern Ireland, with being the first to realise the commercial potential of its geothermal energy.[4] Craig is described as a Belfast whiskey producer and a visionary in energy resources, but the perception back in Belfast was very different. The purchase featured in newspapers there, even *The Times* of London carried it, and Craig's father was far from amused. It was James Craig senior, rather than his youthful son, who was the substantial businessman and he feared public ridicule if it was thought that he had done such a silly thing as to purchase seemingly valueless geysers. He ordered his son to sell the property immediately amid great family tension and it was never discussed again. But James junior inadvertently retained a reputation in Iceland for steadfastness (a quality that even his father might have admired!) because various relatives and friends of his held the property for the next 40 years before it was finally bequeathed to the state of Iceland. I like to see beyond the father-and-son row and envisage that the young Craig did actually foresee that one day 150,000 visitors would flock annually to witness Geysir's inspiring steam eruptions and, more importantly, that sustainable geothermal energy would become a hugely critical support to all aspects of Icelanders' lives.

MacNeice's home was in Carrickfergus, County Antrim, along the northern shore of Belfast Lough. This calm haven gave birth to the *Titanic* during MacNeice's childhood there and its waters divide sharply the Palaeozoic rocks of County Down from those of Mesozoic or younger age in County Antrim. Around Carrickfergus, the basalt cliffs of Belfast have receded through erosion to reveal the underlying clays that Louis recalled as a youngster. Salt has long been mined from these Triassic mudstones at the eastern edge of town and, in MacNeice's time, was exported through its harbour. The harbour walls reveal the finely etched bedding features of Triassic sandstone similar to that present along the shoreline back to Belfast. On the seafront, sturdy Carrickfergus Castle, a handsome building upstaged only in scale by the nearby power station, has safely survived eight centuries on its secure perch upon dolerite exposure. Dolerite comes from the same magma as basalt but cools more slowly in a warmer underground environment and its crystals grow to a size where they can be recognised with the unaided eye.

MacNeice's father, an ambitious Anglican minister, moved the family to England when Louis was ten years old. The mudstone and salt of Carrickfergus was exchanged for the splendid Jurassic limestone of Dorset. He was fascinated by the surrounding scenery and – most of all – "fossils for the picking"; he preferred "the smooth whorls of an ammonite" to identifying butterflies or wild flowers. Indeed when he changed schools to the chalk downs at Marlborough ("from sandstone to flint") he expressed himself as "disappointed in the fossils, if that is the right word for the flint rind of what was once a sponge but now is powder."[5] He would retain a casual familiarity with rock throughout his writing life, including London Clay, limestone and granite.

Nevertheless, he was always happy to hark back to his childhood scenery around Belfast Lough.

> The soil in the kitchen garden was black and littered
> with flints, but in easy distance beneath it lay a stratum
> of thick red clay sticky as Plasticine.[5]

The flint-bearing material had been transported from further north by glaciers and deposited on top of red clay derived from the nearby basalt hills. When he later reflected on his prickly Ulster heritage ("Carrick Revisited"), it was a geological analogy that came to his mind: his heritage was like a boulder stuck in the red Antrim clay.

MacNeice would spend two decades working at the BBC and maintaining his interest in landscape and geology. Indeed having visited some caves to record sound effects, he caught fever as a result of a drenching on a return visit and died prematurely of pneumonia. Did any poet ever have such a geological dimension to their death? As I read MacNeice's work recently, I was taken by his offhand humour, his disarming honesty and his uncertain sense of identity. While I sensed an abiding interest in geology, I certainly felt no proprietorial Protestant grip on basalt, despite what Seamus Heaney would later assert!

That same basalt unifies Antrim with Iceland and other parts of the North Atlantic region. The basalt lava flows on either side of Iceland's Mid Atlantic Ridge display magnetic patterns that indicate their progressively older age with increasing distance from the ridge. The island of Iceland appeared less than 25 million years ago, its volcanic activity being unusually prolific due to an underlying area of extremely hot mantle, a long-lasting "hot spot". Although Ireland is currently a little distant from this exciting action, it still bears the scars of that amazing history. As its crust was ruptured by plate tectonic forces, the northern part of the country was intruded by swarms of narrow dolerite dykes and sills, including that on which Carrickfergus Castle stands. These were the pathways for magma which flooded the surface and formed the extensive basalt lavas of the Antrim coast.

The Antrim coastline featured prominently for a time in a celebrated geological controversy.[6] This concerned whether, with the exception of modern volcanoes, all rocks now regarded as igneous had actually developed through cooling from magma ("vulcanism") or whether, alternatively, they had precipitated from warm seas and accumulated on the seabed ("neptunism"). Rev. William Hamilton (1755–1797), a local clergyman, in 1786 published a creditable vulcanist interpretation of the Giant's Causeway, which is the view now universally accepted. Let me add that his horrific murder in Donegal some years later had nothing to do with the scientific views he espoused. However, the year after his death, a rival geologist, Reverend William Richardson (1740–1820), achieved instant scientific celebrity when he claimed to have discovered ammonite fossils in a dolerite sill on the foreshore at nearby Portrush. If confirmed, this would offer strong support to the neptunist cause. However, further examination revealed that the fossils were actually contained in baked shale bordering the sill rather than in the dolerite itself.

Explore this coastline by commencing near the oval cove of Portballintrae and continue eastwards across the chalky beach of Bushfoot Strand to ascend the basalts at Runakerry Point.[7] At the Giant's Causeway itself, the honeycomb patterns of its foreshore are initially overshadowed by three-dimensional cliffs with slender columns that give rise to such evocative place names as The Giant's Organ, The Chimneys and The Giant's Harp. The cliffs from here to Benbane Head expose a number of individual horizontal lava flows. The tops of some have thick horizons of red lateritic soil, resulting from the tropical weathering of the basalt itself, reflecting the luxuriant climate that existed here some sixty million years ago. But the photogenic lava with distinctive hexagonal pillars down on the foreshore deserves some special comment also. It became ponded in a local valley where its surface was inundated with river water before it calmly cooled to yield a regular pattern of contraction joints (analogous to mud drying and cracking in the sun).

Lacada Point (Port na Spaniagh), provides a grim reminder of a tragic and stormy night in October 1588 when the *Girona*, part of the ill-fated Armada, sank with the loss of all but a few of its 1,300 men. Submarine excavations nearly 400 years later would yield a rich treasure of jewellery, coins, silverware, guns and navigation equipment – all now preserved in Belfast's Ulster Museum. Further along, the basalt cliffs at Bengore Head contain minor hematite and bauxite deposits, the products of extreme leaching of the lateritic soil. I crossed the low-lying basalts around Dunseverick

Castle and reached Portbraddan, where the upper surfaces of lava flows have gas bubbles that are filled with white zeolite minerals.

From here onwards I had views eastwards to the boomerang-shaped island of Rathlin, constructed of basalt, and then the prominent Fair Head dolerite sill. But when I passed through an arch in basalt onto White Park Bay I crossed a fault line which brought me onto chalk, or white limestone, bedrock. That fault was the result of persistent seismic activity, something to which this district was no stranger. I paused to marvel at the white cliffs, but not long enough to collect any of their distinctive cigar-shaped (and coloured) fossils. These are the belemnites that were so beloved of MacNeice. Layers of flint nodules occur at various levels in the chalk, while its lowest beds contain small grains of deep green glauconite and larger grains of yellow-brown phosphate – always attractive specimens to collect. Before finishing, I was determined to visit Carrickarade Island, not only for the exhilaration of reaching it by a loosely-swinging rope ladder but also because it consists of the neck of a volcano that in its day was quite explosive. As a result its interior consists of a jumble of basalt, chalk and other rock fragments set in a matrix of basalt ash. Now I was happy to relax and reflect on how other visitors may have viewed the fascinating coastline I had just traversed.

The literary response to the Giant's Causeway is defined as much by those who didn't visit as by those who took the trouble to come. Samuel Johnson (1709–1784) famously responded when asked if he would visit it:[8] "Worth seeing? Yes; but not worth going to see." Talk about damning with faint praise!

Johnson was a man who never set foot in Ireland, never mind visiting the locality itself, and his words were recorded in 1779 by his biographer, James Boswell (1740–1795). Boswell meticulously noted their conversations and accordingly we can picture Johnson, with an eye to posterity, consciously honing memorable lines that his faithful scribe might transcribe. Together they succeeded in establishing this basalt coastline in the literary mind.

John Keats (1795–1821) has gained an unwarranted reputation for having visited the Giant's Causeway.[9] He did come to Ireland specifically to visit the famous Antrim locality, but never reached it because he deemed the journey too long and prices too expensive. What a pity! This youthful poet, who would die all too soon of tuberculosis, was overcoming the difficulties of his early life, working hard to establish a poetic reputation, and was now experiencing enchanting scenery in places such as the Lake District and Scotland for the first time. Perhaps the Giant's Causeway might even have displaced Fingal's Cave on Scotland's Staffa Island as the backdrop for part of his well-regarded poem, "Hyperion".

"And have I travelled a hundred and fifty miles to see *that*?", the writer W. M. Thackeray (1811–1863) exclaimed to his guide with a mixture of impatience and sarcasm. The Giant's Causeway, "this wild, sad, lonely place", induced fear and terror in him. He considered this strange landscape might have been the very scene of the creation – and it could still harbour prehistoric monsters!

> Does the sun ever shine here? When the world was moulded and fashioned out of formless chaos this must have been the *bit over* – a remnant of chaos?[10]

Thackeray's outraged fantasy may no longer strike a chord with creationists, whose views are given a less strident treatment in the Interpretive Centre here.

The redoubtable Mr S. C. and Mrs A. M. Hall did examine the Causeway Coast in some detail and they have obliged us with a fine account of their journeys.[11] They state that first impressions of the Giant's Causeway are invariably disappointing but that these quickly give way to a sensation of excited curiosity and indeed astonishment and delight. They then provide a physical and geological account that is remarkably detailed and relies on the writings of a Belfast teacher and geologist, James Bryce (1806–1877). Like most other commentators, they also allude to the legendary battle between two giants, Ireland's Finn MacCumhaill and Scotland's

Benandonner, and its mythical role in the origin of the Causeway. They found its guides to be knowledgeable, sure of their geology, trustworthy and safe, quite a change from those they encountered at Glendalough and Killarney who "greet you with a jest, and bid you farewell with a tear".

I checked the response of recent visitors to the Causeway through TripAdvisor[12] and found that the ten most recent reviews were, without exception, fulsome in their praise. A spectacular natural wonder, a beautiful attraction, an amazing and unique experience. Choosing daybreak or sunset would ensure wonderful lighting and less crowding. Many were pleasantly surprised to be able to scramble freely over the columns, but the need to be sure-footed was also remarked upon – a couple of unfortunate accidents were noted. Visitors were urged to put the locality into perspective – and make the visit more enjoyable – by walking the nearby trails or driving the Causeway Coast. This was one of Northern Ireland's top visitor attractions, yet it was possible to visit free of charge provided one avoided the Interpretive Centre. But many had not done this and, in fact, there was much praise for this Centre, newly opened in 2012. Its facilities were exemplary and much could be learned there, including about quarrelling giants!

It is a mark of the abiding popularity of the Causeway Coast that a local prank should get national media attention. *Faulkner's Dublin Journal*[13] reported on 30 May 1788 that the area had been hit by the most violent thunderstorm in living memory, damaging buildings and felling trees. Then a fearful noise came from nearby Knocklayd Hill, the summit of which burst open. Burning matter and hot stones issued as a torrent 150 metres wide and extended downslope for 2.5 kilometres, killing several cattle and destroying many cabins. The tongue-in-cheek nature of this report is revealed by the comment that among the missing persons were the local dissenting minister and parish priest, two of the more expendable members of the community as far as the middle-class newspaper readers of the time were concerned. Surely a reassuringly modest loss given the horrific potential of such an infernal incident! Now where else would benefit from a similar hoax? Perhaps somewhere that might more realistically experience such volcanic events? Thingvellir?

Notes

1. From "The Coming of War", page 685 of MacNeice, L. (2007) *Collected Poems.* Peter McDonald (Ed.). London: Faber and Faber.

2. Auden, W. H. and MacNeice, L. (1967) *Letters from Iceland.* First published in 1937. London: Faber and Faber. The extract on Thingvellir is on page 187.

3. MacNeice, L. (2007) *Collected Poems.* Peter McDonald (Ed.). London: Faber and Faber. Quotations used are from "Valediction" (pages 7-10) and "Iceland" (pages 59-61). I also refer to "Carrick Revisited" (pages 261-262) and "Belfast" (page 25).

4. Ervine, St. John (1949) *Craigavon: Ulsterman.* London: Allen & Unwin.

5. MacNeice's autobiography is MacNeice, L. (1965) *The Strings are False.* London: Faber and Faber. The quotations used here are from Appendix A.

6. Herries Davies, G. L. (2009) "A history of Irish geology". In Holland, C.H. and Sanders, I.S. (Eds.) *The Geology of Ireland.* Second edition. Edinburgh: Dunedin Academic Press, pages 471-485.

7. Lyle, P. (No date) *A Geological Excursion Guide to the Causeway Coast.* Environment and Heritage Service (Northern Ireland).

8. Hill, George Birkbeck (Ed.) (1887) *Boswell's Life of Johnson.* Oxford: Clarendon Press. The extract used is on page 410 of volume 3.

9. Walker, Carol Kyros (1992) *Walking North with Keats.* New Haven and London: Yale university Press.

10. Extracts are from pages 280-282 of: Thackeray, W. M. (2005) *The Irish Sketchbook of 1842.* First published 1843. Dublin: Nonsuch Publishing.

11. See pages 160-169, volume 3 of: Hall, Mr S. C. and Mrs A. M. (1843) *Ireland: Its Scenery, Character, etc.* Volume 3. London: Jeremiah How.

12. http://www.tripadvisor.ie/Attraction_Review-g209948-d189773-Reviews-Giant_s_Causeway-Bushmills_County_Antrim_Northern_Ireland.html Checked on 9 January 2013.

13. *Faulkner's Dublin Journal*, No. 7420, Tuesday 3 June–Thursday 5 June 1788, page 4.

4

Knowing the Place
for the First Time
(Carlow)

*The real voyage of discovery consists not in seeking
new landscapes but in having new eyes.*
– Marcel Proust[1]

The Nine Stones. There are actually nine stones there and I
have counted and even photographed them on occasion.
They form a low trim set of upright rectangular flagstones bordering the roadside. They are not spectacular and their historical
significance is debated, but they form a well-known landmark on
the road crossing the north end of the Blackstairs mountains. It is
a good place to reflect on our perceptions of mountains, not because of its altitude, which is moderate, but because it is isolated.

Robert Macfarlane, raised in a family of climbing enthusiasts, is fascinated with mountains and specifically with the excitement of their dangers. He is candid in describing how he has been propelled into taking unwarranted risks during his many challenging climbs and clearly he is not unique in this. Millions are captivated by the allure of mountains, despite the rising toll of death and injury associated with it. In fact he himself is more driven by the excitement of danger than the prospect of exhileration upon success. On reading the account of the last sighting of Mallory and Irvine on their 1924 ill-fated Everest challenge, he readily admits that he wanted nothing more than to be one of those two tiny dots, fighting for survival in the thin air.[2]

My personal experience of mountains suggests that they are places of work. My earliest geological work involved mapping part of the Wicklow and Blackstairs mountains, systematically traversing their flanks, walking their forests paths, trudging their stream beds and inspecting their lanes and roadways. I was not the only person working there. Many a day I watched enthralled as a farmer guided his sheepdog in rounding up his flock, an otherwise impossible task in this open countryside. I met many forestry workers who understood their environment very well and were sources of great local knowledge. County council workers had many reasons to travel to isolated, mountainous parts, not least to maintain roads. Mountains may also support quarrying operations, although these had shifted to large lowlands operations in limestone areas by the time I started working here. Nowadays access to mountains is driven more by the need to maintain the network of beacons and reflectors that facilitate communications and transmissions.

Many of us want to experience mountains as part of our leisure – perhaps to admire them, maybe to be challenged by them. They can be places of discovery, where we gain insights into nature's diversity or realise the extent or limits of our hiking capabilities. They may also be places of pilgrimage and, where once petitioners left rosary beads now, thoughtlessly, many discard their scratched lottery tickets. Mountains provide us with periods of peace and perspective, as we make joyful journeys in search of spectacular scenery, whether blanket bogs, boulder-strewn slopes or the sheer rock faces of higher mountain ranges. But, fundamentally, mountains for me mean stories, as diverse as the mountains themselves, and in the case of the Blackstairs that story concerns granite.[3]

The Nine Stones is underlain by slates and schists, situated between two substantial granite plutons of contrasting topographic expression, both units of the Leinster Granite. To the south, the Blackstairs Pluton forms the backbone of the Blackstairs mountains, extending as far as the St. Mullins area, while the low ground to the north comprises the Tullow Lowlands Pluton. We are heading southwards for the rocky upper slopes of Mount Leinster, which are covered in blanket bog and highly leached podzols. Accordingly, their practical value is limited to forestry and sheep grazing. However they are a considerable visitor attraction because of their scenic beauty and leisure possibilities. For example, the steep slopes immediately below the Nine Stones are popular with hang gliders because of their rising air currents and their convenience to the nearby road.

Mount Leinster's (800 metres) summit reminds some people of Croagh Patrick's (760 metres) and maybe it is just the memory of similar physical exertion! The latter Mayo peak actually requires trudging up 700 metres while Carlow folks have the advantage of driving to within 500 metres of Mount Leinster's mast. Of course, Croagh Patrick's quartzite is also distinctively different from our granite but both rock types share a common history in that they were not overridden by ice sheets in the Ice Age, but alternatively have been shattered by constant freeze-thaw action. That makes Mount Leinster different from most neighbouring peaks which were scoured of rock debris by advancing ice sheets. When descending its slopes, weary walkers have the advantage of a surfaced roadway used to service its summit transmission mast, a privilege not accorded to more hardy souls on the Reek's slopes!

The Leinster Granite, the largest granite body in northwestern Europe, is an elongate body that stretches from Dalkey on the Dublin coast as far as County Kilkenny. It formed about 400 million years ago as the last act in the complex choreography of plate collision when Iapetus Ocean closed. In this process, the crust of the overridden plate melted and the resulting granitic magma, being less dense than its surroundings, ascended towards the surface. It finally crystallised at a depth of about 5 to 10 kilometres, which is about the same distance below ground as that at which planes fly above it.

Granite plutons develop through a process called incremental assembly, which involves countless small batches of magma moving upwards along seismically active faults over a very extended time period. The magma finds specific horizons where it can accumulate, frequently as flat-lying sheets without underlying deep roots. When this interpretation was applied to the present area, it became clear that a major fault zone, the East Carlow Deformation Zone, which traverses the Nine Stones area, had greatly influenced the emplacement of both the Blackstairs and Tullow Lowlands Plutons. This fault zone contains a series of narrow parallel granite sheets, forming feeders for ascending magma, which welled into convenient low-pressure horizons to give rise to the plutons we see today. This process could have taken a million or more years to complete – not a prolonged event in geological time!

It is good to report that a son of Carlow, Professor Samuel Haughton (1821–1897), was among the key early students of its granite. A man of considerable mathematical and medical skills, he became well-known for his research on animal mechanics and his opposition to aspects of Charles Darwin's (1809–1882) theory of evolution. Carlow town, where Haughton is commemorated on Burren River Bridge, is law-abiding and its former prison has long since been converted into a supermarket with all traces of its gallows obliterated. And so its citizens may not be universally aware that their famous son used his combined talents to produce – for genuinely humanitarian motives – a best-practice guide for the hangman. That Burren River spans both hanging and hang gliding within its modest catchment![4]

Granite is actually a very modern rock whose elements have made mobile communication convenient. Some granites, including those bordering the Nine Stones, have veins containing large white blades of spodumene, a lithium-rich mineral. The use of lithium in batteries for mobiles has facilitated a 100-fold reduction in their weight. However lithium deposited in dried-out desert lakes of South America is commercially more attractive and so Carlow's resources remain untapped. A bluish heavy metal called tantalum is associated in small amounts with these lithium-rich veins and is ideally suited for short-term electricity storage in mobile capacitors. But once more, Carlow's pegmatites are facing daunting competition, this time from pegmatite deposits in Western Australia and elsewhere.

Back at the Nine Stones, take time for lunch before setting off along the gentler slopes of Slievebawn and Tomduff, on the northern side of the road. We are going to see the effects of granite emplacement on the rocks it invades. Before there was any hint of ascending granite, this entire area had been under seawater and muds, silts and sands had accumulated steadily if slowly. In the early stages of plate collision, gigantic stresses deformed and folded these sediments elaborately and a new cleavage was imposed on them. The sandy beds have been metamorphosed to quartzites that still display some lovely folds, with a pattern similar to what might result if someone had roughly scooped up a used tablecloth after dinner. In the softer, dark coloured muddy beds, cleavage displaces the bedding as the rock's major structure. This cleavage arises under intensive pressure when the tiny individual mica flakes of the original mud are re-oriented and recrystallised.

The upper slopes of Slievebawn and Tomduff are quite close to the contact of the Tullow Lowlands Pluton and therefore were metamorphosed further when the hot granite was emplaced via the East Carlow Deformation Zone, Carlow's major locus of ancient earthquake activity. The slates have now become fully recrystallised as mica schist containing visible crystals of andalusite, staurolite, garnet and biotite. The most widespread is undoubtedly staurolite – black, sharply outlined and less than 1cm long. But the most prominent is andalusite and it occurs in oblong pink prisms up to a remarkable 0.5 metres long. Its refractory nature means andalusite is used as a furnace liner, but an exploration programme here over twenty years ago found it was of unsuitable quality. In any event the exploration met with considerable resistance from the community on environmental grounds and the project was discontinued.[5]

Andalusite was first observed at Slievebawn back in the 1840s by Thomas Oldham (1816–1878). At that time he was Director of the Geological Survey of Ireland, an organisation in its infancy and just embarking on the task of mapping the nation's bedrock geology. Oldham would go on to head up the Indian Geological Survey for the latter 25 years of his career, but not before he was involved in a serious dispute with one of his colleagues. Frederick McCoy (1817–1899) was an early recruit to Oldham's organisation and an established specialist in fossils. He found, however, that his best talents were not being tapped by Oldham who had assigned him to Borris, County Carlow, to map rocks with no prospect of yielding a single fossil! Oldham, distantly stationed in Bunclody on the other side of the Blackstairs, had an unsatisfactory correspondence with McCoy on his poor progress. A visit of inspection did not improve matters and I have the impression that McCoy resigned just in time to avoid being fired! But this did not prove ruinous to his career and he would spend 45 years as Foundation Professor of Natural Science in Melbourne. There are varied views of how successful he was in this role but he was awarded a knighthood, a distinction that eluded the Irish boss who might have fired him![6]

As many as 800 volcanoes have been active around the globe in historic times, displaying every gradation from free-flowing basalt lavas to explosive ash eruptions. Although perhaps 200,000 persons were killed in volcano-related catastrophes in the four centuries up to 1914, the comparable figure for earthquakes would be measured in millions. The evidence for Carlow's own volcano stretches from Mount Leinster across the Slaney valley to Shillelagh in Wicklow. Its vent remained below sealevel and built up a considerable stack of green andesite lava flows, still recognisable as such despite their metamorphism to hornblende schist. The volcano also experienced occasional eruptions of ash, as well as persistent earthquake activity. The sequence is now tilted to one side and can be traversed by strolling northwards from Kilcarry Bridge along the Slaney's banks.[7]

I mapped here as a young geologist and, returning on some geological errand about 20 years later, had a most interesting conversation with a farmer who patiently described to me the area's volcanic past. Smoothly moving on to enquire about my own mission, he explained that he had encountered a geologist once, many years earlier and not far from the very spot where we were standing. He indicated that his youthful informant had been very knowledgeable and convincing, a real geologist he said dismissively, with obvious implications for present company. I had already left his company some minutes before my dulled senses recognised my more impressive alter ego!

It was Edward Hardman (1845–1887) who first mapped this area on behalf on the Geological Survey of Ireland and he was certainly an impressive geologist. He subsequently became Government Geologist for Western Australia and made two significant discoveries, gold in the Kimberley area and a pegmatite at Greenbushes. The latter was found to contain lithium and tantalum resources in quantities that Carlow could only dream about and it is still worked to this day. Soon after his return to Ireland he contracted typhoid fever and died, leaving a grieving and impoverished widow who was rewarded by the Western Australian Government with a £500 grant in recognition of his endeavours.[6]

The extent of George Bernard Shaw's (1856–1950) celebrity may have dimmed a little with the passage of six decades since his death, but he truly was a theatrical colossus in his day.[8] His plays were sufficiently accomplished to merit his being awarded the Nobel Prize for Literature and sufficiently successful commercially to ensure that (combined with his wife's wealth) he could maintain a comfortable lifestyle for all of his long life. He must have been gratified to establish a family link, through his father's Kilkenny family, with Macduff of Shalespearean fame,[9] but neighbouring Carlow produced more tangible assets for him when he inherited property there from his mother's family. This he gifted for the common good to Carlow which in turn embraced him as its own.

Carlow's adopted son was a witty, provocative and prolific author who must surely have betrayed some of his affection for the county in his writing. Perhaps if I analysed *John Bull's Other Island* more elliptically I would realise that Shaw's acerbic observations on Irish personality were crafted while strolling the Killeshin Hills. Have I missed some critical geographical allusions in *Pygmalion* that might suggest some of Eliza's family originated along Barrow's banks – perhaps as immune to its flooded February fields as to its September celebration of harvesting success? I may have lost further opportunities for landscape appreciation by not considering exhaustively whether *Mrs Warren's Profession* was practised more in the bleak Blackstairs winter than in the balmy Barrow summer. However, at the age of 88, Shaw informed a correspondent that he had spent only a single day in Carlow in his entire life.[10] Indeed, once he left Ireland at age 20, his subsequent return visits would be distinctly Joycean in their frequency. Nevertheless, the grateful residents of Carlow have properly shown their appreciation of his generosity to the town and its George Bernard Shaw Theatre is now a focal point for the arts there.

Shaw's love of Irish landscape was focused elsewhere.

Its list of attractions include views of the Morne (*sic*) Mountains and Holyhead. It might as well have added the Himalayas and Ceylon. Four thundering lies are better than two when they cost nothing.

This was Shaw's bemused response on being shown an 1847 property advert for his boyhood home on Dalkey Hill, south of Dublin city. In the course of a gracious and good-humoured correspondence with a Dalkey resident, he said:

> Nothing can gratify me more than to be commemorated on the spot where I learned to love Nature and Ireland when I was a half grown nobody.

And elsewhere in that correspondence he gave warm expression to that love:

> I owe more than I can express to the natural beauty of that enchanting situation commanding the two great bays between Howth and Bray Head and its canopied skies such as I have never seen elsewhere in the world. They are as present to me now as they were 80 years ago.[11]

That love for Dalkey Hill is something that I share with Shaw. My Edinburgh uncle was wont to remind me that it was my boyhood walks with him in this very locality that led to my life-long affair with geology. Evidently he would point out the mica flakes of its granite and quote Shaw's ancestral playwright to the effect that there are:

> ... books in the running brooks,
> Sermons in stones ...[12]

No matter that my uncle thought it was Scotland's Sir Walter Scott who said that! I do remember those summertime walks around Dalkey Hill fondly, but less for its granite than for a glimpse of Shaw's own cottage! Assuming he was a Dubliner like myself, I found it easy to make common cause with one so accomplished and famous. So imagine my chagrin when I discovered that he was open to being claimed by Carlow!

Notes

1. Marcel Proust (1871–1922). From "La Prisonnière", the fifth volume of *À la recherche du temps perdu* (*Remembrance of Things Past* also known as *In Search of Lost Time*)

2. Macfarlane, Robert (2003) *Mountains of the Mind*. London: Granta Books.

3. The geology of this district is described in Tietzsch-Tyler, D. and others (1994) *Geology of Carlow-Wexford*. Dublin: Geological Survey of Ireland.

4. Spearman, D. (2002) *Samuel Haughton: Victorian Polymath*. Dublin: Royal Irish Academy.

5. White, Mary (1992) *Mount Leinster: Environment, Mining and Politics*. Dublin: Geography Publications.

6. Herries Davies, G.L. (1995) *North from the Hook*. Dublin: Geological Survey of Ireland.

7. McArdle, P. (2009) "Carlow's volcano". *Carloviana*, 2009 edition, pages 45-47.

8. Holroyd, M. (1997) *Bernard Shaw: The One-volume Definitive Edition*. London: Chatto & Windus.

9. Pilsworth, W.J. (1950) "George Bernard Shaw's connection with Kilkenny". *Old Kilkenny Review*, number 3, January 1950, pages 40-2.

10. Letter contained in the Shaw/Carlow folder of correspondence at the National Library of Ireland, Dublin: NLI MS 2292.

11. Letters (1947–50) from George Bernard Shaw to John Fitzgerald, Dalkey Development Association, 21 Railway Road, Dalkey, County Dublin, concerning the erection of a plaque in his honour at Torca Cottage are contained in the following folder of correspondence at the National Library of Ireland, Dublin: NLI MS 8381. Accessed courtesy of the National Library of Ireland.

12. From Act 2, Scene 1 of *As You Like It* by William Shakespeare (1564–1616).

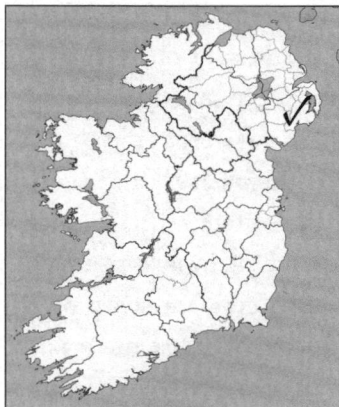

5

MOUNTAINS FOR COMPANY
(Down)

(Geologists) read the ground rules of Earth itself
and tell the time by the planet's body clock.
– Seamus Heaney[1]

Scrabo Hill is as important to the residents of the Newtownards area as, say, Killiney Hill is to those of Dublin; both serve important needs for strolling and contemplation. Scrabo may be less visited but its tower is more imposing than Killiney's obelisk. Scrabo Tower is an impressive tribute to Charles Stewart (1778–1854), the Third Marquess of Londonderry and half-brother of Lord Castlereagh (1769–1822). Charles had had a less than glittering career when suddenly, following his controversial half-brother's suicide, he found himself managing extensive estates and proved to be a well-liked landlord.

Scrabo Hill may be prominent in today's landscape, but 20,000 years ago it was not a sufficient obstacle to prevent advancing ice from overriding it. Those ice sheets, probably several hundred metres tall, crunched their way across the countryside, absorbing soil and loose debris into their bases, and scouring and scoring any bedrock they came in contact with. The ice passed over Scrabo from the northwest plucking away loose material from its summit and leaving a noticeable "crag" or scarp on the downward south-eastern slope. The unconsolidated material on the lower ground further southeast was now protected from scouring due to the cantilever effect of the progressing ice sheet. As a result the soil and debris have been smeared out to produce gently sloping farmland. It is along this "tail" that the approach road to Scrabo Hill has been constructed. Seen from this perspective, this crag-and-tail feature is almost as impressive as its more famous Edinburgh cousin, where the Royal Mile "tail" leads to the Castle "crag".

I had the hill to myself on the morning of my visit. In geological terms it is an outlier, meaning that it is surrounded entirely by older rocks. Its steep sided cliffs are composed of sandstone that, unusually in Ireland, is no more than 250 million years old. This rock used to be known as New Red Sandstone, in contrast to the much older Old Red Sandstone which is extensively developed throughout the south of Ireland and elsewhere. The Scrabo sandstone now has the more romantic name of Sherwood Sandstone, being correlated in age with its (where else?) Nottingham equivalent. Much of it formed in a desert environment and its sand grains have been abraded to spherical "millet seeds". Bedding laminations commonly lie at a high angle to those beneath, mimicking modern sand dunes. In times of flash floods, temporary rivers would carry a great deal of sediment to the area and some siltstones still carry the impressions of rain drops. Impersistent lakes were floored by muds which, whenever the water evaporated, dried out and cracked – features still preserved in the rock record. The area had a diversity of animals whose activities are recorded by features such as burrows. But undoubtedly the prize specimen found at Scrabo is the single footprint of a reptile, *Chirotherium*, which is now on display in Belfast's Ulster Museum.

These features can be well seen in the quarry immediately below Scrabo's tower, where only a few raucous ravens monitored my visit. The buff and pink sandstone is durable and cuts smoothly, so it has long been used in important public buildings, including Belfast's Albert Clock. Sadly it was superseded in time by the richer red shades of Penrith Sandstone from Cumbria, composed of similar sand grains of desert origin. A striking feature of the quarry's back wall is the occurrence of dark dolerite sills, which stand out against the surrounding sandstone. Those sills, which sometimes skip from one bedding plane to another, are rather famous and photos of them adorn many geological textbooks. Dolerite is a tougher rock than Scrabo's sandstone and the hill owes its existence to the protection it afforded.[2]

Descending towards Newtownards, you can look out over the lowlands of County Down – all the way to the Mournes on a clear day. The quiet waters of Strangford Lough stretch away into the middle distance, with the Ards Peninsula fringing it on the left. This country is underlain by sediments of Silurian and Ordovician age – siltstones, mudstones and muddy sandstones (called greywackes). The earliest are dark mudstones which accumulated on an ocean floor and contain thin layers of volcanic ash to add some variety. That ocean was Iapetus, a forerunner of our modern Atlantic Ocean. The latter is still widening today, but Iapetus had reached its maximum extent and now was actually contracting once more. As a result its seabed was eventually fully covered by bottom-hugging density currents carrying sediment off nearby continental shelves and depositing it as greywacke and siltstone. Iapetus closed when one opposing plate overrode the other, in the process scraping up the sediment and assembling it as fault-bounded bundles that are well exposed on the Ards Peninsula coast.

Fault-related seismic activity may have controlled the pace and nature of events here during sedimentation and plate collision, but it also persisted to produce major displacements along later faults. One such fault is the Orlock Bridge Fault which extends from the Ards Peninsula southwestwards through County Cavan to the Slieve Aughty region. This deep-going and powerful fault deformed intensively the rocks it traversed and offset features by as much as 400 kilometres, so if a feature at Donaghadee was ruptured by the initial movement, then part of it might now be found somewhere north of Killaloe!

The southern part of County Down is dominated by granite, but in two distinct and different bodies. The Mournes Granite forms a dramatic and renowned range of coastal hills whose landscape and geology we will shortly celebrate. But first I want to direct your attention to the more subdued country further west, beneath which lies the second body, the Newry Granite. About 400 million years old, it consists of five individual plutons, each representing a separate pulse of granite intrusion. Its development was not always regarded in such straightforward terms, indeed it became embroiled in a major geological controversy on the origin of granite in the middle of the last century.

In her published account of the Newry Granite, Doris Reynolds (1899–1985) characteristically plunged straight to her conclusion: the granite was produced, not by emplacement of liquid magma, but during metamorphism by the transformation *in situ* of its surrounding sediments. Proponents of this view became known as transformists and Doris was their vocal leader. Their process involved hot fluids pervading the rock sequence, introducing alkalis and removing iron and magnesium. Reynolds would later identify the Slieve Croob pyroxenite at its northeast end as the repository of excess iron and magnesium from the Newry Granite. Her paper was delivered at the Royal Irish Academy by an unassuming and quietly erudite geoscientist, but one who would become instantly recognisable to generations of students as the author of *The Prin-*

ciples of Physical Geology, an authoritative text despite its ghastly pink dust jacket. This man, Arthur Holmes (1890–1965), was a towering figure in twentieth century geology and it was he provided the driving mechanism for plate tectonics. And just a few short years earlier he and Doris had got married. They say that opposites attract for, in sharp contrast, she seemed to revel in controversy and was fiercely trenchant in support of her views.[3]

Reynolds' paper was certainly a significant contribution but neither her thoroughness nor the support of her eminent husband was sufficient to win this debate in her favour. The difficulties involved in removing some elements from a mass of rock and at the same time introducing others were never resolved in a convincing manner. By the close of the twentieth century there was hardly a transformist in sight! Granites continue to be regarded as the product of liquid magma. Nevertheless, it is essential to scientific progress that there are people with Doris' determination and courage to continually challenge accepted norms.

The ice that shaped Scrabo Hill originated in the Lough Neagh region and as it streamed across County Down it moulded the underlying boulder clay into dense patterns of drumlins, called basket-of-eggs topography. But when ice reached the formidable obstacles of the Mourne Mountains it was deflected in narrow tongues around them, although some ice also surged across mountainous passes.[4] These mountains are synonymous with outstanding beauty. The skyline is unusually diverse, changing from the flattish summit of Slieve Commedagh to the sharp apex of Slieve Donard and the vulnerably stacked boulders forming the granite tors of Kivitar. Twelve peaks crowd the skyline within as many kilometres, each with summits exceeding 600 metres in height. The surface of the higher ground, with barely concealed bedrock, has a distinctively rough texture which is best enjoyed in slanting sunlight. Lower down, the landscape gives way to bogland and farmland with gentler slopes. They offer a convenient wilderness experience to the residents of Belfast.

The poet Paul Yates (b. 1954) captures the ancient lore, sights, sounds and smells of his mother's home place in the Mournes.[5] Objects he encounters jog his memory, he is at ease with the world of spirits, and granite and solitude are everywhere. The mountains provide companionship, help to set the pace and are undemanding in matching his mood ("A Place"). "Mourne Minded" is more geological in spirit, for in it he envisages erratic boulders being carried out to sea by ice, according as icebergs calve, where they eventually drop to the sea floor

The beauty of Mourne's physical landscape has inspired some memorable images and John Hewitt's (1907–1987) from "The Chinese of Wang Li Shi"[6] is a typical example:

> The Mourne Mountains like a team of bears
> tumbling into the sea,
> the embroidered fields like a monk's patched cloak
> spreading their skirts to every door.

John will feature prominently in the next chapter.

Percy French's (1854–1920) song "The Mountains of Mourne", composed in 1896,[7] has been a long-time favourite of late-night Irish audiences and Don McLean's evocative rendering of it has extended its reach considerably. It may paint a picture of a naïve London-based emigrant wishing for the simple blameless life back in Mourne country, but its language is also accurate: those two simple words of the refrain, "sweep down", seem to aptly capture the majestic manner in which those steep mountain slopes curve smoothly to merge with the surrounding farmland.

Helen Waddell (1889–1965), a remarkably accomplished scholar and thoroughly spiritual person, contemplates a winter walk in her popular poem "The Mournes" (or, "I shall not go to heaven when I die").[8] She longs to be united with a deceased loved one, on whom she stumbles in the unexpected warmth of an imaginary fire-lit room. There is no doubting that she has experienced the peculiar charms of Mourne on her way and indeed she seems to seek reunification with the Mournes landscape as much as with her loved one.

Richard Valentine Williams (1877–1947), using Richard Rowley as his pseudonym, directed his earlier poetry towards the tough life of Belfast's working class. It was only in later life, after he had moved to Newcastle, that he wrote of the Mourne countryside extolling independent rural life and its virtues. But his descriptions of nature are not conventionally framed and he is capable of enlivening relatively simple verse with imaginative precision ("April"):

> The river torrents were white skirts in a gleaming dance,
> the cherry-grove a flight of swans and the larch-wood an
> emerald ring.[9]

These mountains are implicated in the kaleidoscopic range of everyday activities and current events of Northern Ireland. James B. Johnston (b. 1944),[10] is a Belfast poet now settled in the USA. He was always eager to reach the open hillsides and steep granite slopes of the Mournes, leaving behind a city that seemed to brace itself for bombing while searching for peace ("Stone Wall Fences"). Encountering the Mourne Wall he reflects that his then-troubled Belfast was a city divided by stone wall fences and granite hearts. Another meaningful linking of the Troubles with Mourne Granite is in a youthful poem by Kerry Carson (b. 1973).[11] In "Mourne", she plays on the title as both noun and verb, allowing the constant repetition of "Mourne country" to become an unnerving accusation.

Slieve Donard, at 853 metres the highest peak in Ulster, forms the northeastern termination of the Mournes, overlooking both Newcastle and that fertile plain we have already admired from Scrabo Hill. I like to think that Mark Cooper, geologist and poet, had Slieve Donard in mind when he penned "Tread-polished Layers". He has a wonderful way of mingling thoughts about walkers' erosion with geological processes:

> Step down the tread-polished layers.
> Beds of stone, where past sleeps holding secrets.

Such sediments now form the rocks of Silurian age exposed along the Glen River on Donard's lower slopes. If we progress further upwards and reach the open countryside, we are on granite and can imagine solid granite slabs being used for the walking trail: Tracks laid, records played, stacked – many times repeated.

I could have my location entirely wrong, but I still admire Mark's care for the walker: "Step back, take care not to fall."[12]

Mourne Granite is distinctively different from its Newry neighbour and, for example, it shows attractive crystal-lined cavities in places. These are best seen just below the roof level of the granite at Diamond Rocks and while diamond sparklers are regrettably absent, fine specimens of beryl and topaz have been collected here. The Mourne Granite consists of several separate granite pulses emplaced in two contiguous plutons. They intrude the much older sedimentary sequence of greywackes, siltstones and mudstones, all of which are metamorphosed alongside the granite to biotite- and diopside-bearing hornfels. Hornfels is similar to schist but its new crystals are not aligned along the schistosity as in the latter. The granites were emplaced at a high level in the crust over a relatively short period, about 55 million years ago, and each phase had time to solidify before the arrival of the next. The granite's geological history was first determined by a Northern Ireland geologist, J. E. Richey (1886–1968), who was employed by the British Geological Survey in Scotland. We will learn more about him in the next chapter, but for the moment just note that he had a very tolerant family who allowed him map the Mournes during his annual holidays! In a classic interpretation, Richey argued for granite emplacement by cauldron subsidence, where space was created for magma through subsidence of a major block of crust. Recent research has modified this conclusion and suggests that the overall form of the granites is a horizontal sheet which was fed laterally by magma flowing from the southwest. Nevertheless, Richey's conclusions have had a remarkable influence on our perception of how granite is emplaced, an influence that extended well beyond the Mourne Mountains themselves.[13]

That wonderful writer about the Mournes, E. Estyn Evans (1905–1989),[14] states that Mourne granite was exploited as a building stone since prehistory but as an industry it gained life only when shipping made exports possible. By 1800, Annalong and Newcastle ports were handling granite from several convenient quarries. Dressed stone exports thrived in the second half of the nineteenth century and were widely used in lintels, sills and doorsteps. The name of Millstone Mountain records the fact that it supplied many mills with grinding stones, up to an impressive 1.5 metres in diameter. Now restricted largely to tombstone manufacture, many commentators have noted that Queen Victoria herself, when personally choosing stone for the base of her Hyde Park memorial to Prince Albert, passed over this source in favour of the less-used Newry Granite near Castlewellan. However it is quite some time since the value of Mourne was calculated solely in terms of its granite exports.

Notes

1. Heaney, S. (2004) "Bog bank, rock face and the far fetch of poetry". In Parkes, M. (Ed.) *Natural and Cultural Landscapes: The Geological Foundation*. Dublin: Royal Irish Academy, pages 11-17.

2. The following is a convenient guide to the geology of most places mentioned in this chapter: Mitchell, I., Cooper, M., McKeever, P. and McConnell, B. (2010) *The Classic Geology of the North of Ireland*. Belfast: Geological Survey of Northern Ireland.

3. Reynolds, D.L. (1943) Granitisation of hornfelsed sediments in the Newry granodiorite of Goraghwood quarry, County Armagh. *Proceedings of the Royal Irish Academy*, section B, pages 231-267. For a biography of Doris Reynolds, see Williams, F.C. (2009) Doris L. Reynolds (1899-1985). In McGuire, J. and Quinn, J. (Eds.). *Dictionary of Irish Biography*. Royal Irish Academy and Cambridge University Press, volume 8, page 451.

4. See Marshall McCabe and Paul Dunlop (2006) *The Last Glacial Termination in Northern Ireland*. Belfast: Geological Survey of Northern Ireland.

5. Basil Blackshaw (images) and Paul Yates (words) (2005) *Mourne.* Belfast: Tom Caldwell Gallery. I have referred to the following poems: "Mourne Minded" (p. 35) and "A Place" (p. 142).

6. "The Chinese of Wang Li Shi" by John Hewitt appears on page 76 of Longley, Michael and Ormsby, Frank (2007) *John Hewitt: Selected Poems.* Belfast: Blackstaff Press.

7. "The Mountains of Mourne" is included in French, Percy (1925) *Prose, Poems and Parodies of Percy French.* Dublin: The Talbot Press.

8. Helen Waddell's poem "The Mournes" appears on pages 222-23 of Corrigan, F. (1986) *Helen Waddell: A Biography.* London: V. Gollancz.

9. "April" is on page 39 of Rowley, Richard (1940) *Ballads of Mourne.* Dundalk: W. Tempest.

10. "Stone Wall Fences" is on page 23 of Johnston, James B. (1997) *Exile: Poems of an Irish Immigrant.* Knoxville, TN: Celtic Cat Publications.

11. Kerry Carson's "Mourne" is on pages 149-150 of Ormsby, Frank (Ed.) (1992) *A Rage for Order: Poetry of the Northern Ireland Troubles.* Belfast: The Blackstaff Press.

12. Mark Cooper, "Tread-polished Layers". June 2009. Personal communication (November 2010).

13. Richey, J.E. (1927) The structural relations of the Mourne Granites, Northern Ireland. *Quarterly Journal of the Geological Society of London*, volume 83, pages 653-688.

14. Evans, E.E. (1967) *Mourne Country: Landscape and Life in South Down.* Dundalk: Dundalgan Press.

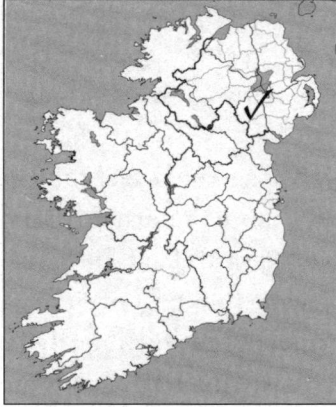

6

Living our Best in the Landscape

(Armagh)

There are no manifestations of the forces of Nature
more calculated to inspire us with feelings of awe
and admiration than volcanic eruptions preceded or
accompanied, as they generally are, by earthquake shocks.
– Edward Hull[1]

The Belfast poet John Harold Hewitt (1907–1987) graduated from Queen's University Belfast and worked until 1957 in the Belfast Museum and Art Gallery before becoming the founding Director of Coventry's Herbert Art Gallery. When he retired he returned to his now-turbulent native Belfast. He described himself as an Ulsterman, an Irishman of planter stock and a socialist. No wonder he was comfortable with ambiguity in both life and poetry!

Seamus Heaney described him as a left-leaning poet of Protestant stock, trying to map out a planter position sympathetic to natives. The terms, planter and native, were used repeatedly by Hewitt in his writing.[2]

As an urban dweller he could feel fulfilled and yet excluded in the countryside. But more importantly he tried to straddle the two landscapes of Northern Ireland, those of planter and native, leading to his never feeling fully part of either. While he revelled in meeting the busy farmers of his own neatly farmed planter landscape, I suspect he enjoyed the native environment just as much, with its easier pace of living and its greater natural diversity. He did not seek deeply hidden meanings in landscape, but he did want to reach out to people in both communities and he craved their acceptance.[3] In "Sunset over Glenaan",[4] planter landscape is described as rich low-lying farmland where:

> economy has drilled the very soil
> into a dull prosperity that year
> by reckoned year continues so.

Native landscape comprises hilly and boggy land that is less intensively farmed by men who may have long memories but are more sociable:

> They take life easier on their hillside farms,
> with time to pause for talk.

Hewitt considered that his love of native landscape should have been sufficient to secure his position in it. But his self-conscious torment implicitly tells us that he did not realistically expect to be accepted equally by both traditions. In "Footing Turf", he contrasts working a bog in wintry weather with haymaking in sunshine. This metaphorically encapsulates for him the differences in circumstances of the two communities of Northern Ireland: the natives would be restricted to less valuable peat digging in poor weather, while the planters would be favoured with good weather and a more rewarding activity. He acknowledged the oppression that Catholics still suffered in the middle of the twentieth century but considered that the labour of planters entitled them to regard their birthplace as their own country.

I do not believe Hewitt when he said that he turned to landscape only because people disappointed him ("The Ram's Horn"). There is no palpable sense in his writing that people and landscape become somehow divorced from each other. People are integral to his landscape and indeed their very activities often classify it for him. He stated in the poem "Landscape" that the countryman could identify different layers in the landscape. These were more mental layers than geological strata and two of them, for example, mapped out land use and land ownership. He may have been frustrated with people at times, whether of his own community or not, but he could not regard them separately from their environment. In recalling his memories of the "Orchard County", his ancestral Armagh, it was on his grandfather he focused because it was he who first introduced him to the wonders of his landscape.

Hewitt had a holiday home in the Glens of Antrim where he could indulge his love of scenery and nature. The flowers and countryside animals all gave him pleasure, but birds were certainly his favourite. All of this meant that his appreciation of what he observed would sometimes have a light touch, particularly as far as geology is concerned. Nevertheless he did not ignore the physical landscape on which nature thrives. For example, he shows a deep interest in rivers and how they shaped our countryside ("Conacre"). Indeed he tended to notice how rocks had been eroded much more than their specific nature. More than anything, rock was something useful and it might become, for example, a pillar. However he was certainly not neutral about the impact that quarrying might have on habitats ("Conacre"). Nevertheless Hewitt appreciated a wider geological context in "Freehold IV: The Glittering Sod" when he saw his part of Ireland as the:

last edge of Europe, cliff against the west
stemming the strong tides with its broken coast.

He returned to this theme in "Conacre", in a rather poignant stanza that also addresses his sense of identity:

Later on
perhaps I'll find this nation is my own;
but here and now it is enough to love
this faulted ledge.

I especially enjoy his description of Northern Ireland as a "faulted ledge" on the margin of the Atlantic. I like to think that he was anticipating, long before the birth of plate tectonics, Ireland's one-time position at a plate edge!

"I live my best in the landscape, being at ease there." When Hewitt wrote these words he had neither planter nor native in mind ("The Ram's Horn"). He was simply expressing his joy of landscape in a straightforward way. Much has been written in recent decades about the importance of territory in creating group identity in Northern Ireland and Hewitt was direct in this regard. He acknowledged the oppression of Catholics but considered that the investment of planters entitled them to regard their birthplace as their own country. He felt that the very sharing of ground should generate sufficient commonality between Protestant and Catholic.

The northern part of County Armagh, where Hewitt's father's family came from, is planter landscape defined largely by the abundant presence of drumlins. It was the accomplished geographer, E. Estyn Evans (1905–1989), who strongly asserted the link between planters and drumlins, contending that such land could only be successfully worked through the strong work ethic of Protestants:

When you see the big drumlins, whether at Rossnowlagh on Donegal Bay or at Killyleagh on Strangford Lough, you may expect to hear the noise of the big drums in the month of July. But the rocky hills which interrupt the drumlins have retained a Roman Catholic population, and this also applies to the badly-drained lowlands of south Fermanagh and central Cavan where the soils are exceptionally sticky: Here a map showing religious distributions is a mosaic of Protestant islands in a Catholic sea.

He went on:

Much of the drumlin country is Orange country. For reasons known to history, the most fertile parts of Ulster were occupied by Protestant planters in the seventeenth century. The deep drumlin soils, previously utilised mainly for grazing, responded to the labour of a Protestant people who saw virtue in hard work.[5]

John Hewitt, a contemporary of Evans and fellow-resident in Belfast, would have had sympathy with this view, but perhaps we will discover an alternative in the next chapter when Patrick Kavanagh's poetry is considered.

The native landscape is concentrated in the southern part of the county, characterised by hilly Slieve Gullion and its granite environs. The land here is rocky and boggy and of marginal agricultural value. So Hewitt's two landscapes, planter and native, have distinctive geological identities within this county, separated from each other by flat-lying countryside underlain by sediments of Ordovician and Silurian age. The north of the county, extending to Lough Neagh's shores, has in addition to its drumlins a rich and fertile bedrock diversity: limestones of Carboniferous and Permian age around Armagh city, and basalts and clays closer to Lough Neagh. The naturalist Robert Lloyd Praeger (1865–1953), who spent his fulfilling life exploring Ireland's landscape, was also impressed by the northern part of the county and Armagh city itself, paved with locally quarried red limestone. He wished that many other towns in Ireland were so well kept, and with an equal appearance of prosperity and well-being.[6]

Slieve Gullion, the nerve centre of the native south, hardly deserves fame, with its modest height, dour shades and untidy shape. Yet its mythology, built around that handsome and courageous hero, Fionn Mac Cumhaill, still weaves a magic spell. When Fionn arrived here, wearied by his adventures, he sought comfort in the deep waters of the summit lake – only to be instantly transformed into a feeble old man. I beseech my readers not to replicate this action because the same effective remedy may not be available to them as it was to Fionn. In his case a local king restored him to his former vigour by offering him a drink from a golden cup – a cup that mysteriously vanished as soon as its contents were quaffed. Some accounts suggest that Fionn's renowned wisdom also came from this powerful drink (pharmaceutical researchers please note!).[7]

Slieve Gullion also inspired a remarkable cluster of Irish-speaking eighteenth century poets. The most popular locally was Art Mac Cumhaigh (c. 1738–1773), a farm labourer whose untimely death was attributed to a weakness for drink, while the most gifted is generally considered to be Peadar O'Doirnín (c. 1700–1769), a hedge-school master whose life was far from comfortable. Their output, preserved in the oral tradition, ranged over many political and social issues of their times, although it was their more romantic themes which proved to have an enduring appeal. Generations of second-level students will have struggled with these, perhaps without realising the enchanting landscape that nurtured them.[8]

The Ring of Gullion embraces not only Slieve Gullion itself but also a necklace of hills that surrounds it. Walk the mountain's summit ridge, for it has not got an obvious singular peak, and you will not be disappointed by the vista. Local farmers suggested to me that the distant views of the Mournes, Cooley Mountains and Dundalk Bay were most deserving of attention, but my gaze was constantly drawn back to that ring of hills. The intervening low ground certainly appears flat-lying and includes the town of Meigh, meaning a plain, but when I walked through it I thought it as hummocky as the back of a dromedary camel!

Our current understanding of how Slieve Gullion evolved starts, as with so many events in Ireland's ancient history, with a volcano and this was certainly an explosive one. Edward Hull (1829–1917) might have been thinking of Slieve Gullion's volcano, now eroded to its very core, when he penned the text that opens this chapter.[1] A magma-filled chamber beneath the volcano released steam under high pressure, shattering the overhead rocks. As a result, its roof was fundamentally weakened and, stimulated by extensive seismic activity, it subsequently collapsed. Magma welled up around the sunken central block, forming a ring dyke which has now been exposed through erosion and is coincident with the low hills of the Ring of Gullion. Thus a classic ring dyke was formed through a combination of earthquakes and volcanic eruptions.

When Slieve Gullion was first surveyed by Joseph Nolan (1841–1902), he astutely recognised that its granite was quite distinct from the surrounding Newry Granite and represented the deep roots of a much younger volcano. When confronted with the bewildering variety of granite and dolerite varieties exposed on the hillside he surmised that the volcanic edifice of the original volcano had somehow foundered into its underlying magma chamber, but he went no further.[9]

We have already encountered the next geologist involved, J. E. Richey, who was the son of a County Tyrone rector and he married a Tyrone woman. Based in Scotland, it seems his wife and daughters were content to visit their relatives in Tyrone while he spent his summer holidays deciphering the geology of other interesting parts of Northern Ireland! He confirmed that Slieve Gullion was the subsurface base of an ancient volcano and concluded that its summit caldera formed when a cylinder of rock subsided along a ring-like set of fractures, giving rise to those circular hills of the Ring of Gullion. The accompanying volcanic outbursts may have left no enduring ash deposits on Slieve Gullion, but they did blanket the entire surrounding countryside and must have been an awesome sight.[10]

The geological diversity of the surrounding Armagh landscape is certainly striking, from predominantly igneous rocks in the south to the sediments and metamorphic rocks of the north. This diversity has, for example, ensured that its northern part would be more fertile. When combined with the more recent products of glacial processes, that variety has led to the range of physical and cultural landscapes we take for granted today and that control the lives of their inhabitants in so many ways. But what was the ultimate cause of such diversity?

The Earth formed from a cloud of dust particles that clustered together under the influence of gravity to form a sphere of boringly uniform composition. This did not last for long, however. Our planet's interior began to heat up due to the radioactivity of its mineral constituents. Its constant rotation gave rise to centrifugal forces that created different layers of distinct composition within the Earth, with denser minerals concentrating towards the centre. The metal-rich core developed an outer liquid part surrounding an inner solid core. The Earth operates as a giant dynamo due to convection in this liquid core, producing an important magnetic shield that now protects the planet's life. The mantle separates the core from the outer crust and consists of relatively dense silicate minerals. Although apparently solid, its material is subject to thermal convection under the influence of radioactivity, and it is this that provides the driving mechanism for plate tectonics. So the Earth's surface is composed of rigid plates, comprising the crust and the upper part of the mantle, that are constantly interacting with each other and their boundaries are loci of earthquakes and volcanoes as a result. The assembly of Earth in this way ensured that it would in effect become a living planet, with eventually an atmosphere, oceans and indeed life. Lateral movements of those surface plates created remarkable changes that had far-reaching effects. Ocean crust was constantly created where adjacent plates diverged from each other. This was the process that formed the Atlantic Ocean and its progress can actually be experienced today on

Iceland. In situations where plates were colliding with each other even the most majestic ocean could be eventually swallowed up. We will consider other outcomes to plate tectonics as we continue our trip around Ireland's counties.

So now the main elements are in place to create the huge diversity of rock that we experience on Earth. Igneous rock would have been forming from the outset – lavas and ashes forming on surface while intrusions of coarse-grained rock such as granite were emplaced at depth. Oceans and atmosphere, both essential to create and protect climates and habitats, were developed partly from Earth-based and partly from comet-derived materials. Soon sediments were forming freely and life had the potential to develop. But Earth needed time – probably as much as two billion years – to lose some of its radioactive heat before its surface became sufficiently rigid to generate plates. Once they formed, then the whole symphony of plate tectonics commenced, with the accelerated production of new igneous and sedimentary rocks. But now, in addition, metamorphic rocks began to develop for the first time as plates were deformed during collision events. Finally, we had reached a point where all varieties of rock had the potential to develop and Earth could blossom in all its geological variety.

Even within the confines of County Armagh, that geological diversity comprehends the outcome of many climatic and environmental shifts – from the oceanic setting in which the county's oldest rocks formed to the shallow tropical seas of its limestone; from the semitropical heat that weathered the region's basalts to the volcanic winter that may have overshadowed violent eruptions of volcanoes such as Slieve Gullion; not to mention that most recent and briefest of episodes, the Ice Age, that so shaped today's physical geography. But I am sure that will not stop any of us from complaining about even the slightest shifts in our own gloriously mild weather pattern. Mind you, if there are seasons to match those two apocryphal landscapes, I feel sure that Hewitt would have no hesitation in designating who might own the sunny landscapes!

Notes

1. From page 1 of Hull, E. (1892) *Volcanoes: Past and Present*. London: Walter Scott.

2. Walsh, Patrick (2009) John Harold Hewitt (1907-1987) In McGuire, J. and Quinn, J. (editors) *Dictionary of Irish Biography*. Royal Irish Academy and Cambridge University Press, volume 4, pages 664-667.

3. John Hewitt's poetry is discussed in the following: Dawe, G. and Foster, J.W. (Eds.) (1991) *The Poet's Place: Ulster Literature and Society. Essays in honour of John Hewitt, 1907-1987*. Belfast: Institute of Irish Studies, Queen's University.

4. Longley, Michael and Ormsby, Frank (Eds.) (2007) *John Hewitt: Selected Poems*. Belfast: Blackstaff Press. I quoted from the following poems: "Conacre" (pages 1-7), "The Ram's Horn" (page 29), "Sunset over Glenaan" (pages 60-61) and "Freehold IV: The Glittering Sod" (pages 133-134). I also referred to: "Landscape" (page 28)," Footing Turf" (page 59) and "Orchard County" (page 110).

5. See pages 29-30 of: E. Estyn Evans (1992) *The Personality of Ireland: Habitat, Heritage and History*. Dublin: Lilliput Press.

6. Praeger, R. L. (1937) *The Way that I Went: An Irishman in Ireland*. Dublin: Hodges, Figgis & Co and London: Methuen & Co. See page 131.

7. See, for example, Mackillop, J. (2004) *A Dictionary of Celtic Mythology*. Oxford: Oxford University Press.

8. The lives of Peadar O'Doirnín and Art Mac Cumhaigh are described by Vincent Morley (volume 5, pages 896-97) and Lesa Ní Mhunghaile (volume 7, pages 358-59), respectively, in McGuire, J. and Quinn, J. (Eds.) (2009) *Dictionary of Irish Biography*. Royal Irish Academy and Cambridge University Press.

9. Nolan, J. (1877) *Explanatory memoir to accompany Sheet 70 of the maps of the Geological Survey of Ireland, including the country around Dundalk and Carrickmacross*. With palaeontological notes by W. H. Baily. Dublin: Her Majesty's Stationery Office.

10. For more information on J. E. Richey, see Byrne, Patricia M. (2009) J. E. Richey (1886-1968). In McGuire, J. and Quinn, J. (Eds.) (2009) *Dictionary of Irish Biography*, volume 8, pages 488-89. His key publication on Slieve Gullion is Richey, J.E. and Thomas, H.H. (1932) "The Tertiary Ring Complex of Slieve Gullion (Ireland)". *The Quarterly Journal of the Geological Society of London*, volume 88, pages 776-849.

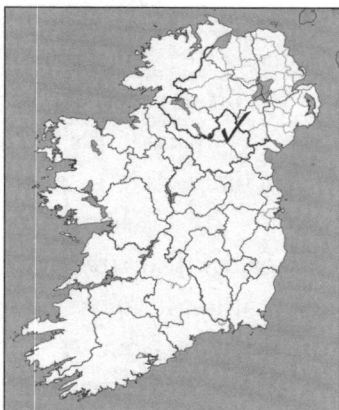

7

MY BURGLED BANK OF YOUTH
(Monaghan)

You flung a ditch on my vision
Of beauty, love and truth.
O stony grey soil of Monaghan
You burgled my bank of youth!
– Patrick Kavanagh[1]

I noticed a general rise in the ground elevation north of Ardee which coincided with the start of the drumlins and I realised I was close to Kavanagh Country. Those drumlins are the product of the last great glacial pulse in Ireland when advancing ice sheets shaped boulder clay into extensive developments of these distinctive hills, extending from Strangford Lough westwards as far as the drowned versions of Clew Bay, well known to far-sighted Reek pilgrims. Over most of Monaghan district, the drumlins are oriented with their long axes trending northwest-southeast, indicating ice sheets moved towards the southeast. The mid-October morning, far from glacial, had drenched the Monaghan fields with dew and the patchy mist would soon lift to reveal the beauty of their rural setting. I imagined that by following in his footsteps I could get a sense of how his landscape influenced the poet Patrick Kavanagh in his writing.

I left Carrickmacross quickly, briefly noting the prominent 1860s church constructed of locally-quarried limestone, its pale grey blocks of uniform rock unmarred by visible fossils. Somewhere on the road to Cormoy, near tree-fringed Capragh Lake, amidst the prominent drumlins that mask any bedrock changes, I crossed from limestone onto the greywackes and shales which underlie the farmland that Kavanagh worked and wrote about. The drumlin pastures, if not rocky, in places have heavy soil and there are low-lying areas with marsh and pretty lakes. However there are also more prosperous areas of well-drained parkland with mature trees. This is the pleasant countryside around Inniskeen, the birthplace of Patrick Kavanagh (1904–1967), in south County Monaghan.[2]

I deliberately deflected northwards and made for Fane River valley and Magoney Bridge. It is entirely unremarkable and yet it deserves some celebrity for it contains evidence of a very strange form of life – and I am not referring to any relatives or acquaintances of the poet! I speak of graptolites, those fossilised remains that seem no more than pencil marks scratched casually on dark shale. When exceptionally well preserved they appear like a narrow hacksaw blade with one side serrated, although Magoney's species is actually a double-edged saw! Colonies of these marine blades attached themselves to floating debris or organisms and roamed the seas as free spirits, feeding on plankton. Their anatomy was actually sophisticated, relatively close to the vertebrates, but they evolved into a biological *cul de sac* from which no modern descendents survive. They were prominent for over 70 million years and the Magoney creatures were alive when they were at their peak.

I wonder what the weather was like on the day that W. H. Baily (1819–1888) first visited here? In addition to some luck, you would need a bright sunny day on which to detect these subtle fossils. Baily was Acting Palaeontologist with the Geological Survey of Ireland at the time and would spend 30 frustrating (indeed infuriating) years in this unsettling grade: yes, he was a competent student of fossils, entitling him to call himself a palaeontologist, but why were his achievements not recognised by his being made permanent, or indeed promoted? By all accounts a difficult man, this disappointment cannot have improved his mood. No doubt before travelling to Magoney he would have already favoured with his attention the limestone exposures on the margins of Kavanagh country, around Dundalk and Carrickmacross – and they would have yielded a rich harvest of corals, crinoids and brachiopods. Older rocks, such as those around Inniskeen, however, tend to be deformed and metamorphosed so that finding fossils in them is much harder. But Baily's painstaking examination of the shale outcrops was rewarded with graptolite specimens that were sufficiently good to establish fairly precisely the age of the rock sequence here. It probably took a week, but that was a good week's work![3]

As south Monaghan seems to have a geological reputation for greywacke dullness, let me assure you that it did actually belch out lava and its faults did quake! Some of those widespread greywacke beds contain significant amounts of volcanic rock derived from contemporaneous eruptions somewhere in this region. There is also evidence for quaking because significant movement occurred along the Kingscourt Fault, with sediments on one side slipping down by a significant two kilometres. Those younger sediments include valuable gypsum beds that are mined to make plasterboard.

Apparently Patrick Kavanagh never tired of saying that leaving the stony grey soil of Monaghan was his greatest mistake and yet he claimed that that same stubborn clay had burgled his bank of youth! He left school at the age of thirteen to assist his father, who was a small farmer and cobbler struggling to raise a large family. Patrick proved to be neither skilled in, nor fulfilled by, this work although he would persevere in it for another twenty years. His intellectual energy was absorbed by his life as a poet, drawing inspiration from both his natural environment and his daily farming tasks.[4]

From the outset, he strove to be both nature poet and farming poet, capturing beauty and usefulness together even in single phrases ("Ploughman"):

> I find a star-lovely art
> In a dark sod.[5]

The Kavanagh farm was in hilly ground, often waterlogged and rushy, while between the hills were some cut-away bogs, including one at Mucker, where the family lived. His brother Peter argued that those fields facing the sun were stony and exhausted, while those facing north were cold, wet and hardly of better quality.[6] No wonder that passers-by, on hearing the land was farmed by a poet, chuckled that he must be a poor one. With delightful self-mockery, Kavanagh allows us believe they thought his poetry must be poor, and not just his land, for his farming neighbours would have had little time for poetic pretension ("Shancoduff").

Kavanagh would neglect neither the pretty lakes nor the backbreaking drumlins but he was quite capable of distancing himself from farming, as he demonstrated in poems like "Inniskeen Road: July Evening". "Stony Grey Soil" is a much-quoted poem that captures the tension between nature poet and farming poet, for clay smothered his love of nature and he became a slave to farming:

> O stony grey soil of Monaghan,
> The laugh from my love you thieved;
> You took the gay child of my passion
> And gave me your clod-conceived.

Kavanagh was fascinated by the place names of his locality. It is remarkable that in the vicinity of Inniskeen there are several town-land pairs of similar name but ending in anglicised versions of *bán* (white) and *dubh* (black). Here are three that I noticed on the Ordnance Survey map:[7] Kinallybane/Kinallyduff, Monaltybane/Monaltyduff and Shancobane/Shancoduff. Kavanagh frequently used contrasting pairs to good effect, for example, white is aligned usually with nature and black with farming. "Shancoduff's" title locates the poem on a specific and steep-sided drumlin that could cast a long shadow, a person on low-lying ground between the hills might never see the sun in winter:

> My black hills have never seen the sun rising,
> Eternally they look north towards Armagh.

Another contrasting pair in Kavanagh's poetry relates to soil and clay, words that to him were often interchangeable. But soil is an ecosystem nurturing a myriad of life forms, much of it unseen, and it represents the practical farming side of a countryside coin. On the other side of the coin, clay consists of subsoil, the weathered product of bedrock, and is relatively devoid of life. Yet it represents nature because it is the essential foundation for soil development and it has been shaped into the drumlins that define the unique quality of the poet's home place. So clay shapes the landscape and makes soil possible, but only fertile soil supports farming. Clay, derived from inert earth yet the basis for the living substance of soil, is a natural bridge between nature and farming. In "The Great Hunger", Kavanagh uses the word clay a lot and where he refers to "clayey hours" of labour he makes clear that his clay is our soil!

Kavanagh claims he gave his youth to farming without receiving any adequate recompense. And yet I would question how real Kavanagh's hardship was as a young farmer. For I have walked this area and am convinced its land is better quality than his writing suggests. His home place is well populated with earnest and dili-gent farmers who leave little land unused. I am not surprised the district is well speckled with attractive and well-kept residences. Even if Kavanagh's holding was below-average quality for the area, my belief is that he was a reluctant farmer and any agricultural land, whatever its quality, would have burgled his bank of youth!

Kavanagh's view of farming drumlins in south Monaghan is certainly more pessimistic than that espoused by Estyn Evans, as we have seen in similar terrain in north Armagh. Evans was careful to say that his analysis could not be applied universally, but he argued that drumlins made the finest farmland provided it was worked by diligent Protestant farmers. No doubt there are some differences in the physical composition of the soil in the two districts, but actually I have the feeling that farmers around Inniskeen, whatever their religion, might be more in sympathy with Evans than with Kavanagh!

Crevasses are great yawning ice fractures that are much respected by climbers traversing glaciers because not alone do they slow down progress but they retain a capricious tendency to open (and even snap shut) without warning. Kavanagh identified some on the slopes of Slieve Donard, which once were ice-covered and it is just possible he was being imaginative ("The Goat of Slieve Donard").[8] But on this occasion it seems more likely that his vision was more earthy than glacial and that he was really thinking of crevices rather than crevasses. Interestingly, his brother, Peter, thought that Kavanagh confused Slieve Donard with Slieve Gullion, which was easily visible from his neighbourhood whereas Slieve Donard, the highest peak in the Mournes, is quite distant. If so, this is a rare landscape lapse on the part of someone known to have climbed both mountains. More challenging peaks occur in Shancoduff where the drumlin hills:

> are my Alps and I have climbed the Matterhorn
> With a sheaf of hay for three perishing calves.

Shancoduff's Alpine steepness reflects the effort required in his daily tasks. He states that his hills made him indifferent to the hardships and thrills of more lofty ranges, even Everest itself ("Monaghan Hills").[8]

It is fair to say that Kavanagh was rarely burdened by fundamental geological considerations, although some geological topics did cross his mind while working. For example, the poem "Kednaminsha"[8] evokes his experience as a quarryman. A dolerite dyke crossed part of his land and he regularly quarried it to maintain road access to fields beyond his bog. This is an example of Kavanagh conveying his appreciation of landscape through his actual experience of it, and for most people it is more meaningful as a result.

Patrick Kavanagh lived in Dublin for the second half of his life, where he struggled to earn a living from freelance journalism. His love of nature did not desert him when he exchanged Monaghan's drumlins for city life. In fact, he rediscovered his roots on the banks of the Grand Canal:

> ... where again I saw the beauty of water and green grass and the magic of light. It was the same emotion as I had known when I stood on a sharp slope in Monaghan, where I imaginatively stand now, looking across to Slieve Gullion and south Armagh.[9]

It is on this same Grand Canal that he is now commemorated on a canal bank seat, where the water seems quite still in summer yet roars "Niagariously" over locks ("Lines written on a seat on the Grand Canal, Dublin, erected to the memory of Mrs Dermot O'Brien"). Niagariously. I wonder if this wonderful adverb has made its way into everyday usage on the other side of the Atlantic! It certainly deserves to.

From Patrick Kavanagh's home in Mucker it is only 3km across the parish to Ballyrush, where the land is better quality and its drumlins more subdued. Here lived Sylvester Duffy's sizeable family and his son, Thomas, now enters our story.[10] Thomas Duffy (1890–1965) was by all accounts good company. He was a tall, well-built man of military bearing and a contemporary newspaper photo reveals his earnest expression and dark hair swept tightly back off a high forehead. He initially pursued agricultural studies but World War I service seems to have quenched his farming ambitions. He completed a natural sciences degree and applied for a position with the Geological Survey of Ireland. His agricultural knowledge of soils would have been advantageous because they were very relevant to the Survey's programme at that time. More difficult to assess is the influence that one of his university tutors might have had on his appointment. He was Professor G.A.J. Cole (1859–1924), who doubled as Director of the Geological Survey and who – perhaps crucially – strongly favoured participation by geologists in Britain's war effort! In any event Thomas, now newly married, was successful and would go on to spend 35 years in GSI while resident in Rathgar. He served in a diligent and praiseworthy manner, his sound judgment and well-honed skills being beneficial to all who called on him in his Hume Street office. In due course his death notice would hint at his family's pride in his geological career.[11]

Born about ten years apart, it seems likely that Patrick Kavanagh, while still living in Inniskeen, was aware of the older geologist. Parishoners in this relatively small parish would all have been known to each other to some degree. For example, Thomas' father had an active role in parish affairs which Kavanagh referred to in family correspondence while light-heartedly coveting a similar status for himself. Also the spirited Duffys do feature in the poem "Epic" and I like to think they were close relatives of Thomas, especially as his townland, Ballyrush, features in the same poem.

Given their subsequent careers, Tom is likely to have thrived at school while Patrick did not. Schooling in the Kavanagh household would have been regarded as a distraction from Patrick's farming duties, while scholastic achievement might have been held in better regard across the parish in Ballyrush. In a rural parish teachers could be expected to pass on information regarding the success of former pupils, but Patrick attended Kednaminsha school while Thomas would have enrolled in the more conveniently located school in Inniskeen village. Both families shared an interest in improving their small farms, so Duffy's early training in agriculture would have attracted admiration in Mucker, where anything that might stimulate the clumsy Patrick would have been seized upon!

Duffy and Kavanagh had some similarities. Both came from small farms and made careers beyond farming. They both had long-standing connections with the Rathgar area of Dublin, Thomas settling there, while the family of Patrick's wife lived nearby. The two might have met occasionally in pubs around Baggot Bridge, which could have been on Thomas' route home from work. But their real point of interaction would have been their shared interest in Inniskeen and their lack of empathy with its residents! It was said of Duffy that "like Patrick he had a keen insight into the land and its people, fully endorsing Patrick's harsh criticism of their former neighbours."[12] This might have engaged them over an odd evening's drinking in Dublin but was evidently not enough to forge an enduring friendship. Each had aspirations beyond the immediate – Kavanagh wished to be considered an intellectual poet, Duffy a man of sound practical advice. I suspect that Kavanagh may have felt more fulfilled by the end of his life, but not by a wide margin. And the scientist who eschewed the limelight, unlike the poet, received no homecoming burial, just a simple grave in Glasnevin Cemetery.

Notes

1. Extract from "Stony Grey Soil". See Patrick Kavanagh (1972) *Collected Poems*. London: Martin Brian & O'Keeffe, pages 82-83.

2. For information on the district's geology, see the following publications: Geraghty, M. (1997) *Geology of Monaghan-Carlingford: A geological description to accompany the bedrock geology 1:100,000 scale map series, Sheet 8/9*. Dublin: Geological Survey of Ireland; McCabe, M. and Dunlop, P. (2006) *The Last Glacial Termination in Northern Ireland*. Belfast: Geological Survey of Northern Ireland.

3. For more information on W.H. Baily see Herries Davies, G.L. (1995) *North from the Hook.* Dublin: Geological Survey of Ireland.

4. For more on the life of Patrick Kavanagh see Quinn, A. (2001) *Patrick Kavanagh: A biography.* Dublin: Gill & Macmillan.

5. Kavanagh, Patrick (2004) *Collected Poems.* Edited by Antoinette Quinn. London: Allen Lane. I have quoted from the following poems: "Ploughman", pages 6-7; "Shancoduff", page 21; "Stony Grey Soil", pages 38-39. I referred to "Inniskeen Road: July Evening", page 15; "The Great Hunger", pages 63-89; "Lines Written on a Seat on the Grand Canal, Dublin, 'Erected to the Memory of Mrs Dermot O'Brien'", page 227.

6. Quotation is from pages 1-2 of: Kavanagh, Peter (2000) *Patrick Kavanagh (1904-1967): A Life Chronicle.* New York: The Peter Kavanagh Hand Press.

7. See Sheet 35 (1:50,000) of the Discovery Series. Second Edition. Ordnance Survey Ireland.

8. The poems "The Goat of Slieve Donard" (page 5), "Monaghan Hills" (pages 33-34) and "Kednaminsha" (page 78) are included in Kavanagh, Patrick (2001) *The Complete Poems of Patrick Kavanagh, with commentary by Peter Kavanagh.* New York: Kavanagh Hand Press.

9. See "From Monaghan to the Grand Canal". In Kavanagh, Patrick (2003) *A Poet's Country: Selected Prose.* A. Quinn (Ed.) Dublin: The Lilliput Press, pages 272-287.

10. The Duffy residence was House No. 8, Ballyrush townland, Inniskeen parish, Barony of Farney, County Monaghan in the Irish Census returns for 1901 and 1911.

11. For information on Thomas Duffy see Herries Davies, G.L. (1995) *North from the Hook.* Geological Survey of Ireland. Following Duffy's death, a death notice and short article appeared in *The Irish Independent* (on Monday 22 November 1965, page 20 and Tuesday 23 November 1965, page 17, respectively).

12. O'Meara, M. (1978?) *Some reminiscences of a long stint in the Geological Survey of Ireland.* Typescript in the records of the Geological Survey of Ireland.

8

THE TIME OF OUR LIVES
(Offaly)

Time passing, time passing timeless.
I am twenty-nine. Only yesteryear I was fourteen.
– Paul Durcan[1]

The margins of melting ice sheets can be noisy places as large blocks of ice collapse onto the surrounding land. In the case of the Irish midlands less than 20,000 years ago, those ice sheets had impressive cliffs, perhaps exceeding a kilometre in height. Water formed on surface during summer would sink along fissures to the base of the ice sheet. There the flowing water would carve out tunnels that allowed the water to drain away. When the ice ultimately disappeared, the sediment that once choked those tunnels would remain as sinuous esker ridges that run across country and bear no relation to local topography. These ridges would have relieved the bleak appearance of low-lying lakelands. However the increasingly milder climate would have encouraged the growth of bogs and forests, and the migration of animals and plants, soon giving us our now-familiar landscape.

Ice sheets are so crisp and sparkling, it is difficult to imagine the untidiness they leave behind. It is not just the eskers, for there is a jumble of additional glacial tills and moraines of varied nature and thickness. These materials all impeded the re-establishment of the drainage pattern that existed before the ice arrived. So there were many poorly drained and flooded areas, and they became occupied by extensive lakes and meandering rivers. The extent of flooding was exaggerated at that time because the Earth's surface, which had been depressed by the huge weight of ice sheets, had not yet rebounded. Those lakelands are no longer obvious for the simple reason that they have been extensively colonised by raised bogs.

However the evidence for the former existence of lakes is compelling and widespread. Firstly, turf-cutters will confirm that clay and silt deposits are commonly found beneath the bog. These pale, laminated sediments consist of alternating silt and clay layers, and with each pair reflecting one year's melting. The silt layer would form during active melting while the finer clay would settle out slowly during the winter months. The sequences of these seasonally-controlled, or varved, sediments do record subtle variations in melting and sedimentation over time and can be used (in a manner analogous to tree rings) to construct a detailed chronology of the receding ice sheets.[7] The second line of evidence can be found in the shape of mushroom stones that occur outside of current lakes. These are limestone boulders whose slender lower portions have been sculpted by shallow lake water over the past 10 to 15 thousand years. The rainwater contribution to lakes consists of dilute carbonic acid, which dissolves limestone, so that the lower portions of partially submerged stones were preferentially eroded below the water line. The most perfect examples, closely resembling edible mushrooms in shape, may occur on the west shore of Lough Ree in Roscommon, but Offaly has the greatest concentration, with 50 per cent of Ireland's mushroom stones.[2]

An extensive cluster of eskers, collectively known as Esker Riada, marks the ancient road linking the bays of Galway and Dublin. Those ridges carried travellers safely across many treacherous bogs and where they were absent, then wooden trackways, or toghers, were built across boggy stretches. The route crossed the River Shannon at the monastery of Clonmacnoise, County Offaly, which made it Ireland's busiest cross-roads. From the neighbourhood of Esker Riada at Tyrrellspass, it is just possible to observe in the distance the volcanic edifice of Croghan Hill (234 metres), a geological feature that is uniquely part of County Offaly. From a distance, the hill has a craggy outline but, up close, this is not matched by any spectacular rock faces, just some scattered volcanic exposures. Its prominence deflected advancing ice sheets so that they streamed around it. Croghan village itself is welcoming and well worth exploring for its unique ecological and cultural heritage.[3]

Croghan Hill represents the roots of an ancient volcano which built up on the Carboniferous seafloor 340 million years ago. At that time, the volcano was probably a lot more intimidating in scale than suggested by the size of the modern hill. Croghan, along with the rest of Ireland, lay just south of the Equator and lime deposits were building up on the warm and fertile seafloor. Its volcano was but one of a series at that time, and not the largest either. There were greater developments in Limerick and various parts of Great Britain. But this was still a formidable event: ashes and lavas accumulated to a thickness of more than 100 metres at Croghan itself and of course they covered an area considerably larger than the hill itself. Initial outpourings on the seafloor led to the formation of a volcanic cone that soon stood proud of seawater. Accordingly the later lavas accumulated on dry land and have columnar jointing (yes, just like Giant's Causeway, if not as spectacular). The eruptions were of two contrasting types. The earliest and the latest were dominated by gentle outpourings of dark-coloured basalt lava. But the intervening eruptions were more explosive and spewed out dense clouds of ash and pumice, which would have covered an extensive surrounding area.

One still-active volcano that may have had comparable eruptions is Vesuvius, overlooking the Bay of Naples. In fact, that pumice on Croghan's hillside might have seemed familiar to Naples residents back in 79AD, as they stared in disbelief at the destruction of their neighbouring towns of Pompeii and Herculaneum. This was an eruption on a greater scale than Croghan has ever witnessed. For that was the year when Vesuvius violently discharged huge quantities of ash and pumice into the atmosphere. Neapolitans would have watched awestruck as the towering ash cloud collapsed on successive occasions sending hot toxic surges of gas and ash towards the doomed towns. Those clouds, called pyroclastic ash flows, moved at an alarming 150 kilometres per hour and contained still-molten particles and pumice. So buildings were almost instantly buried beneath a thick deposit of ash and probably 2,000 residents died of burns or asphyxiation.

What is fascinating about those two tragic Italian towns, Pompeii and Herculaneum, even more than the scale of the disaster, is the fact that since the mid-eighteenth century they have been gradually excavated to reveal the secrets of their vanished past. We can now stroll around the streets and buildings of Pompeii, for example, and learn about life for residents as it was almost two millennia ago – their jobs, how they dressed, where they lived and what they ate.

My uncle Ben, a much-travelled man, was an entertaining host and after dinner he was an enthusiastic purveyor of tales from exotic places like Takoradi and Benghazi. He witnessed many unusual sights, not least the 1944 eruption of Vesuvius, which fortunately was less catastrophic than the 79AD event. His remarkable record of that event was contained in a small glass jar filled with grey layers of Vesuvian sand and ash. Ash had rained down persistently for several days and, having collected some each day, his jar contained a microcosm of the entire eruption and its progress. The ash originated as gas-rich and viscous magma that choked the neck of the volcanic vent until the build-up of pressure caused it to explode. The magma was pulverised into ash in the process, and it was that ash that found its way into my uncle's slender bottle.

That same uncle of mine had a didactic fondness for quoting Charles Dickens (1812–1870) and – with little prompting – he could recite with relish the opening and closing lines of *A Tale of Two Cities.* Sometimes the recitation would come hot on the heels of the flourishing of his precious ash! I wonder if he realised that his hero, Dickens, had an even closer acquaintance with Vesuvius than he himself had. That inimitable story-teller actually ascended Vesuvius by night in 1846, passing lanes and vineyards to a lava field where it seemed "the earth had been ploughed up by burning thunderbolts". Leading a party of interested followers, he reached an exhausted crater issuing hot, sulphurous smoke. Great sheets of fire streamed from the nearby active crater, accompanied by black smoke and showers of red-hot stones and cinders. They stumbled through confusing noise and smoke avoiding crevices as best they could and checking all their number were present still. A few, led by Dickens, climbed to the brim of the flaming crater, conscious of their perilous situation and were overawed by the flashing fire, showers of red-hot ashes and choking smoke and sulphur. Truly a "Hell of boiling fire"! Then they speedily retreated downwards to safety, with blackened skin and scorched clothes.[4]

Long before its crater lit up the night sky here, Offaly had had a fascinating history. The older siltstones which now form the core of Slieve Bloom mountains, and the younger limestones that are spread much more widely over the rest of the county, both accumulated on ancient seafloors over an extended time period. This really is an extended history covering hundreds of millions of years. And yet, as we have seen, its most enchanting phase may have been the recent evolution of lakelands which gave rise in turn to bogland. It is easy to summarise Offaly's geological history in qualitative terms, but any mention of actual ages will inevitably draw us into considering how Earth regulates its calendar.

Some Eastern religions hold that individuals experience time cyclically, with rebirth a possibility, whereas those originating in the Middle East favour a one-way progression moderated by divine interventions. Older readers may be more conscious of the linear progression of irreversible changes in their own lives while young people are liable to be still fascinated by their observations of cyclical environmental changes, such as each year's seasonal changes. Yes, there seem to be two fundamental views, time progresses in either a linear or cyclical fashion. The varved sediments of Offaly's lakebeds offer an excellent example of a cyclical process. When I think of linear time, I am reminded of that painting by G. V. Du Noyer (1817–1869) of the rock cliff behind Waterford railway station. Russet sandstone beds rest upon older mudstones which were deformed into slates and then eroded before a single sand grain accumulated on top of them. There is no suggestion of cyclical processes here, in fact the time gap between mud and sand deposition is probably 35 million years![5]

Two Irishmen are credited with valiant, if ultimately ill-fated, excursions into the realms of geological time. The first was Archbishop James Ussher (1581–1656), a Dublin man of considerable biblical scholarship but now much-maligned because of his 4004BC date for the origin of the Earth.

Ussher's range of knowledge was a marvel in the eyes of his contemporaries and must still arouse admiration because of its depth and diversity. He had an insatiable thirst for knowledge and he amassed such resources of recondite information that many scholars sought his opinion on a great variety of historical and theological problems.

Thus asserted Ussher's 1967 biographer, who further stated that Ussher's well-deserved reputation had, unusually, been validated with the passage of time.[6] But that was before his work was drawn into the highly emotive controversy between Creationists and Evolutionists. While Ussher's work has been properly revised over the past century and more on the basis of compelling scientific evidence, its significance must be fairly appreciated in the context of his time. He was, after all, among the first to actually question the longevity of our planet and to provide a reasoned answer.

The second Irishman was John Joly (1857–1933),[7] who was raised a short distance south of Esker Riada, near Edenderry. He held the Chair of Geology and Mineralogy at Trinity College Dublin for an extended period of 36 years and was an important figure in twentieth century Irish science. He proposed that our planet was about 100 million years old, based on the sodium content of the oceans and assumptions concerning its rate of accumulation. This was much longer than the age of 20-40 million years determined by Lord Kelvin, based on the Earth cooling from an initially molten state. But both estimates became redundant with the discovery of radioactivity. It was Joly who realised it could be applied to dating rock, but when he, along with Lord Rutherford, applied it to finding out the age of the Leinster Granite he derived an age that startled him: 400 million years old – much older than his conception of the age of the Earth itself! Nevertheless it has since been confirmed as a very accurate estimate. When Joly additionally found that the Earth's age might exceed a billion years, he began to question the usefulness of radioactivity. Scientists are obliged to be evidence-led and sadly this aspect of Joly's geological research into radioactivity represents a lapse on his part. When his life-long friend, Henry Dixon, came to write Joly's obituary, he prudently drew a veil over this part of his friend's work.[8] The application of radioactive techniques would eventually determine an age for the Earth of 4.5 billion years, a long way from earlier estimates. However Joly would go on to prove his substantial scientific credentials on several fronts, as for example when he challenged Kelvin's Earth model. Joly argued that in fact the Earth was not cooling down but was heating up due to the energy released through the radioactive decay of its interior minerals. He then went on to propose an elegant and coherent model of how the Earth's crust evolved.

This outstanding scientist behaved more in character when he was briefly diverted by some fascinating trace fossils he collected in the rocks of Bray Head, County Wicklow. Trace fossils are the products of animal activity rather than the fossilised remains of the creatures themselves. *Oldhamia radiata* occurs as thumb-print size impressions on bedding surfaces, composed of discontinuous thread-like ridges radiating from a common centre. They are considered to be the result of a worm-like animal grazing immediately beneath the seafloor. Joly observed frost patterns in frozen mud that reminded him of *Oldhamia* and so he ascribed these trace fossils to frost action. However he then found evidence which invalidated this view and in true scientific spirit he immediately retracted. That did not stop him from celebrating the trace fossil in a rather sad sonnet with the explicit if uninviting title of "Oldhamia".[9] It describes dismal weather on Bray Head and his writing is mournfully in sympathy with it: the sea is in agony, he feels lonesome sorrow. He anticipates what may be a bleak future for humankind, but then refers sarcastically to "promise of the ages!" Comparing the human condition with *Oldhamia*'s wonderful complexity, Joly humbly sees us simply replacing, rather than triumphantly superseding, those long-extinct worms.

It seems that County Offaly has but lightly influenced the annals of Irish literature. In fact we must retrace our footsteps westwards across the county from Joly's Edenderry to the Shannonside town of Banagher to encounter some further evidence of its existence. Banagher is where Anthony Trollope (1815–1882) enjoyed a lengthy sojourn as a Post Office worker. Evidently a diligent and insightful employee, he would go on to occupy a senior position in the British headquarters of this still-fledgling organisation before devoting himself to writing novels. One of his novels, *The Kellys and the O'Kellys*, although composed during his residence at

Banagher, betrays little evidence of Trollope's relationship with the landscape and environment of that district – other than what we can indirectly glean through his treatment of the novel's characters.[10] However he did arrive here in the early 1840s, so his sympathetic thoughts naturally focused on the famine-stricken lives of the ordinary folks he encountered. Yes, Trollope's Irish landscapes were sad, for people do indeed make landscape.

Notes

1. From "Supper Time" on pages 109-111 of Paul Durcan (1991) *Crazy about Women*. Dublin: The National Gallery of Ireland.

2. Dunne, Louise and Feehan, John (2003) *Ireland's Mushroom Stones: Relics of a Vanished Lakeland*. Dublin: Environmental Resource Management, University College Dublin.

3. Feehan, John (2011) *Croghan, County Offaly, Ireland: Cruachán Éile in Uibh Fhailí*. Offaly County Council.

4. My own copy is Dickens, Charles (undated) *Hard Times and Pictures from Italy*. London: Chapman and Hall. Quotations are from pages 263-265.

5. The painting is reproduced as Figure 56 of Anon. (1995) *George Victor Du Noyer (1817-1869)*. Dublin: The National Gallery of Ireland.

6. Knox, R.B. (1967) *James Ussher, Archbishop of Armagh*. Cardiff: University of Wales Press. The quotation is from page 98.

7. Wyse Jackson, P.N. (2001) "John Joly (1857-1933) and his determination of the age of the Earth". In Lewis, C.L.E. and Knell, S.J. (Eds.) *The Age of the Earth: From 4004BC to AD2012*. Geological Society, London, Special Publication No.190, pages 107-119.

8. Dixon, H.H. (rev. Falconer, I.) (2004) John Joly (1857-1933). In Matthew, H.C.G. and Harrison, B. (Eds.) *Oxford Dictionary of National Biography*. Oxford: Oxford University Press, volume 30, pages 428-430.

9. Patrick N. Wyse Jackson (2011) "History of Ichnology: John Joly (1857-1933) on *Oldhamia*: Poetic and Scientific Observations". *Ichnos* volume 18, pages 209-212.

10. Trollope, Anthony (1859) *The Kellys and the O'Kellys*. London: Chapman and Hall.

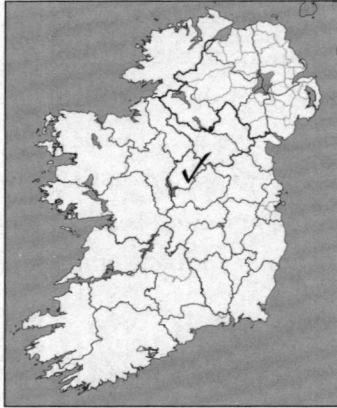

9

Disregarded Beauty?
(Longford)

We shall not cease from exploration
And the end of all our exploring
Will be to arrive where we started
And know the place for the first time.
    – T. S. Eliot[1]

Don't rely on visitors to promote the virtues of your home place, especially if there is any risk that they might be indifferent! Longford has certainly suffered from such dispassion over the years. Samuel Lewis stated that it had little to attract the eye or excite the imagination, being mainly flat and boggy, with some bleak and sterile mountains.[2] Precisely one century later the naturalist, R. L. Praeger, was hardly more positive, asserting that there was nothing to detain the naturalist or antiquary there, it being mostly undulating agricultural land. However Lough Gowna in the north-east was attractive, he said, while in the southwest Longford fronted the Shannon, including the northern part of Lough Ree.[3] This ambivalence has persisted to the present time and has not been concerned exclusively with its landscape![4] But even Praeger has praise for the Shannon, so let's see if Longford can glory in its worthwhile environment. Forming Longford's western border, this majestic river courses through the centre of Ireland and its watershed actually covers 20 per cent of the island of Ireland.

It was the Atlantic, while still in its own infancy, that gave birth to the Shannon. The North American and European continents became separate entities about 60 million years ago and moved slowly apart according as upwelling lava formed the Atlantic's ocean floor. This was a rough and stressful process, with central Ireland's surface tilting southwards, and it was on this sloping surface that Shannon's waters first flowed.[5] Continued seismic activity caused this surface to sag between Lough Ree and Lough Derg, where the river flow is sluggish and the riverside meadows, or callows, are subject to regular winter flooding. Talk of extensive drainage works has long since given way to marvel at the diversity of wildlife in this unique habitat. The symbol of this change has been the corncrake, which returns from Africa each year to breed here, and farmers have modified their hay-making practices to ensure the future of this shy bird is no longer endangered.

There is more evidence further downstream that seismic activity continued to guide the evolution of the Shannon basin. At Meelick, just north of Lough Derg, and again at Castleconnell, between Killaloe and Limerick city, the river cuts through ridges of limestone bedrock where it might have chosen to deflect around these obstacles. But these limestone ridges did not exist when first the river took this course and have since been gradually uplifted by seismic activity while river erosion of bedrock kept pace with it. As a result at Castleconnell the river traverses a limestone gorge with 10 metre-high walls on either side.

Prior to the Ice Age, the Shannon watershed thrived for millions of years in a landscape dominated by karstic limestone. Its bedrock surface, exposed to rainwater, would have been gradually dissolved and subtly sculpted in a manner familiar to Burren visitors – rivers disappearing underground through sink holes and limestone surfaces intensively scored by deep fractures. Those cigar-shaped hills and fragile boulder stacks of other karst districts, such as Vietnam and China, might also have been present here, so parts of Longford might have had the kind of exotic environment that would have enthralled even Lewis and Praeger!

Then ice sheets ploughed their way across Ireland's limestone midlands, exerting considerable influence on its scenery, abrading its peculiarly irregular landscape and burying much of its karstic surfaces beneath glacial deposits. Longford and neighbouring counties would never be the same again. Glacial processes dumped so much material in places that it caused even the majestic Shannon to change course. For one thing, the river now had to make its way through an obstacle course of drumlins along the 20 kilometre stretch between Carrick-on-Shannon and Rooskey. Elsewhere, pre-glacial flow paths became blocked, such as south of Lough Allen, where a gravel ridge was deposited by waters flowing off ice sheets.

Also further downstream before the Ice Age, the Shannon left Lough Derg and then deflected around Slieve Arragh, following the low-lying limestone corridor of the Kilmastulla valley. Now, of course, the river cuts straight through the area of older rocks between Slieve Arragh and Slieve Bernagh. The most recent modification in Shannon's course occurred between Lough Derg and Limerick when the major Ardnacrusha hydroelectric power station was commissioned in 1929. A weir and headrace diverts some of the river's flow in a sweeping arc, keeping to low ground, and gaining an elevation of 30 metres before arriving back at the river in a tumultuous tumble of water that drives the station's turbines.

Its job done, the water is released back into a short tailrace that returns it to the Shannon's course.

The Shannon possesses three major lakes. Lough Allen, with its surrounding Connaught Coalfield, may be the most useful while many would describe Lough Derg as most scenic, but for me Lough Ree wins the title of having the most interesting history. Following the melting of the ice sheets, it doubled its surface area and water levels rose by as much as three metres in a region of impeded drainage. This environment in turn gave rise to extensive peatlands according as the milder climate stimulated rich plant growth. Once more we see a dramatic evolution in the landscape around County Longford, in a history that was far from boring.

Its writers form another of Longford's treasures, not least Padraic Colum (1881–1972). Having moved with his family at age 15 from Aghnacliff, County Longford, to south County Dublin, he subsequently emigrated along with his wife, Mary, to the United States where he pursued a writing and academic career. His poetic reputation rests on his early output, which Colum described as dramatic lyrics based around characters and situations he encountered in the Irish countryside.[6] They may sometimes border on the sentimental, but verses such as "She Moved through the Fair", "Drover" and "Old Woman of the Roads" remain among Ireland's favourites, performed by many who are no longer sure of their composer's identity.

Poet of the countryside he may be, but Padraic disdains any deep involvement with his landscape. He uses place names sparingly and favours localities that allow the reader no intimacy with his own homeplace. Colum is more comfortable using county names or localities of historical, mythological and classical significance. Those place names around Aghnacliff that he does use tend to occur on the County Cavan side of Lough Gowna, in farmland that is somewhat better than that upon which he himself was raised. Some of the most interesting place names cannot be located with any certainty – and neither Google nor the Townland Index provide enlightenment: Cruckmaelinn appears in three separate poems, one of which employs Carricknabauna eight times. Other catchy, almost familiar, place names, such as the Crome hills or the Brenny plain, seem to have no basis in Colum's actual landscape. A comparison is sometimes made with the poetry of Patrick Kavanagh, but he took an evident pride in revealing his familial surroundings and he relished the sound of their names. In contrast, Colum makes little explicit effort to tie his verses to specific localities. This may suit his more sentimental style, lending his poetry an air of mystery and uncertainty, and creating a more universal experience that a wide spectrum of readers may identify with.[7]

Aghnacliff lies in the midst of hilly land of indifferent quality, but with a graceful aspect due to a preponderance of wooded fences. You won't come upon this place by chance, you must seek it out using the tangled web of narrow roads that separates the River Shannon from Lough Gowna. Aghnacliff itself is not exceptional, a small village that saw much housing development during the Celtic Tiger era. Having reached here, do explore a bit further, perhaps the irregular, jigsaw-like shoreline of Lough Gowna or the hummocky ground that rises gradually to culminate in Corn Hill (278 metres), Longford's highest point. The latter is part of Lewis' "bleak and sterile mountains". But it would be hard to deny that Aghnacliff's remote farmland could cast a certain gloom that might overshadow Colum's poetic approach to his countryside.

We get an insight into Colum's relationship with landscape through the personalities and incidents he describes. The boglands scholar cannot expect exciting conversation to lift his depressed lifestyle, whereas comfortable city dwellers seemed unreasonably provided with more than adequate physical and intellectual comforts ("The Poor Scholar").[6] "Old Woman of the Roads" suffers the same dreary life where sunshine and comfort rarely intrude on its poverty-stricken monotony. The "Drover" fares no better, encountering merely winding roads through wet hills and bogs. However he is a man of the world who manages to retain his sanity by thinking of ships and Spanish princesses! The haunting melody of Colum's most popular lyric, "She Moved through the Fair", seems to camouflage its sombre story of a bride's tragic death. Although landscape is not at its heart, this poem certainly evokes the atmosphere of the low-lying Shannon region in lines such as:

Then she went her way homeward with one star awake,
As the swan in the evening moves over the lake.

The poem "Mary Catherine Maguire Colum" was written by Padraic as a dedication to his wife and in it he contemplates the water source for a particular well:

Through what passages
Beneath? From what high tors
Where forests are?

While this might seem to reflect the author's interest in Longford's diversified bedrock geology, in practice I realise it really expresses his intense desire for Mary's presence and wisdom. A prudent poet, for his wife was still alive!

Perhaps I am unwittingly adding to Longford's woes by recounting Colum's litany of bleak hills, desolate countryside, uninviting nutrition and wet, windy weather. In fairness, he does not ignore rivers and lakes and bogs and wells, but he treats them as no more than atmospheric backdrops to the rural experience of his featured characters. Colum never seems to recall the sort of joyful memories of his youthful landscape that we will explore through Oliver Goldsmith's verse in the next chapter. But maybe he was simply a prisoner of his time, when draining the Shannon's callows and exhausting its peat resources were the political priorities. It would be some decades before the value of re-flooding callows and peatland, each now much cherished, would be acknowledged and acted upon. Nevertheless, I would gently chide Colum for overlooking the sweep of his local forest and farmland, not to mention the peace of Corn Hill's summit and the magic of Lough Gowna.

But I admit honestly that there is nothing unique about the rocks of Aghnacliff area, which are about 460 million years old. A similar set of rocks is widespread not only in the Longford–Down region but also throughout the Southern Uplands of Scotland. Between Corn Hill and Lough Gowna they comprise greywackes, mudstones and volcanic rocks which formed on the floor of the Iapetus Ocean, the volcanic rock being ocean crust itself. The black mudstone would have accumulated very slowly from the gentle rain of pelagic mud particles settling out on the ocean floor and this is the rock most likely to preserve fossils, as at Magoney Bridge in County Monaghan. But the dominant rock type, greywacke, occurs in beds which individually were deposited very quickly, perhaps within hours, although there might be a time lapse of decades or centuries between each. These were deposited from bottom-hugging turbidity currents which originated in shallow waters, perhaps at quite a distance. Their mineral composition can tell us much about the source of sediment, even its climate and environment. So if you ascend Corn Hill or stroll around Lough Gowna, do look at the local greywacke outcrops and ponder how such an apparently straightforward rock could carry secrets that can unlock some awe-inspiring complexity and give us real insight into the history of our planet.[8]

Aghnacliff is less than 20 kilometres north of Edgeworthstown, the home of the Edgeworth landowning family. Richard Lovell Edgeworth (1744–1817),[9] who produced 21 children from his four marriages, was an accomplished engineer who devised improved systems of road construction, experimented with new forms of carriages and proposed a telegraphy system between major Irish cities. He is probably best known today for his educational writings. He surveyed the bogs of County Longford along with his son on behalf of the Irish Bog Commissioners, the aim being to increase turf supply through peatland drainage and at the same time increase the available crop-producing land. In this task, Edgeworth worked alongside the young Richard Griffith (1784–1878), who was undertaking his first major assignment in what would be a long and distinguished career.

Richard Edgeworth's daughter became more celebrated than himself in time. She was the novelist Maria Edgeworth (1768–1849), author of such successful works as *Castle Rackrent* and *Ormond*. The latter may now be dated, but it includes the following interesting exchange:

'I hear all the silver mines in Ireland turn out to be lead.'

'I wish they did, for then we could turn all our lead into gold. These silver mines certainly did not pay.'[10]

In fact, Maria was no doubt relaying accurately a dinner table conversation on the emerging mining industry in Ireland at that time. Actually silver was produced from lead mines as a by-product of the lead smelting process. But the lead-into-gold transition remains but an alchemist's dream!

When completing his survey of Longford's bogs I wonder did Richard even momentarily envisage the fascinating discoveries that would one day be made at Corlea Bog, near Lanesborough peat-fired power station? These had nothing to do with fuel utilisation! The bog-causeway, or togher, exposed here is one of the most imposing prehistoric monuments in Ireland. Two sections each of 1km length, linked by an island of dry land, were constructed from hundreds of large oak trees laid on birch brushwood. This causeway was exceptional for its time and must have connected centres of great importance. And we actually know that those oak trees were felled precisely in the year of 148BC, thanks to the distinctive patterns of tree rings that these oaks display. A reference database extending back several thousand years has now been established internationally, allowing us to put a precise date on many events.[12]

How have we done? We have discovered that Longford's landscape is really under-appreciated, for the stories concerned with its development are several and fascinating. They involved an extensive precursor ocean to the Atlantic which closed relentlessly, causing a northerly continent to collide firstly with a chain of volcanic islands and then with another southern continent. The resulting mountain chain was immediately subjected to sustained erosion so that eventually Longford district was inundated by seas. These were distinctly tropical and accumulated an extensive cover of limestone. The opening of the Atlantic Ocean led to the formation of the gently sloping and karstified landscape on which the River Shannon would flow. This river basin would have a major impact on how the region's environment subsequently evolved, how ice sheets developed and then decayed to be replaced by the widespread growth of peatland. This is indeed an awesome landscape which can be expected to influence writers in many different ways. Padraic Colum's interest lay in the atmosphere it created for his Longford characters and his enduring stories of their lives and personalities certainly lifted the spirits of his many readers.

Notes

1. Eliot, T. S. (1944) *Four Quartets*. London: Faber and Faber. Quotation is from "Little Gidding", section V, page 43.

2. Lewis, S. (1837, republished 1995) *A Topographical Dictionary of Ireland*. Baltimore, Maryland: Clearfield Company, volume 2.

3. Praeger, R. L. (1937) *The Way that I Went: An Irishman in Ireland*. Dublin: Hodges, Figgis & Co. and London: Methuen & Co. (Reprinted in 1997. Cork: The Collins Press).

4. See Sheridan, Kathy (2010) My County Longford. In Morris, M. and O'Ferrall, F. (Eds.) *Longford: History and Society*. Dublin: Geography Publications, pages 1-11.

5. The geological development of the River Shannon is treated on pages 198-222 of Mitchell, F. (1990) *The Way that I Followed: A Naturalist's Journey around Ireland*. Dublin: Country House.

6. Colum, P. (1981) *The Poet's Circuits: Collected Poems of Ireland*. Centenary edition with a Preface by Benedict Kiely. Mountrath, Ireland: The Dolmen Press. I have quoted from the following poems: "Mary Catherine Maguire Colum" (page xiii) and "She Moved through the fair" (page 97). I have referred to the following poems: "Poor Scholar" (page 27), "Drover" (pages 41-42) and "Old Woman of the Roads" (page 110).

7. The life and work of Colum is discussed in Campion, E. J. (2012) "Padraic Colum". In McReisman, R. (Ed.). *Critical Survey of Poetry: Irish Poets*. Ipswich, Mass: Salem Press, pages 59-65.

8. Morris, J. H., Somerville, I. D. and MacDermot, C. V. (2003) *Geology of Longford-Roscommon*. Geological Survey of Ireland.

9. Horner, A. (2010) "The contribution of Richard Lovell Edgeworth to the reports and maps of the Bogs Commissioners of 1809-14". In Morris, M. and O'Ferrall, F. (Eds.) *Longford: History and Society*. Dublin: Geography Publications, pages 347-378.

10. Hayden, Mary (1900) "Maria Edgeworth". *Journal of the National Literary Society of Ireland*. Volume 1, part 1, pages 15-42.

11. See pages 242-244 of: Mitchell, F. and Ryan, M. (2007) *Reading the Irish Landscape*. Dublin: Town House.

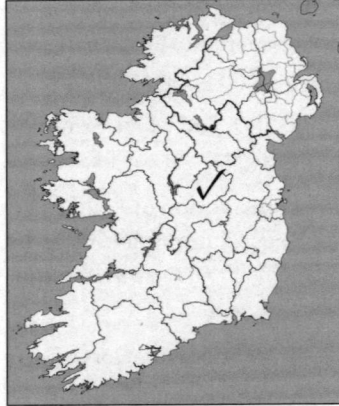

10

HISTORIAN OF THE PENSIVE PLAIN

(Westmeath)

And some run up hill and down dale
Knapping the chunky stones to pieces with hammers,
Like sae many road makers run daft.
They say it is to see how the world was made.
– Sir Walter Scott.[1]

The London literary scene of the late eighteenth century used to fascinate me. Nothing would have pleased me more than to eavesdrop on the conversation in one of the more fashionable coffee houses of that time. I am sure I would have been impressed by Samuel Johnson's (1709–1784) learned contributions, how-ever pedantic, and would probably have been amused by James Boswell's (1740–1795) sycophantic recording of them. Edmund

Burke (1729–1797) might have held my attention with his reasoned discourse on the great events of the day while Joshua Reynolds (1723–1792) might have been an entertaining occasional visitor. But equally I might have felt sorry for another member of that assembly, Oliver Goldsmith (1728–1774), a man not renowned for his conversational fluency or capability. Burke might not have been surprised to learn that one day his own statue would be one of only two to grace the exterior of his alma mater, Trinity College Dublin, but I guess he might have raised his eyebrows in perplexion on hearing that his College Green companion would be none other than Oliver! But then the shrewd Johnson would describe Oliver as a writer "... who left scarcely any style of writing untouched and touched nothing that he did not adorn". These words became Goldsmith's epithet on plaques in both Westminster Abbey and his supposed place of burial at Temple Church in London's legal district. A commemorative tablet at the latter states that he was born at Pallas, County Longford, and was the author of *The Deserted Village*, *The Vicar of Wakefield* and *She Stoops to Conquer*.

The Deserted Village, 432 lines in rhyming couplets, was published in May 1770 and was an instant success. Even his coffee house circle of friends, at times both patronising and dismissive, came to express great admiration for the work. When first I read excerpts of this poem, I accepted them as the nostalgic reflections of an older poet on the pastoral idyll of his own youth. We know that on summer evenings the young Goldsmith was occupied:

> ... taking solitary walks among the rocks and wooded islands of the Inny, strolling up its banks to fish or play the flute, otter-hunting by the course of the Shannon, learning French from the Irish priests, or winning a prize for throwing the sledge-hammer at the fair of Ballymahon.[2]

He may have regretted the passing of a simpler lifestyle but in reality, I felt, he was just mourning the ebbing of his own life. I was very wrong. This is nothing less than a commentary on the widespread environmental damage caused to the English countryside by the dispersal of poor tenant farmers to make way for mansions and parkland for the wealthy. However these verses also warmly echo the poet's happy memories of the Irish landscape where he was raised, specifically the neighbourhood of Lissoy in County Westmeath, just a short distance from his birthplace. He is quoted as saying in 1757:

> If I climb Hampstead-hill, than where Nature never exhibited a more magnificent prospect, I confess it fine; but then I had rather be placed on the little mount before Lissoy gate, and there take in, for me, the most pleasing horizon in nature.[3]

Goldsmith country lies on the eastern shores of Lough Ree, where an intricate pattern of inlets and islands creates an exhilarating patchwork of colours. Grey lake waters are fringed by sandy-coloured reeds, while pastures and broad-leaved woods, themselves sharing many shades of green, vie with each other to touch the water's edge. If only the sun would shine! I had hoped to inspect Lissoy under the warm glow of an auburn sun, but that was not to be. Dr Strean, a local Church of Ireland clergyman, in 1807 identified Lissoy as the inspiration for Auburn. It is located in rolling pastures, although occasional fields contain either outcrop or boulders of the widespread limestone bedrock. Lissoy is simply a townland without village but with a parsonage that Goldsmith knew well – he grew up there. His "little mount" still exists in a nearby pasture, a hill feature that is truly Hampstead-like in its smooth and gentle curves, if not in dimensions!

So this poem may not be about Ireland, but its descriptions and atmosphere have been strongly influenced by the poet's memory of its landscape. The verses exude the glowing warmth of late summer. Lissoy is Auburn and we can imagine its landscape:

Sweet Auburn, loveliest village of the plain,
Where health and plenty cheered the labouring swain,
Where smiling spring its earliest visit paid,
And parting summer's lingering blooms delayed.[4]

Set in fertile farmland with a never-failing river, the village had provided full employment and sound nourishment to a thriving community that enjoyed life to the full, with a satisfying emphasis on evening sports and pastimes. But now the village was destroyed, the land neglected and its peasants have mainly emigrated. He traces the ruins of both the parson's and the teacher's homes, bringing back fond (and much recited) descriptions of both men – the kindly generous pastor, the stern and learned teacher – the characters in sympathy with the warmth of an earlier Auburn! The author himself could no longer hope to retire here among friends.

The poet is scathing about the wealthy who have occupied the land. Having just sufficient for our needs is a blessing, he says, whereas wealth is not. Such a philosophy of frugality was not always evident in Goldsmith's own lifestyle! At its foundation is a generational issue: the fertile legacy of an earlier generation has not been handed on to the next one. Of course, not all agreed with this interpretation and, for example, Lord Macaulay (1800–1859) considered the poem an incongruous mix, where the happy, idyllic past was British while the terrible and decayed present was Irish.[5] But for me, Goldsmith's words argue that we should live in a manner that does not prejudice the ability of future generations to fulfil their own ambitions. In our generation we refer to this as sustainability – Oliver would not have been familiar with this term but he surely understood its deeper meaning and we shall return to it shortly.

The poem is largely devoid of geographical place names, just a single reference to England in addition to Auburn. But then in the closing stages, when he is referring to the dispersal of Auburn peasants as emigrants, he does make mention of three other foreign locations. Goldsmith is emphasising that those displaced and saddened individuals would have to endure unknown terrors and unfavourable climates. So very different from the familiar grassy Auburn landscape of cooling brook and breezy covert!

The first overseas locality is Torno, on the shores of Lake Como, and indeed its grey karstic limestone might remind an alert traveller of Westmeath. The geologically younger Torno limestone experienced a more dramatic history than did its Westmeath cousin, becoming entangled in the collision of the European and African tectonic plates which led to the uplift of the Alps. Goldsmith may have lacked such insights but I suspect that Lake Como was well known to him. In the late 1760s, young James Boswell had recently returned from the Grand Tour and, given Goldsmith's own Italian travels a decade earlier, the pair must have shared many interesting reminiscences. There is no evidence that either visited Torno, although its Villa Pliniana was sufficiently celebrated to have been widely known to readers.[6]

I am not sure we can say the same of Pambamarca. It is an eroded and extinct volcano, much higher (3,900 metres), younger and grander than Westmeath's nearest volcanic neighbour, Croghan Hill. Nowadays, being less than two hours by car from Ecuador's capital, Quito, tourists visit it for its symbolism as a centre of native resistance firstly against Inca and then Spanish invasion. It seems that some of those tourists had already begun visiting in the 1760s and this evidently brought it to Goldsmith's attention.

The Altama is identified by commentators as the Altamaha River, a major river of the American state of Georgia. Formed by the confluence of the Ocmulgee and Oconee Rivers, which both rise close to the Blue Ridge Mountains, its watershed drains 25 per cent of the state. With its subtropical climate and fertile soil, Georgia was favourable for agriculture in the eighteenth century, cotton being its major crop. Unlike the other two locations, Georgia was attracting immigrants at that time, almost exclusively Protestants and potentially including many of Goldsmith's Auburn peasants. So this was a potential destination for his displaced tenants.

Although some have been dismissive of Goldsmith's knowledge of nature, he did have good powers of observation, probably founded on his memories of the Irish Midlands. Goldsmith had a genuine interest in nature, stating that the naturalist "in every plant, in every insect, and every pebble, finds something to entertain his curiosity and excite his speculation".[7] We know that his book shelf contained a rigorous textbook on minerals and fossils.[8] Furthermore, in *The Good Natur'd Man* there is reference to Lisbon's catastrophic earthquake in 1755 and London's seismic shocks some five years earlier. The tedious Mr Croaker contended that this earthquake, having affected other places, was already heading back towards London.[9] It is clear that Goldsmith did not shirk geological topics whenever they were relevant.

There is a depressed band of countryside trending north-south across the central part of Westmeath, perhaps reflecting crustal subsidence associated with the opening of the Atlantic Ocean, and it hosts four delightful lakes. These lakes, shaped by limestone bedrock, define for many people the character of Westmeath and each has its own charms – but only Lough Derravarragh has a great legend. The Children of Lir, victims of a spiteful stepmother, spent 300 unhappy years as swans on this lake. Eventually, with the arrival of Christianity they were restored to an aged human form before they died. But alas no swans were evident during my visit – just a lonely water hen exploring the lake's margin.

Lough Derravarragh limestone was deposited on a Carboniferous seafloor that was far from uniform. While shallow water prevailed over many parts of Ireland, others had deep waters and are termed basins. The Dublin Basin extended westwards from the east coast to embrace Lough Derravarragh and the limestone exposed around the lake is equivalent to the Calp Limestone used in older Dublin buildings. Recurring and strong earthquakes along the many faults of this basin led to the displacement by turbidity currents of large volumes of sediment from shallow water areas. This sediment was re-deposited as thick sequences of limestone and shale. Many limestone beds are graded, meaning that their tops are finer grained than their bases, and this betrays their origin from turbidity currents. A couple of minor volcanic vents were active soon after the limestone formed in the district between the lakes and Goldsmith country. They have an unusual importance in that they brought up rock fragments from the lower crust, perhaps from 30 kilometres or deeper below surface and these fragments, now strongly metamorphosed, have yielded a great deal of information about the nature of the crust beneath Ireland.

Sustainability is as relevant to the lives of present-day Westmeath residents as it was to those of Goldsmith's day. Enduring communities, the basis for sustainability, have always flourished around reliable water sources. The graceful aquaducts constructed during the Roman Empire, long fallen into disuse, are but the symbols for a water supply and disposal system that was both comprehensive and sophisticated. Progress in water management since then has hardly been relentlessly progressive. As recently as the nineteenth century, Dubliners received their water through pipes that were both leaky and made of lead. Westmeath residents rely on groundwater for much of their drinking water. It is stored in cavities in the county's karstified limestone bedrock which, fortunately, is protected by a blanket of boulder clay, peat and alluvium.

Certain waters have always had a special value for us. Their chemical composition is influenced by the rocks they pass through, with limestone, for example, giving a calcium-rich and granite a sodium-rich product. Spa towns developed around some such sources in the mid-nineteenth century and it was from these that the tradition of bottled water emerged. Perrier created a very successful global brand in the 1970s, which was matched in Ireland by the success of home-based competitor brands. Consumption of bottled water has grown enormously so now it vies with soft drinks for sales in North America and Europe. Its popularity is attributed to its convenience, its association with a healthy lifestyle – and perhaps our mistrust of public water supplies. But its very popularity has raised sustainability issues in North America, where 30 million plastic bottles are discarded daily with low recycling rates, delivery costs are increasing greenhouse gas emissions and some aquifers are experiencing huge withdrawals to meet demand.[10]

Bogland is another interesting case of sustainable development. In Westmeath, the main bogland is concentrated along its southern border with Offaly. Often you come upon it unexpectedly; a simple fence or single footstep may separate bog from pastures. We no longer regard peatlands as simply sources of employment and turf supplies as our appreciation of their ecological richness improves. There is a growing demand for bog tourism where visitors can feel the texture of peat and marvel at the rituals of historical bog working. Future generations do not need to forget this heritage in order to view bog as an invaluable ecosystem (or even a carbon sink!) and strive to regenerate it on that basis.

There is no doubt that Goldsmith's Auburn seems more attractive than Colum's Aghnacliff, although both share essentially similar Midlands countryside. Samuel Lewis was not easily seduced by scenery in his topographical survey of Ireland, yet he was unusually impressed with the loveliness of Westmeath:

> The surface of the county, though nowhere rising into tracts of considerable elevation, is much diversified by hill and dale, highly picturesque in many parts, and deficient in none of the essentials of rural beauty, but timber. In its scenery it ranks next after Kerry, Wicklow, Fermanagh and Waterford.[11]

This seems like strong praise for one Midlands county over the others and it may be optimistic. Consider this alternative snapshot of the Midlands region:

> Yes, the newspapers were right: snow was general all over Ireland. It was falling on every part of the dark central plain, on the treeless hills, falling softly upon the

Bog of Allen and, farther westward, softly falling into the dark mutinous Shannon waves.[12]

Viewed from Dublin, the Midlands have sometimes been regarded as simply an unnecessary obstacle separating the capital from Galway. Galway of fun and craic, of university times and fond holidays and garrulous Galway races, of Aran Islands and Clarinbridge oysters and Gaeltacht rites of passage. The quotation above is from the climax of James Joyce's celebrated short story, "The Dead", and reflects a deep dichotomy between the imperfectly living of Dublin and the tragically dead of Galway. Gretta Conroy is impatient with the gap between Dublin and Galway and wants, through some unfathomable quantum leap, not just a 3D union with Galway but especially a 4D union with her long-dead first love, Michael Furey. But the bland Midlands (and perhaps her uncomprehending husband Gabriel) get inconveniently in the way! The monotony of a Midlands smothered in snow suggests a sameness that allows us to imagine being instantly transported between Dublin and Galway. No time is wasted on the boring Central Plain in between, so that at a stroke both the cheer of Goldsmith and drear of Colum have been obliterated!

Notes

1. This opinion of geologists is attributed to Sir Walter Scott (1771-1832). No source was found – it is not included in his *St. Ronan's Well* as sometimes alleged!

2. Quoted from page 27, volume 1, of Forster, J. (1875) *The Life and Times of Oliver Goldsmith*. Sixth edition. London: Chapman and Hall.

3. Quoted from page 133, volume 1, of Forster, J. (1875) *The Life and Times of Oliver Goldsmith*. Sixth edition. London: Chapman and Hall.

4. These are the opening lines to Dr. Goldsmith (1770) *The Deserted Village, a poem*. London: Printed for W. Griffin, at Garrick's Head, Catharine Street, Strand.

5. See page 154, volume 1, of Forster, J. (1875) *The Life and Times of Oliver Goldsmith*. Sixth edition. London: Chapman and Hall.

6. I explored Google for information and background on the various locations.

7. Quoted from page 259 of Gwynn, S. (1935) *Oliver Goldsmith*. London: Thornton Butterworth.

8. A catalogue of Oliver Goldsmith's books begins on page 496 of volume 2 of Forster, J. (1875) *The Life and Times of Oliver Goldsmith*. Sixth edition. London: Chapman and Hall.

9. See page 9 of Goldsmith, Oliver (1768) *The Good Natur'd Man: A Comedy as Performed at the Theatre-Royal in Covent Garden*. London: W. Griffin.

10. For a wide-ranging and fascinating study of humankind's relationship with water, see Salzman, James (2012) *Drinking Water: A History*. New York: Overlook Duckworth.

11. Quoted from page 698, volume 2, of: Lewis, S. (1837, republished 1995) *A Topographical Dictionary of Ireland*. Baltimore, Maryland: Clearfield Company.

12. These are among the final sentences of "The Dead" from Joyce, J. (1914) *Dubliners*. England: Penguin Books in association with Jonathan Cape, pages 173-220.

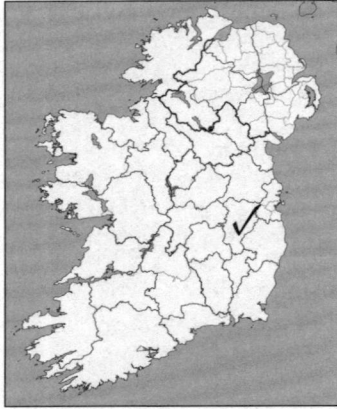

11

AGELESS SOLITUDE
(Kildare)

Happy the man whose lot it is to know
the secrets of the Earth.
– Euripides[1]

Kildare is rightly a source of endless fascination for its discerning residents yet Dubliners persist in regarding it as either a dormitory or a corridor county! Two transport corridors bifurcate westwards from Dublin city, opening up a rich triangular plain across County Kildare. The forerunner of the M4 motorway established the trend to the northwest and was subsequently strengthened by the Royal Canal and the Dublin–Sligo railway line. The southwesterly-directed corridor is less prominent because the Grand Canal wanders considerably from the tighter lines of the road and rail links with Cork and Limerick. Indeed, the only pro-trusions on Kildare's plains form a series of low hills, including Grange Hill (226 metres) and the Hill of Allen (202 metres), that trend northeastwards along the zone between the Grand Canal and the rest of this corridor. Together these hills make up the Kildare Inlier, an area of older rock surrounded by Devonian sandstones and Carboniferous limestones. Prolonged seismic activity along its northwestern margin ensured the inlier remained standing proud throughout its history, so that quaking activity which might prove catastrophic elsewhere has actually sculpted a haven of peace here.

Those hills of the Kildare Inlier are neither impressively high nor steep, yet they are prominent in this low-lying country and their historical significance far exceeds their physical elevation. The Hill of Allen was the legendary stronghold of Fionn Mac Cum-haill and his warriors, Na Fianna, personalities we have already encountered at Slieve Gullion. Their mythology is a cherished part of Kildare's heritage and indeed as an epic it ranks among Europe's finest. Unperturbed by this background, Sir Gerald George Aylmer constructed a folly, Aylmer's Tower, on its summit around 1860. The hill itself is made of stone that yields excellent aggregates and, given its proximity to the greater Dublin area, its western flank has been extensively quarried over many years.

The Kildare-born poet Desmond Egan (b. 1936) has published a sequence of 16 poems, which are numbered rather than titled, to voice his deep anger at the impact of this quarrying on his cher-ished landscape.[2] He feels the spiritual loss resulting from quar-rying and, hoping visitors won't notice the scars, he invites us to explore its hillside and get lost in what he calls its ageless silence ("No. 7"). Even passing motorists experience its calming effect ("No. 1"). He feels our successors won't easily forgive the destruc-tion caused by extracting rock that has been here for hundreds of millions of years. Quarrying, it seems, is the price of progress and we are uncaring of the cultural void the quarry will leave ("No. 1"). As a society, we place no more value on the hill, he asserts, than on a book of poems ("No. 14"). Those making authoritative pronouncements on the merits of quarrying are unlikely, he would lead you to believe, to be well acquainted with poetry!

I myself found solitude on the Hill of Allen. It was easy to enjoy Allen's woodland trails, to imagine those gallant Fianna warriors at hunt or play here and to empathise with the workers who trekked from surrounding villages to labour on Aylmer's elegant Tower. From this tower's summit I found the quarrying was largely screened from view by the hillside contours. Indeed the westerly vista is of the immense Bog of Allen, contrasting pleasantly with a varied patchwork of tillage and peatland to the east. It is of course the possibility of the entire hill being removed that is of most concern to Egan. Aylmer's Tower may actually have limited the future extent of quarrying here and it does seem to find favour among local residents. On the weekend prior to my visit, more than 120 people visited the Tower as part of National Heritage Week and recorded only positive impressions in the visitors' book. I don't doubt they were mostly locals for neither hill nor tower has even a solitary sign to attract the attention of an inquisitive stranger.

The other hills in this area have their own stories to tell, but it is Grange Hill and the Hill of Allen that interest us most.[3] Both are composed of dark green andesite lava and it is speculated that they may once have briefly formed volcanic islands that protruded above the waters of that long-vanished ocean of Iapetus. We know the age of that lava is almost 450 million years from the fossils of animals – brachiopods, gastropods and trilobites – that lived in the surrounding shallow seas. These fossils are particularly well preserved in limestone on Grange Hill, so this rather than Allen is the hill favoured by geologists. Its most celebrated fossils are trilobites, an extinct group of arthropods whose external skeleton protected them from predators. These creatures are oval-shaped, related to crabs and have a similar size range. At the start of the current millennium they became fashionable due to Richard Fortey's engaging book *Trilobites!*[4] He does not hide his fascination with these animals – their sophisticated eyes, branched limbs and ability to thrive in a variety of habitats and climates. They evolved as diverse and complex creatures at the start of the Cambrian Period, forming part of what is referred to as the Explosion of Life. They rapidly became successful and abundant, occupying many marine ecosystems. Fortey comments:

> Trilobites survived for a total of 300 million years, almost the whole duration of the Palaeozoic era: who are we Johnny-come-latelies to label them as either 'primitive' or 'unsuccessful'? Men have so far survived half a per cent as long.

They would finally become extinct in a mass extinction event 250 million years ago, an event that fledgling dinosaurs saw as an opportunity to occupy and dominate many favourable habitats!

Yes, all life suffers ups and downs, and this applies equally to the trilobites. Indeed those Kildare fossils represent creatures that had been witness to one such planetary hiccup: global cooling. I am referring to events towards the end of the Ordovician Period, a time we will return to again in these pages. At this time, about one-third of the way through the life history of trilobites, polar ice sheets spread towards the tropics, absorbing increasing quantities of seawater and causing sea levels to fall. In these changed environmental and climatic circumstances, there was widespread disruption of habitats and mass extinction prevailed over as long as a million years. The trilobites were not immune from this devastation and suffered a spectacular reduction in their diversity: about 40 per cent of their genera became extinct in what was one of the great mass extinctions recorded on Earth.

If the Hill of Allen marks a potential source of solitude on Kildare's eastern flank, we will shortly find another on its western border. But will the county's centre be a contrasting scene of desolation? Actually Kildare's central plains owe much to the impact of a relatively recent polar climate. When ice sheets start melting, their water drains away in two distinctively different ways and these are displayed respectively in the north and south of this county. When water is channelled along fractures in the ice sheet it builds up substantial thicknesses of sand and gravel which, when the ice has finally gone, remain on the landscape as distinctive esker ridges. Esker Riada is a spectacular example and it can be traced across the northern part of County Kildare. Its surroundings were largely hummocky low-lying land that supported an untidy if widespread patchwork of lakes. As the climate ameliorated and growth of bogs started, these areas must have had an enchanting variety of wild-life. But the south of County Kildare was no less favoured. Here, large lakes developed in front of the ice sheets themselves and were dammed by local landscape features. We can imagine such lakes by looking at the modern Blessington Lake, which was created by erecting an artificial dam. But Glacial Lake Blessington, 10,000 to 15,000 years ago, was even more extensive and due to damming by ice sheets rather than concrete! Similar circumstances led to the development of another large lake at the Curragh. The higher ground surrounding such lakes is commonly marked by dry chan-nels formed by meltwater flowing from them. The dry channel at Glending on the R410 west of Blessington is but one of many in Ireland, but it is also Kildare's finest! Meltwater flowing into such lakes deposited huge quantities of sand and gravel which over time built up to considerable thicknesses. So when the lake finally drained away, extensive sandy deltas were exposed in both areas, forming flat-lying and well-drained landscape where bogland did not subsequently develop. These deltas became a source of aggre-gates for Dublin's construction sector but, even more famously, formed the favourable foundation for celebrated racecourses at the Curragh and Punchestown. As a result, the peace and calm of that impersistent polar lakeshore has facilitated the development of a bloodstock industry that attracts global envy!

Did Paul Durcan pluck the village Moone out of the night sky when he came to write that captivating poem, "The Haulier's Wife

Meets Jesus on the Road Near Moone",[5] or was he determined to locate it firmly within the bounds of County Kildare? If so, he was unusual among Irish poets! But that is not to say that Kildare lacks literary links. James Joyce, for example, spent time at Clongowes Wood boarding school and I believe its environment did have some influence on his writing. Moone and Clongowes skulk uneasily along the county's eastern border and to find another literary association we must cross to the opposite boundary.

Gerard Manley Hopkins (1844–1889), English poet and Jesuit priest, may only have been an occasional visitor to Monasterevin, but he left his mark on County Kildare where he is remembered in the Hopkins Summer School, an annual assembly of literary enthusiasts and Hopkins scholars under the watchful eye of Desmond Egan.[6] Hopkins was raised in comfort by parents who encouraged both his writing talent and fascination with nature. On entering religious life he abandoned poetry at least temporarily, feeling it might be in conflict with his priestly vocation. Never a completely contented person, his conversion to Catholicism had already caused a rift with his family and subsequently his Jesuit superiors were never entirely comfortable with his literary output. No wonder he was subject to periods of depression, which can only have been exacerbated by his unwise posting in 1884 to what is now University College Dublin where he found himself entirely out of step with the political views of the city's Catholics. He was an isolated figure, estranged from his family, religion and country, and now in Ireland equally distant from citizens of his adopted country and practitioners of his chosen religion. In "To Seem a Stranger"[7] he says bleakly:

> To seem the stranger lies my lot, my life
> Among strangers.

He disliked Dublin and would seek occasional solace in the homes of wealthy and sympathetic Catholics, especially the Cassidys of Monasterevin, to restore his mood and health. Sadly, he

contracted typhoid fever and died in June 1889, being buried in the
Jesuit plot at Glasnevin Cemetery. Hopkins gained a posthumous
reputation as an important Victorian poet who linked themes of
religion and nature together in his often melancholic works.

Monasterevin, for long a milestone on the Dublin–Cork route,
is now by-passed and chiefly remembered as a one-time home of
the singer John Count McCormack and for the 1976 kidnap of in-
dustrialist Tiede Herrema, who was held captive in the town. With
its tangle of roads, waterways and bridges, Monasterevin hides its
former economic strength well. This was largely centred around
a distillery on Main Street, which by the time of Hopkins' visits
was annually producing 250,000 gallons of whiskey, and a brewery,
producing St. Patrick's Pale Ale. Both were owned by the Cassidy
family and each would finally close down in the 1930s.[8]

On his Christmas 1886 visit to the welcoming Cassidy sisters at
Monasterevin House, Hopkins threw his energy into starting "On
the Portrait of Two Beautiful Young People", a poem inspired by a
portrait of local children, in which he is dejected about the passing
of beauty over time.[9] Aside from that, he had pleasant undemanding company, both in the house and the town, and yet although
this poem does briefly refer to the Barrow River, he does not peer
out the window in search of poetic inspiration or solitude. So the
man whose early poetic impulses had been stimulated by natural
beauty now seems to cut himself off from the balm of nature and
landscape and rural life.

Solitude has long been sought in natural wilderness. Many
find it easier to discover their relationship with God in such an
environment. The wilderness might be a mountain, desert, island
or even your urban garden, while God might don a bewildering array of theological mantles depending on individual prefer-
ences. Ireland possesses its share of inspiring wildernesses, but
none more remote than Skellig Michael off the coast of Kerry.
So I am intrigued that the Kerry-based poet, Paddy Bushe (b.
1948), when writing of Hopkins, imagines him as a forlorn over-

night pilgrim there ("Hopkins on Skellig Michael").[10] The boatmen wonder how he will fare on that windswept rock pinnacle. But Hopkins does climb to the lofty monastery, marvels at its reliable water wells and kneels to pray at the high cross. But that evening he experiences a violent storm that forces him to retreat to the island's lighthouse for shelter. Nevertheless he survives a tortured night on this mystical island and his mood recovers sufficiently for him to exchange pleasantries with the boatmen on the homeward journey.

In real life the priestly poet might have refreshed himself by simply taking a stroll along the Grand Canal! Monasterevin House, his holiday home but now a convent, stands on one of the town's principal streets only a few 100 metres from the canal harbour. Heading southwards, the canal hugs the western edge of the Barrow valley and enters a cut in boulder clay. Here the stroller enjoys the tranquil blend of nature and canal water, unconscious of life's continuing pace beyond the tree screens. Further along, the canal occupies an embankment where walking would be a more bracing experience in winter and the sound of traffic passing on the nearby road might have been more intrusive. The water does not seem sufficiently murky to protect its pike and bream from the silent swoops of a watchful heron. Perhaps such primal struggles unsettled the sensitive English poet, reminding him of the unsavoury events elsewhere in the country that he found so unpalatable. He might alternatively have focused on the mellow swan and mallard cruising slowly together for company or the water hen rising noisily from canal bank reeds. His holiday respite might have been deepened had he allowed himself to experience the sharpness of a frosty morning, the ruggedness of the surrounding bogland, the changing weather over rail and canal lines, the repartee of local residents or the beauty of the Barrow valley. How sad! His wearying life, uninspired by Irish landscape, seems to have sapped his ability for light-hearted, melodic and uplifting verse such as this earlier poem ("Spring")[7]:

Nothing is so beautiful as spring –
When weeds, in wheels, shoot long and lovely and lush;
Thrush's eggs look little low heavens, and thrush
Through the echoing timber does so rinse and wring
The ear, it strikes like lightnings to hear him sing;
The glassy peartree leaves and blooms, they brush
The descending blue; that blue is all in a rush
With richness; the racing lambs too have fair their fling.

Notes

1. Attributed to Euripides (c. 480-406 BC).

2. Desmond Egan (2001) *The Hill of Allen: A Sequence of Poems.* Newbridge, County Kildare: The Goldsmith Press.

3. Report on geological sites in County Kildare accessed on 3August 2013 at: http://www.gsi.ie/NR/rdonlyres/0298E392-2EDD-4818-80BE-CBA415ED7332/0/Kildare_section3_part1.pdf.

4. Fortey, Richard (2001) *Trilobite! Eyewitness to Evolution.* London: Flamingo. The quotation is from page 21.

5. This poem is on pages 3-7 of Paul Durcan (1985) *The Berlin Wall Café.* Belfast: The Blackstaff Press.

6.http://gerardmanleyhopkins.org/Hopkins_International_Literary_Festival_2013.pdf accessed 8 August 2013.

7. Gardner, W.H. (Ed.) (1948) *Poems of Gerard Manley Hopkins.* Third edition. Oxford: Oxford University Press. I have quoted from "To Seem the Stranger" on page 109 and "Spring" on page 71. I have referred to "On the Portrait of Two Beautiful Young People", pages 169-170.

8. For information on Cassidy's Whiskey see http://www.irelandwhiskeytrail.com/?pg=cassidys_distillery_monasterevan_kildare.php (Accessed 10 August 2013).

9. White, Norman (2002) *Hopkins in Ireland.* Dublin: University College Dublin Press.

10. Paddy Bushe (2001) *Hopkins on Skellig Michael.* Dublin: The Dedalus Press. "Hopkins on Skellig Michael" appears on pages 57-68.

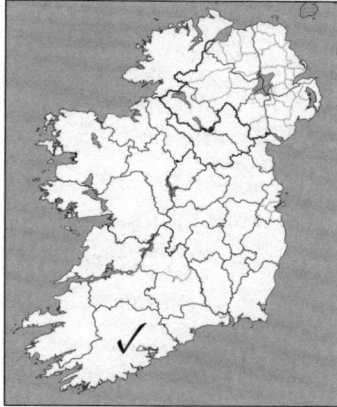

12

COAST OF COPPER
AND CALAMITY
(Cork)

*There was wealth in this country of his, ready for the
taking, and only the laziness of his fellow-countrymen
prevented them from enjoying it. He looked upon it as
a duty, something (he) owed to his country and to the
Almighty, to glean the hidden wealth from Hungry Hill
and give it, at a price, to the peoples of the world.*
– Daphne du Maurier[1]

Nowadays it is tourists rather than emigrants that create the
footfall along Cobh's seafront but the indications remain, including the offices of the Cunard and White Star lines, that this was
once a busy transatlantic port. *RMS Titanic* provided, of course, its

most famous departure, but I wanted to reflect on the experience of the typical departing emigrant so I walked up to St. Colman's Cathedral. Chances are that I retraced the paces of many intending passengers anxious to kill some time or pray for a safe arrival in North America. Perched above the port, the construction of this cathedral started in the 1860s although *Titanic*'s single 1912 visit would be already a tragic memory before the spire was completed. Richly adorned with cut stone, its exterior favours Dalkey granite and its interior Bath oolitic limestone.[2] But my attention was soon drawn to the waters of Cork Harbour below, as I envisaged clamouring relatives waving encouragement from shore while a departing ship rounded Haulbowline and Spike Islands and disappeared into the channel of the River Lee beyond.

What better place than the cliffs above Crosshaven to observe those liners as they built up speed and made their way through the harbour's mouth. As each vessel swept out into the open Atlantic, many passengers would have lingered on deck to savour their final images of Cork. This is the very part of its urban area to which residents and visitors alike come for a better understanding of its geology. Even a casual visitor to this city will notice the colourful use of building stones: the pale grey of the limestone contrasts with the greens and reds of the sandstone. The story of how these very different rock types evolved can be gleaned during the course of an enlightening excursion along Cork's coastline around Crosshaven and Ringaskiddy.[3]

Composed of rocks whose age spans between 300 and 400 million years, the Cork district would have looked very different at that time. Even the modern mountains of west Cork, however awesome, would have been no match in terms of scale and grandeur for the backdrop of rocky peaks that would have marked the distant skyline then. A series of major rivers eroded these mountains, carrying a steady supply of sediment to deposit it on the floodplains that existed where Cork now stands. Those floodplains were subsiding within the major Munster Basin so that it could accommodate a very thick set of sediments – one of the thickest formed at this time anywhere on the Earth's surface. Basins are areas where sediments accumulate more thickly than in surrounding areas, usually because their floors slip downwards along faults and thus keep pace with sedimentation. In the Munster basin the sediments were characteristically red sands, giving rise to the classic Old Red Sandstone, but in truth the spectrum of materials was much greater, mudstones as well as sandstones, and with purple, green and grey colours. Those green and grey colours became more prominent later and heralded the onset of rising sea levels. As the land was relentlessly inundated, the nature of sediment changed: instead of quartz sand grains and clay minerals, the seabed received layer upon layer of carbonates, which would in time be transformed into grey limestones. This was not just a Cork event, for the sea would extend eventually over all of present-day Ireland and indeed further afield. But Cork harbour area does display in an exceptional manner the changing products of this great transition. Soon after the rock sequence was laid down it was compressed into tight folds whose crests have been eroded and allow us examine the full rock sequence. So Cork's east-west-trending ridges are underlain by sandstone and its parallel valleys by limestone. This is a fine example of a district where topography reflects underlying geology.

During this period another environmental change was asserting itself and this one would be unique to Cork Harbour and areas south of its latitude. This involved a change from the regionally extensive lime deposition taking place across Ireland to contemporaneous clay deposition further south. The most southerly Carboniferous limestones are found at Ringaskiddy and only mudstones occur further south. These are now metamorphosed to slates. So the modern visitor in going southwards from Ringaskiddy to Crosshaven is crossing the margin of a newly evolving basin, called the South Munster Basin and only partly coincident with the earlier Munster Basin of Old Red Sandstone fame. That southwards change reflects the transition from shallow seas where lime deposition prevailed to deeper basinal waters which received silt and mud, a change that was sustained through persistent seismic activity.

The rocks of Cork Harbour featured in some fundamental discussion in the first half of the nineteenth century as the scientific parameters for Ireland's geological maps were being established. The merits of various mapping techniques were being evaluated and modified based on emerging experience and the practices proven elsewhere. For example, the principle of superposition was becoming widely accepted, which held that an overlying bed was younger than that on which it was laid. But the importance of employing only properly trained geologists was also clear, because this principle would not apply, for example, to deformed sedimentary sequences where older beds might be thrust over younger ones. Also, the folly of correlating beds solely on the basis of their composition was being recognised and, accordingly, all red sandstones could not automatically be assigned to the pre-Carboniferous Old Red Sandstone, because they might equally be of post-Carboniferous age and belong to the New Red Sandstone. Alternatively, the value of diagnostic fossils to date rocks accurately was now seen by most geologists as critical.

So while with hindsight it seems self-evident that the Ringaskiddy limestone is the same age as the Crosshaven mudstone, its unravelling 150 years ago involved some of Ireland's key geologists in extended debate. But it was left to Joseph Beete Jukes (1811–1869), a much travelled and talented geologist, in 1864 to finally establish that the mudstones and limestones of Cork Harbour were of the same age. It was simply the case that they formed in different marine environments and Jukes on his travels had actually observed a modern example of such a transition. This was an example where diverse overseas experience outshone the views of geologists whose careers were mainly within the confines of Ireland. However even Homer nods at times and Jukes fell foul of Britain's geological establishment when in a wrongheaded manner he insisted on applying a Cork solution to Devon's problems.[4]

Coastal outcrops are not reliable indicators of offshore geology. This is especially so here, for a short distance offshore the seabed is underlain, not by typical Cork sandstones and limestones, but by thick sequences of relatively young sediments. These include the white chalk so typical of parts of the Antrim coast. It is sandstone underlying this chalk that contains the valuable natural gas of Kinsale Gasfield, Ireland's first commercial offshore field. Augmented by two smaller satellite discoveries, it has been supplying the national gas grid as well as supporting electricity generation and production of ammonia-based fertilisers.[5]

The Kinsale gasfield occurs in one of several basins that occur in Ireland's offshore and are analogous to, but much younger than, the Munster Basin onshore. The 1996 Corrib discovery in the Slyne Basin off the Mayo coast, occurs in deeper seawater and further offshore than the Kinsale Gasfield. The fact that its gas occurs a further 3.5 kilometres below the seafloor makes its economic extraction a considerable challenge. There are additional basins even more isolated from shore out in the Atlantic, the Rockall and Hatton being the best known, where exploration has been less intensive and no commercial discoveries have been made to date. These offshore basins all developed in response to stretching and rupturing of the continental crust according as the Atlantic Ocean began to form. At the far edge of these basins lies the margin of the continental shelf, where seabed falls away steeply to greater depths and, in the absence of sediments, the hydrocarbons potential dwindles also.

Returning ashore once more, I am curious to realise that not all Cork poets feel enthusiastic about their landscape. However many, including Patrick Galvin (1927–2011), do advert to their physical surroundings in order to create a context or atmosphere for another unrelated topic. When Galvin writes poetry concerning his native city we feel the energy and essence of inner Cork city life around the mid-twentieth century. He takes the time to situate us in the physical landscape of Cork city, with its sights and sounds and smells, but there is no doubting that the underlying human story in each poem is what grabs his attention. In "The Wall", his affinity with his then residence, Ballycotton in east County Cork, is magnified by an imaginary process whereby the Earth swallows up both sun and stars only to be itself consumed by Ballycotton! He uses a marvellous economy of language to conjure up multiple images of Picasso-famed Gernika, extending from the pain of its war-ravished past to the ambivalence of its current tourist influx ("The Oldest Man in Gernika"). We sense Galvin's impatience with any environmental description that does not pay its way in adding significant value to his dominant theme.[6]

There is another Cork. It is further west in the county, defined by rugged rocky mountains of sandstone that underpin some splendid scenery. These mountains are of Old Red Sandstone, part of the extensive Munster Basin and they are marked in places by the products of both volcanic and seismic activity: the Black Ball Head intrusions are examples of the former, the major Killarney-Mallow Fault in north County Cork a well-known locus for the latter. Copper deposits are widely dispersed across the extensive peninsulas west of Skibbereen and formed from copper-bearing fluids which circulated in the basin during or shortly after sediment deposition. Most deposits proved to be disappointingly small and mines based on them often failed. To see the remains of the most successful of these mines, take the road from richly-vegetated Glengarriff along the Beara Peninsula, south of the Caha Mountains and their highest point, Hungry Hill (685 metres), past the commercial fishing port of Castletownbere and do not divert until you are close to Dursey Island, the peninsula's most remote location. One day I had intended taking the cable car across to this island but found it was out of service due to maintenance, so I turned north and explored Allihies instead. I invite the reader to do the same.

Copper deposits at Allihies, also called Berehaven, formed the basis of enduring mine operations for much of the nineteenth century. The copper ore comprises the mineral chalcopyrite (fool's gold) which is hosted in white quartz veins that are usually little more than a metre thick. They are invariably steeply disposed so that mining quickly followed them down to significant depths. Miners worked in cramped conditions to extract the ore which was then hoisted to surface by steam engine. The remains of distinctive steam engine houses on the hillside are prominent reminders of, and indeed tribute to, Cornish mining technology. The ore was crushed on surface and screened so that its copper content was increased to an average of about 10 per cent copper before being shipped to Swansea for sale. In good years about 5,000 tons of ore would be sold at about £10 per ton, although copper prices were subject to fluctuations. The economic significance of the operation can be gauged from the fact that it employed about 1,000 workers, including women and children.

The Allihies mine was operated for much of the nineteenth century by the Puxley family of nearby Dunboy Castle.[7] John Lavallin Puxley (1772–1856) established the enterprise and managed it for over forty years. It was a remarkable achievement to run this major operation successfully in a remote part of Ireland and never miss a dividend payment. After his death, other family members ran the operation until 1869 when the family sold its interests in the venture. Copper grades declined during the 1870s, mining costs increased and there was no prospect of steady copper prices. Mining finally ceased in 1884 although sporadic interest was shown in reviving it up until the mid-twentieth century.

If you wish to dig deeper into relationships within the Allihies mining community of the nineteenth century, then you could do worse than relax with Daphne du Maurier's (1907–1989) entertaining novel *Hungry Hill.*[8] She transferred the mine's location 25 kilometres eastwards along the peninsula to the more evocatively-named hill of the novel's title. John Lavallin Puxley of course dominates the novel's early part and is re-christened Copper John Brodrick, more suited to the cinematic version that would be released immediately after World War Two and that would draw renewed investor attention to the area. The mine would create employment for the poor of the district while providing for the welfare and security of his own family. He was an astute risk-taker with vision and energy. Tough but fair-minded, he had great determination that many saw as high-handed. Nevertheless, any feelings of resentment towards him were tempered with grudging respect. In truth, his Irish (although not necessarily British) workers lived in squalid conditions and worked in a hazardous environment, all for meagre wages.

We can capture something of the work experience of Allihies miners through the writing of Leanne O'Sullivan.[9] Her poem "Man Engine", a mix of the surreal and historical, opens as a worker hears the sound of blasting as she approaches the mine from Castletownbere. She descends underground using the man engine, a steam-powered system that transports miners in stages. O'Sullivan recreates the noise and the danger very well: unless miners were agile in boarding and leaving the chamber of the man engine, they could fall to certain death. The shaft becomes a "cankerhole", a foul area with poor air, because the choking dust clouds from an earlier blast have not been dissipated by the inadequate ventilation. She imagines her silhouette frozen in this thick smog and can barely detect a miner's candlelight ahead, where miners are drilling the face in preparation for further blasting. She is soon rewarded with the sight of golden yellow copper ore in this face. But now she receives a cautionary tap on her shoulder and hears ominous warning sounds, courtesy of the Tommyknockers,[10] the legendary Cornish mine-dwelling dwarfs who alert sympathetic workers to imminent danger. This strikes terror into every miner's heart for a disastrous fall of ground is now inevitable and some miners are already trapped. A fatalism settles among workers as they embark on the inherently dangerous task of shovelling overhead broken rock, but somehow they manage to emerge safely on surface by the end of the shift.

When mining ceased in 1884, most workers had little option but to emigrate and many chose the copper mines of Butte, Montana, where their descendents are still conscious of their Beara roots. The mining world had changed dramatically over the life of Allihies mine. Prior to 1840, Swansea was at the centre of the global copper trade, based on smelting British and Irish ores. But after 1840 the rich copper mines (and higher wages!) of the Great Lakes region, Chile and Australia increasingly attracted the hard-pressed miners of Britain and Ireland. But the Irish miners tended to restrict their travelling to USA and Australia.

The theme of transatlantic emigration seems to unite our two parts of County Cork. While West Cork offered constant employment during the life of the mine, eventually its miners joined the queue of less skilled passengers to board vessels back in Cork Harbour for westward migration. Having left all sight of land behind them, they might not have been conscious of crossing the edge of the continental shelf – but that is really when they left Ireland! It would be here in international waters, before reaching the safety of North America, that an international tragedy unfolded 30 years after the last of the Beara miners had passed by. *RMS Titanic*, the icon of the White Star Line, managed to get beyond Ireland's sedimentary basins and had crossed the Mid-Atlantic Ridge before disaster struck and it sank. It was seabed exploration off Newfoundland (and not just the filming of that wonderful film *Titanic*) that famously led to the discovery of its wreck.

Notes

1. Quoted from page 15 of Daphne du Maurier (1943) *Hungry Hill*. London: Victor Gollancz.

2. Noted in Irish-language leaflet available in St. Colman's Cathedral in September 2013.

3. See Field Trip 2 (Cork Harbour region, County Cork) in Meere, P., MacCarthy, I., Reavy, J., Allen, A. and Higgs, K. (2013) *Geology of Ireland: A Field Guide*. Cork: The Collins Press, pages 58-86.

4. See pages 16-27 of Lamplugh, G.W., Kilroe, J.R., McHenry, A., Seymour, H.J., Wright, W.B. and Muff, H.B. (1905) *The Geology of the Country around Cork and Cork Harbour (explanation of the Cork colour-*

printed drift map). Memoirs of the Geological survey, Ireland. Dublin: His Majesty's Stationery Office.

5. Information on Ireland's offshore hydrocarbon resources is contained in www.pad.ie.

6. Greg Delanty and Robert Welch (Eds.) (1996) *New and Selected Poems of Patrick Galvin.* Cork: Cork University Press. I refer to the following poems: "The Oldest Man in Gernika" (pages 28-30) and "The Wall" (pages 31-32).

7. Williams, R.A. (1991) The Berehaven copper mines. British Mining No. 42. A monograph of the Northern Mine Research Society.

8. Daphne du Maurier (1943) *Hungry Hill.* London: Victor Gollancz.

9. Leanne O'Sullivan (2013) *The Mining Road.* Northumberland, UK: Bloodaxe Books. "Man Engine" appears on pages 38-42.

10. For more on Tommyknockers see http://www.theastralworld.com/mythical-creatures/tommyknockers.php (Accessed 3 October 2013).

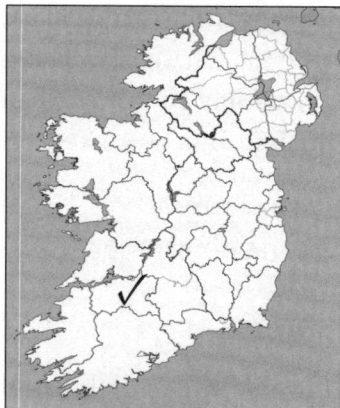

13

SHIFTING SHORELINES
(Limerick)

Lives of great men all remind us
We can make our lives sublime,
And, departing, leave behind us
Footprints on the sands of time.
— H. W. Longfellow[1]

Gerald Griffin (1803–1840) became best known as the author of *The Collegians*, a novel based on the scandalous events surrounding a lurid murder tragedy that took place on the shores of Shannon's estuary when he was a youth. Of course, it could be argued with merit that his reputation lies not in the novel itself but in the fact that it has since been adapted as both opera and play – the latter still featuring today thanks to Dion Boucicault's (1822–1890) enduring success with *The Colleen Bawn*. But for me, I am happy to think of him as the Bard of Shannon Estuary.[2]

I still feel joy in recalling the progress of President John F. Kennedy's (1917–1963) triumphal Irish tour in 1963, right through to his final lyrical lines regarding the River Shannon, with which I had not then been familiar:

> 'Tis, it is the Shannon's stream,
> Brightly glancing, brightly glancing,
> See, oh see the ruddy beam
> Upon its waters dancing![3]

So when I found myself in Boston in later life, it was natural that I would visit the John F. Kennedy Presidential Library and Museum, devoted to JFK's life and presidency.[4] And there on display, to my further joy, was the very scrap of paper where he had scribbled those lines of Gerald Griffin, recited for him the previous night by his dinner companion, Sinéad Bean de Valera (1878–1975), wife of Ireland's President. "'Tis, it is ..."? This repetition was surely a mistake, perhaps Sinéad had simply repeated it for emphasis and he had misunderstood. But if so, then JFK had still delivered his words, whether redundant or not, in an effortless manner. It turned out that this repetition was no mistake, Griffin had intended to start his tribute to Shannon that way. Indeed repetition is actually an inherent part of the poem's charm, which captures a returning exile's enchantment on seeing the river once more.

Gerald was familiar with the stretch of estuary from Limerick city almost as far west as Tarbert, for he resided at various times close to both extremities of it. The western outskirts of Limerick city consist of low-lying limestone pastures with occasional parkland and forest. They encompass the valley of the River Maigue, celebrated for picturesque Adare village as well as its eighteenth century poets who would surely have admired Griffin's lyricism:

> Oh, sweet Adare! Oh, lovely vale!
> Oh pleasant haunt of sylvan splendour,
> Nor summer sun, nor morning gale,
> E'er hailed a scene more softly tender.[5]

Looking eastwards, Griffin would have seen the ruins of Carrigogunnel Castle perched on a rocky prominence and overlooking the Shannon's shipping lane. It sparked his imagination, "Rock of the Candle" being a literal translation of the Irish form of the castle's name:

Rock of the Candle! It is well for thee –
Fresh blows the wind around thy lofty breast,
From thy bold height thy chieftain's eye may see,
Each freighted bark that seeks the billowy West.[6]

Carrigogunnel's rock is no less exotic than the cargo of those vessels for it is volcanic, forming part of Limerick's fiery past and dating from about 325 million years ago. Comparable to contemporary events at Croghan Hill, County Offaly, the Limerick eruptions were more widespread and their products underpin a distinctive part of the county's landscape. They involved several centres in two distinct phases that were separated by a period of limestone deposition. The original volcanic vents, much less assertive than in Offaly, spewed out mainly lavas and rarely if ever thrust their heads above the waterline!

West of Foynes we enter the hilly country marked by mudstones that overlie the limestone. On reaching Loghill I am surprised by the roadside notice that gives its Irish form as Leamh Choill, meaning dull or insipid forest! Mind you, much of the bedrock I have crossed is not inspiring, being black mudstones with few fossils. These formed in seawater that was progressively shallowing and the youngest sediments have increasing amounts of siltstone and sandstone beds that reflect the formation of a delta environment on which coal seams would develop. The uppermost sandstones represent sands formed on the delta surface and have fireclays, essentially fossilised soil horizons that underlie coal seams. But the coal itself, although carbon-rich anthracite, is thin, impersistent and not economically viable.

At a height of fully two metres, Ted Nevill (1925–2006) was a giant of a man but with a disarming and genial disposition. An academic and textbook author, he completed outstanding research on Irish coalfields over many years. His study of fossils in coal-bearing rocks required him to undertake painstaking and tedious examination of muddy exposures where decorum of dress and demeanour were easily forfeited. The work he remembered most fondly himself was that he undertook in Griffin's boyhood country around Loghill. But its scenery provided little enchantment to Ted:

> When you leave the prosperity of the limestone plain and climb into sterile (uplands) territory, you probably encounter one of the places that was made by God – last. You meet with subsistence and lonely living.

He writes of:

> the wilds of West Limerick, whose every inch I trod in search of coal and of an elusive fossil.[7]

An English geologist had requested he collect fossil specimens of a particular fresh water mussel found here. Its strategic importance had recently emerged and his friend wanted to be the first to publish a monograph on it. Ted knew it occurred in black shales above an anthracite bed, however he was still seeking a fossil horizon that was no more than 15 centimeters high in a substantial sequence of apparently uniform shales: not quite a needle in a haystack, but not far off! Nevertheless, he persevered until nightfall, digging and hammering constantly, and ultimately with considerable success. He gathered a dozen robust slabs each with several fossil bivalves having exquisitely preserved ornamentation:

> they looked as though they had housed living creatures in the not-distant past.[7]

Just what the English palaeontologist would need for some state-of-the-art research. Well pleased with himself, Ted was making his way home when by sheer coincidence he encountered a newly-arrived American geologist who had precisely the same objective as his friend: she also wanted to be the first to publish detailed descriptions of West Limerick's unique and ancient mussels! And remarkable man that he was, Ted generously provided her with half of his precious spoils although, being a discreet man, he did not record his friend's subsequent reaction to what must have been very unwelcome news!

The Griffin family settled at Loghill and it was from here around 1820 that, unusually, his parents emigrated to the United States, leaving their older children behind. Gerald subsequently lived with his remaining siblings at Adare and Pallaskenry before himself emigrating to London in 1823. Success in writing came disappointingly slow however and he was dogged by hardship and ill-health. But in darker days he could still fondly remember the happy feeling when viewing the Shannon from above Loghill:

> Know ye not that lovely river?
> Know ye not that smiling river?
> Whose gentle flood,
> By cliff and wood,
> With wildering sound goes winding ever.
> Oh! often yet with feelings strong
> On that dear stream my memory ponders,
> And still I prize its murmuring song,
> For by my childhood's home it wanders.[8]

Some of his work only reached the bookshops after his death, including *Tales of the Jury Room*. This recounts how members of a jury, on finding themselves confined to a single room overnight, entertained each other with story, recitation and song, including many of his well-cherished songs such as "Aileen Aroon". His poetry reflects not only his love of nature but also a deeply religious temperament which came to increasingly dominate his final years. Despite being at the height of his success, in 1838 he turned his back on his life as a writer and joined the Congregation of the Christian

Brothers. Assigned to the North Monastery School in Cork city, he foresaw a dedicated career in the service of that city's poor, but he tragically contracted typhus and died prematurely in 1840.

It is interesting that when his brother, Daniel, came to write his biography he could not mask his own lack of enthusiasm about Shannon's scenic virtues. Was he, and perhaps even Ted, unwittingly influenced by that uninspiring translation of Loghill? Having described its surrounding landscape, Daniel continues:

> Yet these beauties are considerably diminished by the absence of lofty mountain scenery along its shores, and by its vastness, which makes any such features as do exist, as well as the woods and plantations with which it is too scantily furnished, shrink into nothing.[9]

The invigorating and popular Brendan Kennelly (b.1936), a retired academic at Trinity College Dublin, is a modern poet of the Shannon Estuary. He grew up at Ballylongford, County Kerry, on the Shannon's hilly southern bank west of Loghill. The poem, "Lislaughtin Abbey", inspired by the riverside monastic ruins in his homeplace, sombrely focuses on the birds, the river and the dead, but mainly the dead! He is unsettling when he describes the river as containing the rich juice of the dead – something he strangely repeats in "God's Eye". However Kennelly is correct because groundwater seepage from cemeteries can contaminate nearby streams and wells. He embraces a spiritual approach and speaks of the anticipating dead, suggesting those buried in the Abbey are awaiting resurrection. But he foresees no sense of resurrection in nature here, and neither river nor birds offer any hope of renewal. On the other hand, Lislaughtin's fertile ground preserves those dead who are content to await salvation through Christ's suffering and resurrection.[10]

Brendan Kennelly's boyhood home was immediately downstream of where the Moneypoint Power Station now stands, just where the estuary widens to embrace the sea ("Lislaughtin Abbey")[10]:

> the Shannon moves with ease
> towards a mighty union with
> Atlantic mysteries

But where does ocean start and land finish? It seems an obvious question to answer, especially if we ignore the fourth dimension of time. It is equally a very important question considering that as much as 40 per cent of mankind live close to the seashore, drawn by a myriad of industrial, social and sporting activities – not to mention the seawater's sheer enchantment. So what controls the sea level, does it depend on changing volumes of seawater (perhaps driven by changes in polar ice sheets) or vertical movements of the land surface (the result of, say, subsidence or earthquakes)? Seamus Heaney wisely ignored those complexities and posed the dilemma in a more eloquent fashion:

> Did sea define the land or land the sea?
> Each drew new meaning from the waves' collision
> Sea broke on land to new identity.[11]

If we cast an eye backwards through time, we will find that Ireland's familiar coastline is a relatively recent attribute and history would suggest we should not overly rely upon it. Global sea level is a matter of current concern in the context of ongoing climate change but it is a mere plaything in the casual arms of our planet and its level is much influenced by the nature and pace of plate movements. Of course these movements also establish the course and intensity of ocean and air currents and these in turn determine the global pattern of climate, environment and human habitation. It is interesting to appreciate that the entire globe is so intimately attuned with the ordinary lives of its residents!

It is clear that Ireland's coastline may vary considerably over time. Let's explore the fourth dimension in more detail, starting when the Old Red Sandstone was being deposited and Ireland was dry land, with an arid climate and major seasonal rivers.[12] By the close of this era, seawater was already lapping against the most southerly parts of the country and in the early part of the succeeding Carboniferous Period it would advance relentlessly across Ireland, with just a few hills here and there exposed above sea level. The prevailing tropical climate and shallow water depth gave rise to the widespread beds of richly fossiliferous limestone that are common across the country. Basins developed in certain areas where more muddy sediment was abundantly deposited in deeper waters, areas such as south Cork and the Dublin region. The Shannon Estuary itself developed along Iapetus Suture, here marked by a deeply-ingrained fault over which the Shannon Basin formed. Faults cause thinning and subsidence of the crust and thus permit basins to accommodate considerable quantities of sediment. Fault systems actually evolve through time through the preferential growth of fewer and longer faults. This process becomes self-perpetuating because bigger faults have greater associated earthquakes which in turn advance the growth of more successful faults.[13] It sounds reminiscent of natural selection in biological evolution – another hint of the interconnectedness of our existence on Earth!

Nothing is permanent on the Earth's surface, and soon the Carboniferous sea was in retreat southwards, and newly-exposed land steadily became prominent once more. Right across Northern Europe, from Ireland to Poland, enduring coastal swamps preserved luxurious tropical vegetation in their quiet waters which, when fossilised, would give rise to coal seams of great economic value. Unfortunately the plants which formed Ted's Limerick anthracite made far too fleeting an appearance to have any practical value! Soon plate movements further south in Europe led to Ireland's surface being uplifted once more and thus any coal resources that had accumulated were now eroded away.

As the Atlantic Ocean widened, basins on the continental shelf would continue to subside and receive volumes of sediment whereas onshore the hilly nature of the countryside meant there was little deposition. The major seafloor spreading here and elsewhere led to a global rise in sea level – 200 to 300 metres above current levels in the case of Ireland. This was the time when thick deposits of chalk formed over this part of Europe: Ireland was whitewashed although, just as in the case of the earlier coal seams, much of it would be subsequently removed by erosion. Mind you, life on Earth may have felt premonitions of disaster at this stage for, in a very short period of two million years, drastic climatic and environmental changes would wipe out 75 per cent of its species! Although there is strong evidence to implicate a comet's impact as the culprit, some contemporary and very intensive volcanic eruptions may not have been entirely innocent.

But now the northward pressure of Africa against Europe led to the growth of the Alps and this had consequences across northern Europe, with much of Ireland being uplifted as dry land while its offshore basins continued to subside and fill with sediment. We were soon on the threshold of the Ice Age when sea level would fall globally because of the quantity of seawater locked up in ice sheets. The melting of the ice sheets de-stressed the Earth's crust, giving rise to surface rebound but not in any consistent way so some coasts have drowned valleys while others have raised beaches. And what the future holds is not hard to forecast. We have been progressing steadily if a bit haphazardly northwards across the Earth's surface for perhaps a few hundred million years and there is no sign of any impending change. This means, I am afraid, that the long-range weather forecast is rather arctic!

Notes

1. Quotation from "A Psalm of Life" on page 9 of H. W. Longfellow (1868?) *The Poetical Works of Henry Wadsworth Longfellow*. London: Frederick Warne & Co.

2. For information on the life and writings of Gerald Griffin see W. S. Gill (?1941) *Gerald Griffin: Poet, Novelist, Christian Brother*. Dublin: M.H. Gill & Son Ltd.

3. See pages 306-307 of "The Eighth Juryman's Tale: Mr. Tibbot O'Leary, the Curious" in Gerald Griffin (1887?) *Talis Qualis; or, Tales of the Jury Room.* Dublin: James Duffy & Sons.

4. See www.jfklibrary.org.

5. Stanza No.3 (pages 60-62) of: Daniel Griffin (1979) *The Life of Gerald Griffin, with an introduction by Robert Lee Wolff.* New York & London: Garland Publishing. Reprint of 1857? Edition.

6. See page 258 of "The Seventh Juryman's Tale: McEneiry the Covetous" in Gerald Griffin (1887?) *Talis Qualis; or, Tales of the Jury Room.* Dublin: James Duffy & Sons.

7. W.E. (Ted) Nevill (1987) *'Ted', His Fossils and Friends.* Cork: University College Cork. The quotations are from pages 30, v and 35 respectively.

8. See pages 381-382 of "The Tenth Juryman's Tale: Antrim Jack, and His General" in Gerald Griffin (1887?) *Talis Qualis; or, Tales of the Jury Room.* Dublin: James Duffy & Sons.

9. See page 32 of Daniel Griffin (1979) *The Life of Gerald Griffin, with an introduction by Robert Lee Wolff.* New York & London: Garland Publishing. Reprint of 1857? Edition.

10. Terence Brown and Michael Longley (Eds.) (2011) *The Essential Brendan Kennelly: Selected Poems.* Tarset, Northumberland, UK: Bloodaxe Books. I quote from "Lislaughtin Abbey" (pages 29-30) and refer to "God's Eye" (pages 31-32).

11. "Lovers on Aran" is on page 34 of Seamus Heaney (1966) *Death of a Naturalist.* London: Faber and Faber.

12. David Naylor (1998) *Irish Shorelines through Geological Time.* John Jackson Lecture 1998. Occasional papers in Irish science and technology, number 17. Dublin: Royal Dublin Society.

13. Walsh, J. (2000) *The Long term Effects of Earthquakes: Revealing the Hidden Charms and Tremors of Ancient Fault Systems.* John Jackson Lecture 2000. Occasional papers in Irish science and technology, number 21. Dublin: Royal Dublin Society.

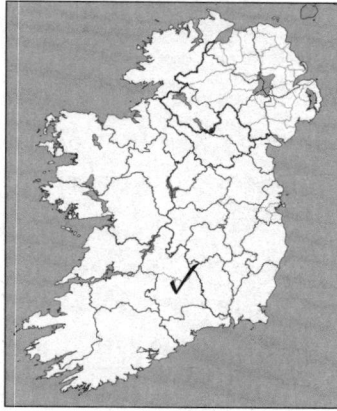

14

Sermons in Stones
(Tipperary)

And this our life, exempt from public haunt,
Finds tongues in trees, books in the running brooks,
Sermons in stones, and good in everything.
– William Shakespeare[1]

Mitchelstown Caves are hosted in limestone in the low ground between the Galtee and Knockmealdown mountains. The Old Cave is called Desmond Cave because it briefly sheltered the Earl of Desmond after the failed 1601 rebellion. When the New Cave was discovered during quarrying in 1833, it immediately became the main attraction. Caves develop where descending rainwater dissolves limestone along joints and bedding planes, so that the partings gradually open out to form galleries and chambers. It is the continued dripping of that water, enriched in carbonate from its attack on overhead limestone, that leads to the spectacular deposition of carbonate. Robert Lloyd Praeger was impressed by the results at Mitchelstown Caves. He describes some remarkable forms which both descended from above and rose from the floor, including pillars, bosses and curtains. The material itself was often snowy crystalline calcite which glittered in the candle-light. He drew particular attention to "cave pearls", hard pebble-like accretions which formed where water dripped into small pools.[2]

Praeger goes on to describe the cave-dwelling fauna, with bats and blind insects occupying even the most remote parts of the cave. He is fascinating when he moves on to discuss the fossilised remains found in some Irish cave systems, not just Mitchelstown caves themselves. These are fossils preserved beneath stalagmites or unconsolidated clay beds and they include many animals that are long ago extinct in Ireland – the spotted hyena, African wild cat, lemming, reindeer, bear and wolf. What a spectacular range! He also mentions the ungainly woolly mammoth, the frozen remains of which are still occasionally recovered in Siberia. However exotic these animals might all be, the most celebrated of extinct Irish mammals, and not forgotten by Praeger, is surely the Giant Deer, formerly mis-named the Irish Elk. Its most impressive attribute, antlers up to three metres across, seem to inspire admiration and greed in equal measures and have been highly prized as trophies. Ireland holds the largest European concentration of its remains, sometimes found in caves but more usually in lake clays underlying bogland. Giant Deer roamed the post-glacial landscape in the relatively short period from 12,000 to 10,600 years ago before becoming extinct in Ireland, at least a millennium before *Homo sapiens* arrived. So it seems that humanity is blameless in their demise, now widely regarded as due to the climate and vegetation changes that followed the end of the Ice Age.[3]

The Kilmastulla valley, away in the north of the county, is the kind of gentle landscape which must have nurtured Giant Deer in their prime. Rising in the neighbourhood of Nenagh, its river proceeds southwards to the base of Silvermines Mountain before turning westwards to follow its base, the line of the Silvermines Fault, and eventually join the Shannon River. The valley is floored by Carboniferous limestones which have been warped downwards along an axis parallel to the valley itself. The district has long been known for its silver production, usually derived as a by-product of lead mining. The Silvermines Fault is implicated as a key influence on the development of both metals, which have been produced here for maybe a millennium and not always peacefully – many English miners lost their lives here in the 1641 rebellion. The major product in recent decades, until the operation closed in the early 1980s, would have been zinc. Prior to the twentieth century only limited amounts of zinc were sold for the chemical and medical sectors, but new twentieth century industries such as galvanizing gave this metal a new lease of life. Another modern product here is barite, a dense inert mineral which was discovered here as long ago as the 1860s. But it was only exploited commercially a full century later when it became an essential component of drilling mud for the UK offshore sector.[4]

The approach to Slievenamon summit is through Kilcash, a locality renowned in Irish environmental history because of the poem of that name, written anonymously around the eighteenth century, allegedly admired by W. B. Yeats (1865–1939) and translated by many, including Thomas Kinsella (b. 1928):

> Now what will we do for timber
> with the last of the woods laid low?
> There's no talk of Cill Cais or its household
> And its bell will be struck no more.[5]

The poet laments not only that planters had demolished the woods but that nature in all its aspects – birds, game, vegetation – had been hugely diminished as a result. This is a modern insight, that all elements of our environment are interdependent so if we interfere with one aspect, there is no telling how others will be impacted. But the good news is that Kilcash has since been restored to all its glory! It forms rolling grassland on the north shoulder of the River Suir valley and even has some proud conifer stands. It gives way to a subdued ridge from which rises the smooth dome-like contours of Slievenamon itself, its slopes darkened by extensive heather. A trail is signposted to the summit and it is worth persevering for the panoramic views as well as the rocks that lie there!

Slievenamon may now be a low mountain, but in the Devonian it lay on the edge of a major lowland, the Munster Basin, that received a strong supply of sediment from further north, and accumulated on lake beds and along river systems. The resulting rocks on the Slievenamon summit, dominantly red and green in colour, are conglomerates and sandstones that are pebble-rich and formed in a river system. Indeed when the more muddy sediment dried out it developed mud cracks so that the next river flood would incorporate broken mud fragments in the newly forming sand bed. You will find narrow quartz veins that may have some well-formed transparent quartz crystals. These developed long after the rocks themselves, at a time when this region was deformed by plate movements taking place further south in Europe. But you will also notice white quartz pebbles contained in some sandstone beds. The quartz in these pebbles is older than both sandstone and quartz veins and is evidence that rocks, like many modern substances, are regularly recycled.

A curious consequence of Slievenamon's domed outline is that it is impossible to monitor its slopes from the summit. This must have been a drawback for the legendary Fionn MacCumhaill in his search for a bride. In the interests of fair play, he had arranged a contest for the many aspirants on the slopes of Slievenamon, announcing that he would position himself at the summit and marry the first woman to reach it. But he could not easily see how his favourite, Gráinne, was faring, so he secretly bestowed a winning advantage on her. It is not clear how well this successful betrothal suited her because it would not be long before she famously fell under the spell of one of Fionn's warriors, Diarmuid![6]

One writer who was captivated by Slievenamon was the Mullinahone Fenian and journalist, Charles Joseph Kickham (1828–1882).[7] He was a man who was passionate about redressing Ireland's ills, writing as he was at a vexed time of famine, emigration and insurgency. The novel *Knocknagow* is considered his best work with its portrayal of life in nineteenth century Ireland. Some of his poetry describes the beauty of the countryside around his native Slievenamon. These were sentimental lyrics, with a haunting appeal especially for emigrants, and his love of place shines through most clearly in "Carraigmoclear", Carrigmaclea on Ordnace Survey maps. This poem expresses the tormented thoughts of a departing emigrant who is leaving behind his loved one as well as unfinished insurgency against Britain. The place names he savours are locally significant landmarks and his use of them reflects his intimate knowledge of the Slievenamon district:

> How oft have I wandered, in sunshine and shower,
> From dark Kyleavalla to lonely Glenbower;
> Or spent with a light heart the long summer's day,
> 'Twixt See-Finn and the Clodagh above Kyleatlea;
> But than wood, glen, or torrent, to me far more dear
> Is thy crag-crowned forehead, old Carraigmoclear![8]

Kickham's landscape is peopled with insurgent heroes who were defeated either at Carrigmaclea in 1798 or Ballingarry in 1848. This theme is so powerful it almost (but not quite!) eclipses memories of rambles here with his loved one! The hillside is so pleasant in summer that a young woman might sleep in the pleasant sun traps between boulders that one encounters on mountain slopes, but how could he mistake sandstone for granite?

The forced emigration of a young tenant farmer also forms the theme for Kickham's best-known ballad, "Slievenamon". The farmer abandoned his loved one in the process so that now, although he is living comfortably abroad, his mind:

> … flies far away, by night and by day,
> To the time and the joys that are gone –
> Ah! I never can forget, the maiden I met,
> In the valley near Slievenamon.

But while in anguished despair ("Oh, my love – shall I never see you more?"), he still manages to address a patriotic consideration: "my land – will you ever uprise?" The addition of this noble sentiment may have diluted the romantic impact of the poem on his loved one, but we are not told the outcome!

"Patrick Sheehan" was a very influential ballad concerning a wounded veteran from the Crimean War, forced to beg once his meagre and temporary pension had been exhausted:

> My name is Patrick Sheehan,
> My years are thirty four;
> Tipperary is my native place –
> Not far from Galty-More;
> I came of honest parents –
> But now they're lying low –
> And many a pleasant day I spent
> In the Glen of Aherloe.

Kickham uses the tranquillity of Galtymore and Aherlow to create a contrast with the soldier's harsh condition, imprisoned in Dublin for begging. The public response was so strong that, not only was he released from jail, but the British Government conceded him a life-pension!

The Arra and Silvermines Mountains, on opposite sides of the Kilmastulla valley, are composed of similar Silurian sediments, although each represents the detritus of a separate continent. The front edges of these approaching continents, as Iapetus Ocean finally ceased to exist, crashed into each other along a line close to that of the Silvermines Fault. This fault itself is but a shallow expression of the huge deformation that was occurring at depth, which in itself suggests a causative link with the formation of Silvermines ores, albeit 100 million years later. After all, such deep-going faults could channel hot water capable of scavenging metals from the deep crust and steering it upwards to the seafloor.

Those mountainous Silurian sediments bear testament to the rigours of continental collision, because they have been transformed into slates. These started life as mudstone, dominated by tiny plates of clay minerals aligned parallel to the bedding. During the increased temperature and pressure during collision, individual clay mineral platelets were rotated and recrystallised as larger plates to form the new thorough-going rock fabric that is slaty cleavage. Where well developed, as around Portroe village in the Arra Mountains, the rock can be thinly split to make slates suitable for roofing. The quarries there were an important local industry from the 1820s to the 1950s, producing high-quality slates. The occurrence of regular joint sets was particularly important because it minimised the proportion of waste involved. Larger slates attracted a premium out of proportion to their size, the value of Princesses being 25 times that of Commons (€1,000 as against €40 in today's currency) – and quite right too![9]

It was at Devilsbit Mountain, northeast of Silvermines Mountain, that the well-known environmental author and geologist, John Feehan, made a remarkable discovery. As a young scientist, he was researching Silurian muds which had accumulated at a time when life on land was far from exciting, mainly lichens, spiders and possibly scorpions, with some algal mounds clustered around shorelines. John found impressions of small delicate plants which are called *Cooksonia*. These were not spectacular to behold, just simple stalks with bifurcating branches that ended in spore-filled spheres. They had no flowers or leaves, indeed their very greenness was uncertain for they had rapidly become extinct. But these were not just any old plants, but examples of the Earth's earliest land plants. Indeed with an age of 425 million years, it is generally agreed that these Tipperary specimens are among the oldest examples known![10]

Tipperary poet Dennis O'Driscoll (1954–2012) lived a full century later than Charles Kickham, but their birth places were no further apart than 20 kilometres. Born in Thurles, he was raised close to the scenic uplands of Silvermines mountain and yet he found little poetic inspiration there. Working in the Civil Service in Dublin, his poetry had two recurring themes, a preoccupation with death and the tedium of everyday office life. But while he enjoyed landscape incidentally, perhaps while travelling, he does view it unconventionally. He sees winter hills as suffering from head colds, fields that are exhausted and snow capped mountains as burned meringue ("Time Sharing").[11] Coming home from work, his wife and himself are renewed, simply by passing through their favourite stretch of roadside trees, a canopy of branches ("Friday"). "The Bottom Line", a long review of the successes and disappointments of his career, could be O'Driscoll's urban response to Patrick Kavanagh's rural epic, "The Great Hunger". But his urban struggle allows him little opportunity to enjoy nature or savour local scenery. On a typical golf outing, he communes with nature only between fairway and rough.

All of this does not prepare us for O'Driscoll's sophisticated appreciation of mountain landscapes, where he richly links the scientific with the spiritual. In "Sermon in stones", O'Driscoll takes his title from *As You Like It* ("And this our life ... finds ... sermons in stones ...")[1] where William Shakespeare (1564–1616) extols the virtues of a pastoral life. Mountains, he asserts, glean their knowledge:

> from rifts and faults
> and shifting plates,
> a faith moving
> across millennia,
> sermons in stones
> handed down
> in granite seams.

Then O'Driscoll becomes more spiritual:

> Mountain peaks
> aspire to wisdom.
> Passing like molten
> glass through fire
> and water, they thirst
> for knowledge
> pure as driven snow.

He seeks answers by:

> scanning their
> weathered folds
> as if each
> shimmering outcrop
> hinted at some
> bedrock insight,
> gold reserves of truth,
> looking to their
> carbon-dated strata
> for the longer view.

Outcrops do indeed provide insights into the formation of both bedrock and mountains, although not necessarily involving carbon-dating (which would be too short term), so they really do harbour gold reserves of truth.

Addressing biodiversity ("All"), O'Driscoll suggests that all life forms, whether living or dead are just as enduring as meteorites. Even extinct species dwell among us, just as alive as our next-door neighbours. This 4D view of life's evolution, including its death and extinction, is breathtaking and shifts the poet's narrative on death to a new level. In "Looking Forward", the poet quotes approvingly the evolutionary biologist, Stephen Jay Gould (1941–2002), to the effect that modern order is largely a product of contingency, meaning that it has emerged coincidentally without a pre-ordained plan.

Irish place names never feature prominently in his work, not even Tipperary names, nor can we learn much of the poet's attitude to landscape by how he describes his home place. In "Thurles", he complains of its wet miserable weather, capturing it in depressingly clear terms. I am saddened by his loveless reference to a boring childhood and he seems relieved to return to city life without having revealed much of his feelings. Seventeen years later, he returns to the theme of "The Home Town" and still finds it and its residents quite ordinary. Only the family headstone (death again!) in the local cemetery claims him. But where are his happy childhood memories, the collection of small incidents that defines a person's youthful experience? Did he have close school companions? Did his neighbourhood have any outstanding personalities? His overriding attitudes to his office life and to death have influenced his thinking about his home town. But when he has chosen to do so, he has demonstrated a sophisticated appreciation of environment and its geological foundation, and found a refreshing way of expressing it.

Notes

1. Quoted from Act 2, Scene 1 of *As You Like It* by William Shakespeare (1564-1616).

2. See pages 324-326 of Praeger, R.L. (1937) *The Way that I Went: An Irishman in Ireland*. Dublin: Hodges, Figgis & Co and London: Methuen & Co. (Reprinted in 1997. Cork: The Collins Press).

3. See the following for more information on extinct mammalian fauna: http://news.nationalgeographic.com/news/2004/10/1006_041006_giant_deer.html (Accessed 3 November 2013).

4. An excellent starting point for studying the geology of Ireland's base metal mines is Kelly, J.G. and others (Eds.) (2003) *Europe's Major Base Metal Deposits*. Irish Association for Economic Geology.

5. This translation of "Cill Cais" is by Thomas Kinsella and appears on pages 330-331 of Seán O Tuama (Ed.) (1981) *An Duanaire – An Irish Anthology. 1600-1900: Poems of the Dispossessed*. With translations into English verse by Thomas Kinsella. Philadelphia: The University of Pennsylvania Press.

6. For background see, for example, entries by Ríonach Uí Ogáin on Fionn MacCumhaill (page 390) and Fionn Cycle (pages 389-390) in Brian Lalor (General Ed.) (2003) *The Encyclopaedia of Ireland*. Dublin: Gill & Macmillan.

7. William Nolan (2009) Charles Joseph Kickham (1828-1882). In James McGuire and James Quinn (Eds.) *Dictionary of Irish biography*. Royal Irish Academy & Cambridge University Press, volume 5, pages 168-171.

8. Maher, James (Ed.) (1942) *The Valley near Slievenamon: A Kickham Anthology*. Printed by *Kilkenny People*. The poems quoted here are "Slievenamon" (pages 60-61), "Carraigmoclear" (page 76) and "Patrick Sheehan" (pages 88-90).

9. Anonymous (1861) *Explanations to accompany Sheet 134 of the map of the Geological Survey of Ireland, illustrating parts of the counties of Clare, Tipperary and Limerick*. Dublin: Alexander Thom and Sons; Hodges, Smith and Company.

10. See D. Edwards and J. Feehan (1980) "Records of Cooksonia-type sporangia from late Wenlock strata in Ireland". *Nature*, 4 September 1980, volume 287, pages 41-42.

11. Dennis O'Driscoll (2004) *New and Selected Poems*. London: Anvil Press Poetry. I have quoted from "Sermons in Stone" (page 232) and referred to the following: "Time Sharing" (page 42), "Thurles" (page 43), "Looking Forward" (pages 71-73), "All" (page 132), "Friday" (page 158), "The Bottom Line" (pages 89-113), and "The Home Town" (pages 257-258).

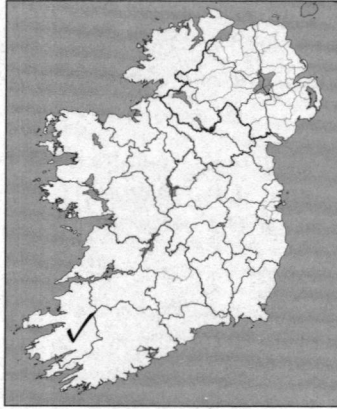

15

THERE IS SOMETHING ABOUT VAL!

(Kerry)

Everything here is above. The rock rears above us,
we are above the sea, the sea is above the depths.
– Macdara Woods[1]

They never found the skeleton on Valentia Island, no matter how hard they searched. But, for the forensically inclined, I have to report that a very fine set of footprints was discovered. The culprit moved across the sandy beach with a sluggish stride and was not acting alone, for the footprints of others were judged to be present. The strange thing is that as of now we have no reports of any crime having been committed. If it was a crime scene then its environment was very strange, with a sparse vegetation of ferns, mosses and horsetails, and no sign of any grass. Nor was it a companionable place for neither mammals nor even dinosaurs had appeared as yet – mainly a lot of bothersome insects! The footprints were sufficient evidence to allow palaeontologists to deduce that their owner was a metre-long amphibian, probably similar to modern-day salamanders.[2]

It is time for me to introduce you to Val, the world's earliest known amphibian, who enjoyed Kerry's warm climate all of 385 million years ago and whose criminal record was entirely unblemished. The climate was very hot, for at that time Kerry was in the realm of the southern hemisphere's tropics, devoid of any soothing shade unless Val fortuitously stumbled upon some coastal cave. The only excitement came in the form of occasional flash floods which carried quantities of sediment from the Caledonian mountains further north. It was one such flood that buried Val's footprints for posterity. If in search of company, she could have returned to the sea where there was already abundant fish life as well as a variety of molluscs, corals and brachiopods – but hardly the kind of life that would tempt Val to revert to the marine!

If you ever get a chance, do have a look at those footprints but choose a calm day and for preference visit when the sun is low. They occur on sea cliffs directly north of Valentia Island's well-known slate quarry. You may begin to doubt Val's dimensions, for the footprints seem too close together. In fact, the set of footprints has been shortened by a full 40 per cent, due to the huge compression the rocks suffered later as a result of the collision of the European and African plates further south. Those steps still have gigantic significance and are certainly on a par with Neil Armstrong's on the surface of the Moon back in 1969. For this salamander was the first animal to emerge on dry land, to breathe in the fresh Kerry air and to use all four feet to get around efficiently. There are few equivalent tracks anywhere else on Earth that are as old and as extensive. Valentia can be proud of its oldest ancestor!

Having reached Valentia, we are already well on our way to Skellig Michael. Surely one of Ireland's most spiritual and beautiful islands, it rises as a stark sandstone pyramid on the distant horizon as the boat approaches from Portmagee. Its World Heritage Status reflects the historical significance of its monastic site – and its puffin colony is not bad either! Its sister island, Little Skellig, hosts Europe's second largest gannet colony. We have already eavesdropped on the hypothetical visit there by Gerard Manley Hopkins, so now for a more contemporary view let's consider the recent visit by a group of poets to this remote island.[3]

Anyone who has visited Skellig Michael will appreciate that the sea trip is an inherent part of the day's experience and Theo Dorgan and John F. Deane were certainly impressed, if not overwhelmed, by it. The former, with uncertain sea legs, envisaged the islands as yachts. Derek Mahon wrote about two failed attempts, one historical, to reach the island due to stormy weather. As a frequent visitor, Paddy Bushe was engrossed with the vagaries of the weather, realising that he himself could be enclosed by the weather, and not just Skellig. Having been storm-bound there for four days, he contrasted its agitated atmosphere with the orderly lives of its monks. Nuala Ní Dhomhnaill wondered whether they stoically endured the harsh weather for the sake of suffering. John F. Deane envisaged the monks in procession and imagined them petrified forever in the rock. He regarded the island as a living being, with rock as its skeleton and Christ as its blood.

Visitors to Skellig Michael face an ascent of more than 600 steps in order to reach the monastic settlement. John F. Deane didn't find the climb easy, but the music of Russian composer, Modest Mussorgsky (1839–1881) sustained him! Macdara Woods found the rhythm of the steps entrancing and he became positively ethereal. Bernard O'Donoghue saw both the birds and monks making nobler choices than we ourselves might today. In one poem, Paddy Bushe devoted a stanza to the antics of each of thirteen types of birds. But gannets are foremost and both Seán Lysaght and John F. Deane observed them hunting for dinner. Deane mused forlornly that death might become a friend here for both monks and birds.

Indeed few referred to the bliss and solitude that many visitors experience, underlining the complexity of island life.

Eiléan Ní Chuilleanáin was impressed by the survival techniques that the monks developed, such as rainwater collection. Kerry Hardie thought the monks' life of mortification was unnatural until she experienced the island's spiritual calm. John F. Deane saw the settlement as a hiding place for the suffering soul. Indeed issues of faith and unbelief form a strong thread in many poems, Theo Dorgan saw the island as God's citadel and St. Michael, its patron, as a warrior saint. Macdara Woods felt comfortable in the monastic public space, which reminded him of walled Italian hill-towns, while Derek Mahon was repulsed by the intellectual isolation he sensed among the monks.

Skellig Michael is not the only famous locality in Kerry. Killarney is the gateway to the Iveragh Peninsula and its islands, being close to the famous Lakes of Killarney and east of the rugged Magillycuddy Reeks, Ireland's highest mountains.[4] The attractive combination of mountains, woods and lakes has made Killarney a focus for writers and visitors for more than 200 years. The socio-economic conditions of the country and its unfortunate peasants may have been their dominant theme, but some writers did also appreciate its landscape.[5] Arthur Young (1741–1820), agricultural economist, journalist and traveller, in 1776 stayed at Muckross House on the peninsula separating the main Lough Leane from Muckross Lake.[6] The lakeshore, with its fertile limestone bedrock, he found enchanting and its cultivated land formed a pleasant contrast to the surrounding mountains. He considered Innisfallen, the most prominent island in the main lake, to be idyllic with its undulating slopes, green lawns and great variety of trees. For him the Lakes of Killarney were simply incomparable!

His views on the surrounding mountains were not so clear-cut. Those he encountered on the way from Kenmare he regarded as immense, their rocky surfaces were grotesque and overall they filled him with terror. Tomies (735 metres) and Shehy (571 metres) mountains, on the southwestern shore of Lough Leane, were no different, their steep jagged profiles being considered savage and dreadful. This was sandstone country of bare rocks, very different to the main lakes area. However Shehy's beauty was redeemed a little by its wooded slopes. A torrential river which flowed along a rough river bed was considered unpleasant by Young, yet he was greatly taken with O'Sullivan's Cascade, on the lakeshore below Tomies. However, by the time he departed Killarney he had mellowed his views, thinking Tomies and Shehy were no longer threatening, and perhaps his views were softened by the changing weather and daylight patterns. Indeed Eagle's Nest, a relatively low ridge between Shehy and Torc mountains, was initially considered unworthy of applause but finally he could praise its impressive slopes overlooking some lower forests. And then there was Torc mountain (535 metres) itself, which certainly caught his attention and he returned more than once to praise its noble outline and the splendid shoreline beneath it.

For Young, mountains were acceptable when smooth, but ugly when too vast or jagged. His ideal was where mountains were relieved by farmland, woods or gardens. There has been some recent discussion of changing attitudes towards natural landscapes, from the apparent abhorrence of the eighteenth century to the romanticism of the nineteenth.[7] It is argued that in the eighteenth century "useless" terrain such as mountains was regarded as ugly while productive areas such as farmland were considered beautiful. If Young's views were taken as representative, then we would have to acknowledge that the position was more complex than that. In the case of mountains, their scale, steepness and outline all determined whether they were considered ugly or beautiful. On lower "useful" ground, he seems equally delighted with gardens and woods as he is with farmland although surely the latter's productivity would far outweigh that of gardens and perhaps woods? However we should concede that Young was no more rational than the rest of us and that our feelings towards landscape could be greatly influenced by our changeable moods, the prevailing weather – or the presence of hungry peasants in nearby wretched cabins.

Arthur Young was right to state that Killarney's past was volcanic. He describes the Devil's Punch Bowl on Mangerton mountain (839 metres) as one of perhaps several volcanic craters in this area and considered that they ejected the brown boulders found on limestone bedrock in the area. While there are no actual craters – extinct or otherwise – lurking in these mountains, there are certainly beds of volcanic rock exposed in the cliffs at the Devil's Punch Bowl. In fact a series of rhyolitic lavas and ashes can be traced in bedrock from the Mangerton area eastwards to the County Cork boundary. So Killarney experienced some volcanic events and, judging by the nature of the rock sequence, they must have been quite explosive. Young's comments are interesting because the study of volcanoes was in its infancy then and it would be another decade before the volcanic pedigree of even the Giant's Causeway was widely recognised. Nowadays, the Devil's Punch Bowl is considered to be a corrie developed by erosion during the Ice Age and those brown boulders are glacial erratics.

Heading towards Killarney town, Young passed the mines at Ross Island which extracted copper ores from the limestone bedrock, noting they had been abandoned, more from ignorance in the workmen, than any defects in the mine. With this casual sideswipe at blameless miners, Young dismisses a mine with a most interesting and distinguished history. For this deposit may have produced the very first copper ores ever mined in Ireland, almost 4,500 years ago, and which were smelted for use in Bronze Age artefacts. The mine did produce ores intermittently at various times since then, most recently in the period 1707–1829, so its output actually outlived Young's visit.[8]

Fast-forwarding to the allegedly romantic mid-nineteenth century, in 1842 William Makepeace Thackeray (1811–1863)[9] took a boat out on Lough Leane and admired the mountains, islands and trees. He was impressed by O'Sullivan's Cascade, quite a sight, and found the splendour of the lakes overpowering. Muckross Lake was more beautiful than the main lake – or was it? He was confused, so pretty was the scenery! He enjoyed the wonderful lakeshore views, the bays, vegetation and rocks. And the distant purple hills made as pretty a landscape as the eye could see. He seemed to identify the favourite spot of Sir Walter Scott who had already visited Killarney. Torc waterfall he found most handsome: it was wild not fierce, but had enough savageness to make the view piquant.

Very soon after Thackeray's visit, Killarney received a pair of travellers, Mr and Mrs Hall, with a history that might have illdisposed them to the district's charms. For Mr Hall's father, Col. Hall, had re-opened the Ross Island mine back in 1804, but without commercial success. Nevertheless the Halls were completely enchanted by 1850s Killarney in its many dimensions.[10] The day spent ascending Carrauntwohill (1,041 metres), Ireland's highest mountain, on horseback was one of great enjoyment, while the view from the more accessible Mangerton mountain was the most magnificent sight they had ever witnessed. No ambivalence about mountainous scenery here! Torc Waterfall was incomparable, fed by water flowing from the Devil's Punch Bowl, while the lakes were all equally splendid. Well, perhaps nature had not created its best in Lough Guitane, which was surrounded by rude and barren hills.

But Killarney certainly benefited from the attention of popular British writers including Alfred Lord Tennyson (1809–1892), who visited Killarney twice in the 1840s and would do so again in 1878. It was Killarney that provided him with the inspiration to compose "Blow, Bugle, Blow":

> The splendour falls on castle walls
> And snowy summits old in story:
> The long light shakes across the lakes,
> And the wild cataract leaps in glory.
> Blow, bugle, blow, set the wild echoes flying,
> Blow, bugle, answer, echoes, dying, dying, dying.

Strangely enough, when the Halls experienced bugle echoes one evening on Lough Leane, it brought to their minds John Milton's (1608–1674) poem "Sweet Echo" rather than Tennyson's recent composition.[11]

Some commentators[7] argue that popularity of scenic landscape grew in the mid-nineteenth century as an antidote to the stresses of an increasingly urbanised way of life. If so, there is no doubting that the completion of convenient transport routes really helped, whether it be Killarney's railway or the Coastal Road to its main rival destination, the Giant's Causeway. The latter, with its stacks of basalt columns, held more than scenic fascination for visitors, depending on whether they looked to them as either evidence of Creation or of volcanic activity. The Giant's Causeway experienced further controversy at the end of the nineteenth century when it was fenced off and a charge imposed on visitors. In contrast, Killarney's simple appeal rested in unrestricted access to its scenic beauty which was regarded as the common heritage of humanity.[12]

Killarney's scenic beauty is based on its combination of limestone lowlands and sandstone mountains. The contact between the two rocks is a fault which lies close to the base of Torc Mountain and can be traced eastwards to County Cork, as a splay of the major Killarney–Mallow Fault Zone. The fault follows the railway line between Killarney and Millstreet, separating the rugged, freely-draining hills of sandstone to the south from the flat, subdued and poorly drained countryside to the north. The latter's bedrock is predominantly mudstone which overlies the Carboniferous limestone while the sandstone corresponds with Old Red Sandstone. In the Torc Mountain area, the sandstone has overridden the limestone along this fault plane and the vertical displacement may be as much as three kilometres. The fault zone marks the northern limit of strong deformation arising from the end-Carboniferous collision of the two tectonic plates in central Europe – the same collision that cramped Val's footsteps down on Valentia Island!

Torc Waterfall is worth visiting for two reasons. Firstly, the waterfall itself, with rapids both before and after it, is situated in a sandstone-lined ravine whose visual impact lies somewhere between impressive and awesome. I was fortunate that my January visit came when the river was in full spate. Secondly, you have the opportunity to follow paths above the waterfall in search of scenic views. If you do so, be prepared for a reasonable uphill hike because viewpoints are scarce within woodlands where trees and rhododendrons struggle for supremacy. But there are some great viewing positions and I met a couple descending from one who were so excited by what they experienced that they felt obliged to share it with me. The view was breathtaking! I think that "breathtaking" is at least a notch above impressive or awesome and it is justified! You can feast your eyes on Muckross House Gardens, headquarters of Killarney National Park, leading to wooded Muckross Peninsula, Muckross Lake and Lough Leane, Innisfallen and Ross Island. The sprawling metropolis of Killarney lies in the background with its northern hinterland of low hilly ground.

Do not depart from Torc without at least glancing at its sandstone bedrock. Traditionally called Old Red Sandstone, there certainly are some red beds present. There are rusty brown and buff varieties as well. But actually most of the sandstones here are green in colour and this is due to their content of chlorite, a mica mineral of metamorphic origin derived from the weathering of the old Caledonian mountains further north. As I examined some bedding surfaces, I was fortunate to note some slender plant fronds and I reflected once more on Val and her diet. Had she lived say 10 to 15 million years later she might have found nourishment in this very vegetation. But whatever food was available, I do hope that Val found it flavoursome.

Notes

1. Quoted from "Timesis" by Macdara Woods, see pages 171-184 of Paddy Bushe (Ed.) (2010) *Voices at the World's Edge: Irish Poets on Skellig Michael*. Dublin: The Dedalus Press.

2. Matthew Parkes (2004) *The Valentia Island Tetrapod Trackway*. Dublin: Geological Survey of Ireland and National Parks and Wildlife Service.

3. Paddy Bushe (Ed.) (2010) *Voices at the World's Edge: Irish Poets on Skellig Michael*. Dublin: The Dedalus Press. The following authors are referred to: Paddy Bushe ("Skelligs birds", "Stormbound"), John F. Deane ("Night on Skellig), Theo Dorgan ("Sailing to the Edge"), Kerry Hardie ("A High Tradition"), Seán Lysaght ("Gannets"), Derek Mahon ("A Fine Soft Morning on Sceilg Bay", "At the Butler Arms"), Eiléan Ní Chuilleanáin ("Vertigo"), Bernard O'Donoghue ("The Skelligs Listeners") and Macdara Woods ("Timesis").

4. Pracht, M. (1997) *A geological description to accompany the bedrock geology 1:100,000 scale map series, sheet 21, Kerry-Cork*. Dublin: Geological Survey of Ireland.

5. Glenn Hooper (2005) *Travel Writing and Ireland, 1760-1860: Culture, History, Politics*. Basingstoke, Hampshire: Palgrave Macmillan.

6. Arthur Young (1970) *A Tour in Ireland 1776-1779*. Volume 1. A.W. Hutton (Ed.). Shannon, Ireland: Irish University Press. See pages 343-362 for his description of Killarney.

7. Christian Keller (2003) "The theoretical aspects of landscape study". In Timothy Collins (Ed.) *Decoding the Landscape*. Third Edition. Galway: Centre for Landscape Studies, pages 79-97.

8. William O'Brien (2004) *Ross Island: Mining, Metal and Society in Early Ireland*. Bronze Age Studies 6. Department of Archaeology, NUI Galway.

9. William Makepeace Thackeray (2005) *The Irish Sketchbook of 1842*. First published 1843. Dublin: Nonsuch Publishing. For Killarney district see pages 101-122.

10. Hall, Mr and Mrs S.C. (1858) *A Week at Killarney*. London: J.S. Virtue.

11. Popularly known as "Blow, Bugle, Blow", Tennyson's "The Splendour Falls on Castle Walls" appears on page 264 of Tennyson, Alfred, Lord (1918) *Poems of Tennyson*, with an introduction by T.H. Warren. London: Humphrey Milford and Oxford University Press.

12. Irene Furlong (2008) "The landscape for all – no penny-in-the-slot at the Giant's Causeway". In Una Ní Bhroiméil and Glenn Hooper (Eds.) *Land and Landscape in Nineteenth-century Ireland*. Dublin: Four Courts Press, pages 63-77.

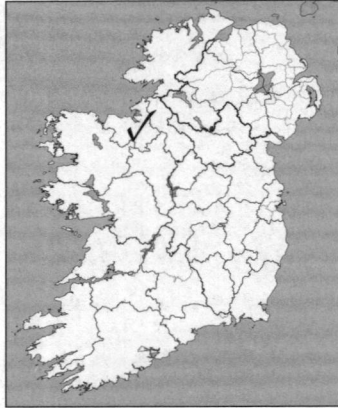

16

EMERALD ROCK
(Sligo)

There is a waterfall
Upon Ben Bulben side
That all my childhood counted dear.
– W. B. Yeats[1]

William Drennan (1754–1820),[2] Belfast-born Presbyterian, patriot and poet, chose well. In 1795 he published a new ballad, "When Erin First Rose", in which Ireland was described for the first time as the Emerald Isle, thereby assigning to his homeland as emblem one of the most precious of gemstones – but one of which we could not claim a single native specimen! No wonder his choice was widely adopted! Emerald is a special variety of beryl, a mineral that itself is not uncommon. It does occur in the granites of Donegal and Mournes, but it is dull and turbid, and has relatively limited aesthetic value. When beryl contains traces of chromium and vanadium it is transformed into a gemstone of satisfyingly deep green colour which is universally prized for its durability and rarity. The main source of gem-quality emerald has long been Colombia, which is one of several countries that might feel entitled to adopt the gem as its national emblem. Emerald may be an affectionate and popular appellation for Ireland, but clearly it would be inappropriate to designate it as our national mineral. Ireland already has well recognised national emblems such as the harp and shamrock, but their wide acceptance should not deter us from designating an important rock or mineral as national emblem. I believe it should be a rock, and that rock should be limestone.

Limestone is the foundation for Ireland's much-vaunted greenery, it provides critical nourishment for soils and so it truly is Emerald Rock! It is the most extensive rock type on the island, covering almost half of it, and presents itself in a wide spectrum of varieties. It nurtures some of our most sensitive ecosystems, such as the turloughs, or winter lakes, to the west of the River Shannon. When quarried and dressed it has been used in some of our best-known buildings, from Dublin Castle to the monastery on the Rock of Cashel. A great deal of it has been quarried in recent decades for the manufacture of aggregates for our motorways and construction. It contains a range of metal ores, especially of zinc and lead, which have been mined intermittently for more than a millennium in various parts of the country. At least as important is the fact that many counties draw significant quantities of their drinking water from the aquifers of this abundant bedrock. Limestone defines some of our most iconic landscapes, from the Burren pavements to the callows near Clonmacnoise and the cliffs of Sligo. Should we expect any more than this of a national emblem?

Where better to promulgate limestone as our national rock than in Sligo, which is strongly associated with the well-liked poet and dramatist, William Butler Yeats (1865–1939).[3] The limestone areas of County Sligo and Gort in County Galway are his important landscapes – he is the Lyricist of Limestone! Raised in Dublin and London, he spent sufficient of his youthful summers in Sligo to ensure it featured in his work throughout his life. After being awarded the 1924 Nobel Prize for Literature, he became an eminent public figure in Ireland and went on to produce some of his most influential poetry. Scenic landscapes were sacred to him and he savoured their beauty and solitude:

> For years to come it was in my thought, as in much of my writing, to seek also to bring again into imaginative life the old sacred places – Slievenamon, Knocknarea – all that old reverence that hung – above all – about conspicuous hills.[4]

He often regarded landscape as symbolic of other themes, such as his happy childhood. Visitors are now drawn to Knocknarea and Lough Gill for Yeats' narrative just as strongly as for the landscape itself.[5]

Lough Gill features in some of Yeats' most popular poems and "The Stolen Child" is a good example:

> Where dips the rocky highland
> Of Sleuth Wood in the lake,
> There lies a leafy island
> Where flapping herons wake
> The drowsy water-rats.[6]

That rocky highland might be Dooney Rock, just as the island might be Innisfree. An incident reminded the London-based poet that the local Sligo river of his childhood was sourced in Lough Gill and this was the inspiration for "The Lake Isle of Innisfree". In this poem, he longs for the solitude of Innisfree, a bushy and rocky island in this lake, where he dreams of an ascetic existence:

> I will arise and go now, and go to Innisfree,
> And a small cabin built there, of clay and wattles made:
> Nine bean-rows will I have there, a hive for the honey bee,
> And live alone in the bee-loud glade.

His peace would be gradually restored through his daily interactions with nature and even in his urban life he can still recall his
idyllic island environment:

I hear lake water lapping with low sounds by the shore.

Stand on the beautifully wooded Dooney Rock on the southern
shore of Lough Gill and, looking beyond this lake, you can appreciate the restricted extent of Yeats Country, with the table mountain
of Knocknarea and the steep cliffs of Benbulben both visible. I arrived when the latter was mist-covered and displayed a vertical
segment of rainbow just where I fancifully imagined that Glencar Waterfall might be. Wouldn't Mr Yeats have been intrigued!
Dooney Rock itself is composed of rather featureless limestone,
but behind it rises the craggy spine of the Ox Mountains with their
metamorphic gneisses, formed at great depth from sediments dating back a billion years, and locally containing intrusions of granite and serpentinite. These ancient rocks have been exhumed by
seismic activity along a major southwesterly–trending fault that
separates them from Yeats Country limestone and which can be
traced as far as Westport.[7]

Significant developments of Dooney Rock limestone are confined to the course of this fault, where periodic earthquake-in-
duced subsidence encouraged its accumulation. In fact elsewhere
the limestones of Yeats Country are varied, occurring in several
distinctive layers, and we will confine our attention to just two,
the younger being composed of thickly-bedded limestone that
forms the cliffed uplands of the Benbulben range and Knocknarea.
In contrast to this, the second and underlying layer comprises in-
terbedded shale and limestone that forms coastal exposures with
spectacular evidence of contemporary animal life.

In his adult life Benbulben mountain was a significant landmark on Yeats' Sligo horizon, holding for him treasured memories
of clambering its streams in search of prospective fishing loca-

tions. When he was disheartened by "decrepit age" ("The Tower", section 1), he fondly remembered:

> when with rod and fly,
> Or the humbler worm, I climbed Ben Bulben's back
> And had the livelong summer day to spend.

Yeats described the nearby waterfall at Glencar more than once, but his earliest is surely his most beguiling ("The Stolen Child"):

> Where the wandering water gushes
> From the hills above Glen-Car,
> In pools among the rushes
> That scarce could bathe a star,
> We seek for slumbering trout
> And whispering in their ears
> Give them unquiet dreams.

He is enchanted by this river that feeds Glencar Waterfall before its waters tumble into Glencar Lake. In winter's slanting sunshine, I could discern that large chunks of mountainy limestone had become detached and slid downwards along the lubricating shales beneath. This happened only after the melting of a buttressing Ice Age glacier which had gouged out and steepened the lower slopes, and was also responsible for creating the Glencar Waterfall itself. Over thirty years after his initial enthusiasm, Yeats would still yearn for that waterfall ("Towards Break of Day"):

> There is a waterfall
> Upon Ben Bulben side
> That all my childhood counted dear;
> Were I to travel far and wide
> I could not find a thing so dear.

I sense echoes of Goldsmith's Auburn in the open-eyed wonderment and lyricism of this!

Those hills are secure childhood memories although, as far as I know, Yeats never walked their slopes in adulthood. But he did ordain that he be buried beneath Benbulben, his grave marked by a simple gravestone of local limestone with these words ("Under Ben Bulben"):

Cast a cold eye
On life, on death.
Horseman, pass by!

This simple and celebrated epithet reflects his quiet resignation at approaching death. Yeats is not usually portrayed as a humble man but it must be said that his grave, with its unexceptional location within the cemetery and modest-sized headstone, eschews any triumphal or garish suggestion. In fact the visitor could easily miss it!

Yeats loved the seashore and was fascinated by the sea's rhythmical movement. In "The Fiddler of Dooney", the fiddler delights in his power to entertain people but he leaves us in no doubt that he exults just as much in the seashore itself. Yeats remained enchanted with the edge of the sea, yet it is remarkable that he is silent about much of the Sligo coastline, which is just a short drive from his beloved Benbulben. Perhaps he simply wished to avoid the unpleasant memories associated with localities such as Streedagh Point, where more than 1,000 sailors of the Spanish Armada drowned after their vessels were shipwrecked here in 1588. Those who managed to scramble ashore must have thought themselves fortunate, until they encountered the hostile British soldiers and unsympathetic Irish residents, who between them slaughtered most survivors mercilessly. But the evidence of death stretches much further back in time to the formation of the bedrock itself. The limestone and shale here became the graveyard for a tropical marine fauna, including sea lilies, corals and brachiopods, whose remains accumulated on the seafloor. Most impressive are the solitary corals whose skeletons form curved stems 0.5 metres long and weather out prominently on bedding surfaces, looking for all the world like segments of fossilised serpents. It is just possible that that explains the origin of the nearby place name, Serpent Point, which has a similarly spectacular fossil display! Had Yeats realised this, it would have made him even more comfortable in this magical landscape.

Knocknarea (350 metres) is a prominent headland that juts out into the estuary of Sligo Bay. Dark brown heathery moors give way downwards to a trellis of small green fields, but the ascending walker is soon aware of limestone bedrock underfoot. This is a fairly uniform grey rock that has prominent clumps of fossilised colonial corals and chert, a black lustrous material. It is the same limestone layer that forms the top of the Ben Bulben range. Knocknarea's summit is marked by a cairn including some granite gneiss boulders that were transported by ice from the Ox Mountains. Yeats sustains a glacial climate here in "Red Hanrahan's Song about Ireland". Wind may be colourless, but we have no difficulty feeling the chill of a cold black wind which causes the withered thorn-trees to snap in a bleak winter landscape.

The Gort area of east Galway became important for Yeats after he met Lady Augusta Gregory (1852–1932), playwright and landowner, in the 1890s. Their blossoming friendship led to their jointly founding the Abbey Theatre, his frequent summer visits to her home at Coole Park, outside Gort, and his eventual purchase of Thoor Ballylee, a nearby Norman tower house. Yeats' strong attachment to this limestone landscape certainly confirms him as Ireland's Lyricist of Limestone!

The Gort Lowlands have tended to be overshadowed by their more famous westerly neighbour, the karst limestone uplands of the Burren. They are also floored by karst limestone but have experienced much more prolonged weathering and dissolution by rainwater. They have many turloughs, impersistent lakes which shrink dramatically in summer, when they are marked only by dry swallow holes. Rivers tend to run underground for stretches along open fractures, re-appearing at irregular intervals as upwelling springs. During the Ice Age, unlike the Burren, these lowlands were extensively blanketed by hummocky deposits of boulder clay.[8]

The focal point of the Gort Lowlands is undoubtedly Coole Park, although its house is long since demolished. Its mixed woodlands form a nature reserve of international importance, with turloughs, some limestone pavement and a variety of wetland ecosystems. Coole Lough, the turlough with celebrated swans, is fed by a river with no surface outflow, being drained by underground flow along fractures and caverns in the bedrock limestone. Gort limestone is a dour grey variety which formed in a marine environment that had strong wave action so that most skeletal remains were comminuted before being preserved in fossil form. There is nothing of the excitement of Streedagh shoreline with its dazzling display of fossils! However Coole Park did have its own intellectual excitement, the evidence being still present in the Walled Garden. I am referring to the bark of the expansive copper beech which contains the carved initials of visiting writers such as George Bernard Shaw, Douglas Hyde, John Millington Synge, Sean O'Casey – and, of course, W. B. Yeats.

The poem "Coole and Ballylee, 1931" gives a description of the natural landscape of these two localities, linked by underground river. An underground river of itself might be considered unexceptional in this karst area, but surely this link between his Thoor Ballylee and his patron's Coole Park had huge symbolic importance for Yeats! It might even have encouraged him to give additional consideration to his physical environment. Yeats quickly developed a love for the natural environment of Coole Park, which seems to have reliably assuaged him in troubled times. Two decades, later, in "The Wild Swans of Coole", he would use the "nine-and-fifty swans" there to memorably capture the magic of Coole:

But now they drift on the still water,
Mysterious, beautiful;
Among what rushes will they build,
By what lake's edge or pool
Delight men's eyes when I awake some day
To find they have flown away?

But, of course, there is also a darker theme running through the poem, that of Yeats' advancing age – while the swans seem timeless.

Opinion remains divided on the extent of Yeats' commitment to natural history and landscape appreciation. He has been viewed as disinterested on the basis of his less than comprehensive environmental descriptions,[5] and this may be unfair because we all tend to be influenced by our own particular landscape narratives. So should I bring a group of friends to inspect a rustic bridge, the angler will be alert for the splash in the river, the birdman will watch for the kingfisher, I may be forgiven for noticing the bedrock outcrop on which the bridge is built, while the engineer will be fascinated by the bridge's design and construction. But there is no doubt that Yeats developed a sceptical approach to science, one that was in sympathy with prevailing attitudes in newly independent Ireland,[9] and so he preferred to dwell on more mystical topics.

However, he is unlikely to have entirely abandoned his early interest in natural science[9] and Seamus Heaney regarded him as being close to the natural landscape. In reflecting on Yeats' poem, "The Man and the Echo", Heaney saw poets and geologists at their most heroic because they both ask a question of the stone.[10] I cannot disagree with anyone who sees geologists as heroic! Having said that, the key to Yeats' appreciation of landscape is its relationship with the communities it nurtures and, writing in 1903 of the Gort lowlands, he regarded one as an extension of the other:

There is still in truth upon these great level plains a people, a community bound together by imaginative possessions, by stories and poems which have grown out of its own life, and by a past of great passions which can still waken the heart to imaginative action.[11]

We don't need detailed descriptions of Benbulben or Gort landscapes to realise that Yeats relished the time he spent in them. He took pains to express that enjoyment eloquently throughout his poetic career and usually in an unobtrusive manner. He treasured fond memories of Sligo's mountains and continued to actively enjoy Coole's less demanding scenery! But wouldn't he be delighted if he knew his humble limestone were elevated to the status of Emerald Rock! Why not?

Notes

1. From "Under Ben Bulben" by W. B. Yeats. See pages 325-328 of W. B. Yeats (1983) *The Poems, a New Edition*. Richard J. Finneran (Ed.). London: Macmillan London.

2. Stewart, A.T.Q. (2009) William Drennan (1754-1820). In McGuire, J. and Quinn, J. (Eds.) *Dictionary of Irish Biography*. Royal Irish Academy and Cambridge University Press, volume 3, pages 461-463.

3. Brown, T. (2009) William Butler Yeats (1865-1939). In McGuire, J. and Quinn, J. (Eds.) *Dictionary of Irish Biography*. Royal Irish Academy and Cambridge University Press, volume 9, pages 1087-1093.

4. See page 124 of W. B. Yeats (1972) *Memoirs: Autobiography – first draft journal*. Denis Donoghue (Ed.) London: Macmillan.

5. Pat Sheeran (2003) "The narrative creation of place: The example of Yeats". In Timothy Collins (Ed.). *Decoding the Landscape*. Third edition. Galway: Centre for Landscape Studies, University College Galway, pages 148-162.

6. W. B. Yeats (1983) *The Poems, a New Edition*. Richard J. Finneran (Ed.) London: Macmillan London. I quoted from the following poems: "The Stolen Child" (pages 18-19), "The Lake Isle of Innisfree" (page 39), "The Wild Swans of Coole" (pages 131-132), "Towards Break of Day" (page 185), "The Tower" (pages 194-200) and "Under Ben Bulben" (pages 325-328). I also referred to "The Fiddler of Dooney" (page 74), "Red Hanrahan's Song about Ireland" (pages 81-82), "Coole and Ballylee, 1931" (pages 243-245) and "The Man and the Echo" (pages 345-346).

7. For the geology of the Yeats Country see Anon. (2008) *Landscapes, Rocks and Fossils: The Geological Heritage of County Sligo*. Sligo County Council and the Geological Survey of Ireland.

8. Mike Simms (2001) *Exploring the Limestone Landscapes of the Burren and the Gort Lowlands*. Belfast: Burrenkarst.com.

9. J. W. Foster (1997) "The culture of nature". In Foster, J.W. (Ed.) *Nature in Ireland: A Scientific and Cultural History*. Dublin: The Lilliput Press, pages 597-635.

10. Seamus Heaney (2004) "Bog bank, rock face and the far fetch of poetry". In Parkes, M.A. (Ed.). *Natural and Cultural Landscapes: The Geological Foundation*. Dublin: Royal Irish Academy, pages 11-17.

11. The quotation is from page 213 of the essay, "The Galway Plains", in W. B. Yeats (1961) *Essays and Introductions*. London: Macmillan & Co.

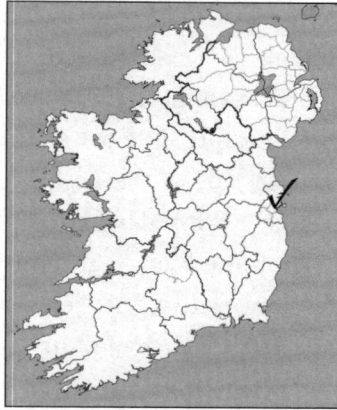

17

O Rocks! Give Us
the Plain Words
(Dublin)

All quiet on Howth now. The distant hills seem. Where we.
The rhododendrons. I am a fool perhaps. He gets the plums
and I the plumstones. Where I come in. All that old hill
has seen. Names change: that's all. Lovers: yum, yum.
– James Joyce[1]

A significant number of visitors to Howth village find their way
to the Cliff Walk that encircles Howth peninsula clockwise
from the village as far as Sutton. Walkers are traversing Dublin's
oldest rocks – Cambrian sandstones, greywackes and siltstones,
dominantly green in colour, as well as some prominent quartzite
beds ("Howth Stone"). Some beds seem chaotically jumbled because they were disrupted and re-deposited by strong earthquakes.

Ireland's Eye is composed of similar rock but the more distant Lambay Island is Dublin's own volcano, composed of dark green andesite lava with abundant light-coloured feldspar crystals.[2] As we proceed, it is sometimes possible to see the mountains of the Lleyn Peninsula on the far side of the Irish Sea. Now Dublin Bay has come into view, which is floored by the same limestones which underlie Dublin city. Soon the Baily Lighthouse forms the northern extremity of Dublin Bay, with a fine view across to its southern shores around Killiney Bay. The skyline of serrated peaks, from Bray Head to the Sugarloaf, comprise rocks similar to those on which we are treading, while the rounded hills further west are of granite.

Killiney Beach played a prominent role in the study of quakes. This is where Robert Mallet (1810–1881) in 1849 demonstrated through a controlled explosion that the ground could transmit seismic waves. An engineering graduate, he developed his family's foundry into a successful business that supplied ironwork for railways and construction. But his intellectual passion became the study of earthquakes and he was first to publish a global map and catalogue of their distribution. He also created the first map showing the intensity of damage caused in December 1857 following the disastrous Naples earthquake.[3]

Yes, we are now walking in full view of the Wicklow and Dublin Mountains.

> There they were, as if I'd never left them; in their sweet and stately order round the Bay – Bray Head, the Sugarloaf, the Two Rock, the Three Rock, Kippure, the king of them all, rising his threatening head behind and over their shoulders till they sloped down to the city.

These were the affectionate thoughts of the young Brendan Behan as he first hungrily glimpsed his native city on his ship-board return from borstal in England. In his mind, he had all the church spires counted and he lingered over each suburb around the Bay, from Dun Laoghaire to Howth Head. He struggled to identify Kilbarrack with its cemetery, where so many of his relatives were buried and which he called the healthiest graveyard in Ireland. His love and knowledge of his native place were evident.[4]

The northside suburbs are underlain by variable thicknesses of glacial till – the boulder clay commonly found beneath the soils of Dublin gardens. It is prominently exposed on Howth peninsula and was deposited in at least two stages, the earlier from an ice sheet that occupied the Irish Sea and the later from a major ice sheet that moved southeastwards across Howth Head, scoring rock surfaces as it went. Howth subsequently became an island as sea levels rose during ice melting and it was the action of tides and currents over the past 5,000 years that re-united it with Fingal by constructing a linking tombolo of sand and gravel.[5]

Homer's story of Ulysses was played out in the eastern Mediterranean between the longitudes of Sicily and Rhodes. *The Odyssey* describes Ulysses' prolonged and hazardous voyage home to Ithaca on Greece's west coast following his successful siege of Troy. He would lose his fleet of twelve ships and every one of his 600 fighting men before triumphantly reaching home himself.[6] Not many people realise (I could be the only one!) that when Joyce selected a context for his Dublin-based novel, *Ulysses*, it was his abiding interest in geology and its boundary with astronomy that moved him to choose Homer's epic. For one thing, the key bedrocks in both environments are the same, igneous rock and limestone. Holiday-makers may return from the Mediterranean with fond memories of limestone-fringed beaches or the awesome volcanoes of Italy and the Aegean, but Dublin will not be found wanting on either score![7]

While I could simply point to Lambay Island's volcano, I prefer to remind you that granite, that great Dublin stone, represents molten magma that solidified before it could reach surface in volcanic expression. So just a few more kilometres upwards pushing and the rock underpinning Killiney's scenery, with its pretensions to Sorrento grandeur, might have seemed truly Italian (minus the sunshine!). Now I realise that readers might find it invidious to compare creamy Mediterranean limestone with cold dark Calp Limestone visible only in dank quarries on the edge of Dublin! But what a fascinating stone that Calp is! It has been used so much in constructing the city that it is part of Dublin's very fabric. Its sedimentary features speak of an environment where its deposition has been punctuated by periodic seismic activity – a variation on the theme of Howth's rock sequence. What Dubliner would trade such a meaningful rock for the flashiness of a creamy version that requires sunshine to bring it to life?

Astronomy was the hobby of Leopold Bloom, *Ulysses'* central character, but his thoughts stray easily between geological and astronomical topics. The novel is set on 16 June 1904, now immortalised as Bloomsday, and Bloom's transit across the façade of Trinity College Dublin prompts him to reflect on matters astronomical. He recalls Professor Joly, evidently Charles Jasper Joly (1864–1906),[8] who in 1904 held the joint position of Andrews Professor of Astronomy at Trinity and of Royal Astronomer of Ireland. Bloom, anxious to ingratiate himself with this erudite gentleman, thought he might visit him at his observatory. In the Ithaca episode, Bloom demonstrates many constellations to Stephen Dedalus, the younger man he is shepherding towards his home, and reflects on the wonder of cosmic evolution.

Charles Joly was a second cousin of Professor John Joly (1857–1933) who was seven years his senior, outlived him by a quarter century and ultimately was more celebrated. They shared a similar family background, their father in each case being a Protestant rector in County Offaly. Both cousins had achieved professorships at Trinity by 1904 although, in Charles's case, Bloom might have been surprised to learn that his reputation rested less on his astronomical work than on his mathematical research. For example, he prepared a new edition of William Rowan Hamilton's (1805–1865) classic work on quaternions. His principal astronomical initiative was a 1900 expedition to Spain to study a total eclipse of the sun.

We have already encountered Professor John Joly among the eskers of Offaly. Irish citizens owe him a special debt of gratitude because he was responsible for establishing the Irish Radium Institute, one of the first to treat cancer patients with radioactive doses.[9] His work on the newly emerging topic of radioactivity gave him new insights into the origin of the Earth itself, which had been thought to have cooled from an originally molten state. Indeed Bloom's thoughts loosely took their cue from this earlier model, ranging over the Earth's origin as a spinning gasball:

> Gas, then solid, then world, then cold, then dead shell drifting around, frozen rock like that pineapple rock.[10]

Joly concluded that the Earth was actually heating up due to the radioactivity of its interior, but Bloom had yet to adjust to this new insight – although Joyce himself might have been well aware of this paradigm shift in thinking.

It is just possible that Bloom confused the two Joly Professors in his mind for, in the Ithaca episode, after discussing cosmic evolution, he strays into strictly geological territory by referring to eons of geological periods recorded in the stratification of the Earth. But why blame this on Bloom, maybe the confusion was in Joyce's own mind! By the time he was writing this, Charles had long since died of typhoid and at the same time John's academic star had risen inexorably. It would have been easy for him to become confused between the two Joly professors, for John the geologist did some astronomy and Charles the astronomer did surprisingly little! So the confusion would have been very understandable.

Africa has been plunging beneath Europe for 70 million years along a complex plate margin spanning the Mediterranean and giving rise to many volcanoes, none of which had erupted since the late nineteenth century. But just two years beforehand, in May 1902, the town and harbour of St. Pierre, on the Caribbean island of Martinique, were devastated by the eruption of the Mont Pelée volcano. Its entire population, save for a convict confined to a dungeon, were killed. With this catastrophe so vividly in the public mind, it is remarkable that Joyce pens no description of a volcano, for Homer's hero visited many volcanic isles. But it seems entirely appropriate that granite, which with a little extra effort might have been extruded as lava, should be the first rock we encounter in *Ulysses*, around Sandycove Martello Tower. Leopold and Molly Bloom both remember fondly picnics and parties held in the nearby granite mountains. Joyce does not ignore volcanic scenery and the attractive Bay of Naples, with which the "almost-volcanic" view from Dalkey across Killiney Bay is compared, does feature. Bloom, recalling Molly's forthcoming concert in Belfast, might also have recalled Belfast's dark hills composed of the same lavas that gave us the Giants Causeway.

The Mediterranean, where the geological tussle between Africa and Europe occurs, is subject to many quakes. Although there had been no catastrophic quakes in the years preceding 1904, in writing *Ulysses* some years later, Joyce would have had hindsight of seismic events in the intervening period: not only of the 1906 San Francisco disaster which killed 700, but of the utterly calamitous series of Messina and Reggio di Calabria earthquakes at Christmas 1908. These quakes and their related tsunamis would destroy both cities and kill up to 160,000 persons.

Dublin does periodically experience minor quakes, such as that of July 1984 centred on the Lleyn Peninsula, which registered 5.4 on the Richter scale. But Dublin has never felt anything remotely like the seismic shock that struck Barney Kiernan's pub soon after 5.00 p.m. on 16 June 1904. The tension which had been building between Bloom and the Citizen would be released in a seismic wave! When the pub occupants formed the mistaken impression that the departing Bloom had just been enriched by a handsome win on a racehorse, this was the last straw for the Citizen. Emerging from the pub with a biscuit tin, he flung it with such force after Bloom's carriage that he precipitated the seismic event causing eleven successive shocks! Joyce infuses this quake with wide-ranging and catastrophic consequences. All the fine buildings around the Law Courts collapsed and a violent storm transported objects to the extremities of the country. Witnesses "observed an incandescent object of enormous proportions hurtling through the atmosphere at a terrifying velocity ..."[11] It was reported that Dunsink had recorded this unique seismic event, although this observatory did not possess the means to do so, neither then nor since!

"Am I walking into eternity along Sandymount Strand?"[12] Stephen Dedalus entertained feelings of continuity and stability as he strode the southern side of Dublin port and walked along South Wall. But the Bull Wall on the opposite side of the Liffey estuary, and particularly the Bull Island extending away from it, might alternatively have evoked thoughts of change, for it has evolved substantially over recent centuries. Vice Admiral William Bligh (1754–1817), mainly remembered for his command of the mutinous *Bounty*, surveyed Dublin Bay and Port in 1801.[13] His hydrographic map showed the true extent of the Bull Island which had grown through the eighteenth century according as harbour works changed the pattern of sediment deposition. The island would continue to evolve after Bligh's visit, not only with the eventual construction of the Bull Wall in the 1820s but also the causeway at St Anne's Park in the 1960s. So now we have a splendid nature reserve of sand dunes fringed by Dollymount Strand on its seaward side and giving way to intertidal marshes and flats on its landward side. But given its history we no longer view it as something of permanence and its very fragility makes it popular with visitors, both human and avian.

Natural resources such as minerals and coal are no strangers in *Ulysses*. The keeper in the Eumaeus episode, reputedly the old Invincible rebel known as Skin the Goat, argues that Ireland was as well endowed with resources, especially coal, as any other country, including Britain, but the latter had sought to impoverish Ireland through penal taxes. This was some claim given that Britain's vast coal resources had underpinned its huge industrial development. But minerals were seen as a sure path to prosperity and in the Ithaca episode, Bloom mused that he could be independently wealthy if only he could find a gold deposit – "a goldseam of inexhaustible ore".[14]

Bloom gives a list of Ireland's scenic attractions and it is interesting that many have a strong geological dimension:[15] Lough Neagh "with submerged petrified city", Cliffs of Moher, Giants Causeway and Connemara. He then goes on to mention four limestone-based localities, the Aran Islands, the Golden Vale of Tipperary, the pastures of Royal Meath and the Lakes of Killarney. Limestone owes its origin to the warmth of a tropical sea and is often replete with fossil remains. *Ulysses* has many additional references to limestone areas – Lough Owel which Bloom's daughter visited, the Burren close to Ennis where his father owned a hotel, and Gibraltar, that rugged block of limestone guarding the entrance to the Mediterranean. But when it comes to appreciating the beauty of nature, no-one does it better than Molly Bloom. I have inserted slashes and emphases to slow down your reading and help you enjoy this exuberant text, but feel free to ignore them.

> *God* of heaven / there's *nothing* like nature / the wild mountains / then the sea and the waves rushing / then the beautiful country / with fields of oats and wheat and all kinds of things / and all the fine cattle going about / *that* would do your heart good / to see rivers and lakes / and *flowers* / all sorts of shapes and smells and colours / springing up *even* out of the ditches / primroses and violets / *nature* it is / as for them saying there's no God / I wouldn't give a *snap* of my two fingers for all their learning.[16]

The secret of Joyce's geological insights was all down to his first impressions on that fateful morning of Bloomsday! When he emerged from his residence at Shelbourne Road, it was Beggar's Bush Barracks that first met his gaze. Built in 1827, this barracks was a recruiting depot for the British Army and soon housed over 250 officers and men. Nowadays it has a similar number of residents, but all domiciled in modern apartments, and in additon half that number work in Government offices, including the Geological Survey of Ireland. As far as I know, Beggar's Bush does not explicitly feature in *Ulysses*, but I associate it with Bloomsday because the sunshine that morning would have picked out in its stonework the two native rocks of Dublin: granite and limestone. The more gracious granite has been used sparingly in the buildings, mainly around the arched entrance, while the humbler grey limestone has been employed extensively in the guardhouses and surrounding walls. Granite of the Southside and limestone of the Northside were fused together in this Dublin building so effortlessly that it inspired city-wide thinking on Joyce's part and allowed him to create one of the classics of the twentieth century.

Notes

1. Quotation from page 374 of James Joyce's *Ulysses* (Nausicaa). Quotations from *Ulysses* in this chapter are from Joyce, J. (1969) *Ulysses*. Harmondsworth, Milddlesex, England: Penguin Books. Naming of *Ulysses* episodes follows conventional usage as given in: Gilbert, S. (1955) *James Joyce's Ulysses: A Study*. New York: Vintage Books.

2. Wyse Jackson, P., Stone, J. Parkes, M. and Sanders, I. (1993) *Field Guide to the Geology of Some Localities in County Dublin*. Dublin: Department of Geology, Trinity College Dublin and ENFO – The Environmental Information Service.

3. Leaney, E. and Byrne, P.M. (2009) Robert Mallet. In McGuire, J. and Quinn, J., (General Eds.). *Dictionary of Irish Biography*. Royal Irish Academy and Cambridge University Press, volume 9, pages 321-323.

4. See page 378 of Behan, B. (1958) *Borstal Boy*. London: Corgi Books (reprinted 1967).

5. Mitchell, F. 1976 *The Irish Landscape*. London: Collins. Sutton is described on pages 131-2.

6. There is no scholarly consensus on the precise route taken by Ulysses. Tim Severin's conclusions, based on his exploration and research, are interesting: Severin, T. (1987) *The Ulysses Voyage*. London: Hutchinson.

7. I drew on the books by Stuart Gilbert (1955) and Frank Budgen (1934), two friends of Joyce's, for commentaries and personal interpretations. Budgen, F. (1934) *James Joyce and the Making of Ulysses*. London: Grayson & Grayson. Gilbert, S. (1955) *James Joyce's Ulysses: A Study*. New York: Vintage Books.

8. Byrne, P.M. (2009) Charles Jasper Joly, 1864-1906. In McGuire, J. and Quinn, J. (General Eds.) *Dictionary of Irish Biography*. Royal Irish Academy and Cambridge University Press, volume 4, pages 1020-1021.

9. Wyse Jackson, P.N. (2009) John Joly, 1857-1933. In McGuire, J. and Quinn, J. (General Eds.) *Dictionary of Irish Biography*. Royal Irish Academy and Cambridge University Press, volume 4, pages 1021-1022.

10. *Ulysses*, Lestrygonians, pages 166-7.

11. *Ulysses*, Cyclops, pages 342-3.

12. *Ulysses*, Proteus episode, page 43.

13. See further information on Bull Island and Capt Bligh in Gilligan, H.A. (1988) *A History of the Port of Dublin*. Dublin: Gill and Macmillan, pages 89-96.

14. *Ulysses*, Ithaca episode, page 640.

15. *Ulysses*, Ithaca episode, pages 647-8.

16. *Ulysses*, Penelope episode, page 703.

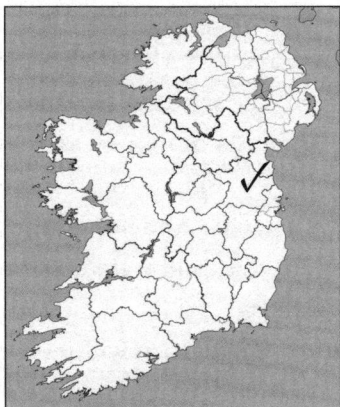

18

ROCKS TOO CAN BE OUTSIDERS!
(Meath)

... but that's the way it is for lowlanders will call
a small incline a mountain and mountain-men mention
a hill and point to Everest.
  – Peter Fallon[1]

The Book of Job, perhaps 3,000 years ago, lists four important metals at that time:

Silver has its mines,
and gold a place for refining.
Iron is extracted from the earth,
the smelted rocks yield copper.[2]

These same four metals are still in common use and are considered strategically important for modern life. In County Meath,

the Beauparc mine near Slane produced the historically important copper, but nowadays it is a relatively new metal, zinc, that
is mainly exported from the modern Navan mine. The mining industry invests large amounts of money and employs increasingly
sophisticated technology in the search for new sources of metals to support society's needs. And sometimes, if we are mindful
enough, the rocks themselves will yield up some useful clues as to
where we should look next.

The Iapetus Suture Zone is a will-o'-the-wisp feature that
meanders beneath the Meath countryside, unguided by physical
features and apparently without influencing the pattern of human
habitation. Its formation 430 million years ago culminated in the
rise of the Caledonian mountain chain, which was eroded during
Old Red Sandstone times and then inundated by the sea during
the Carboniferous. The seafloor began to subside more rapidly
in some places, leading to the formation of deeper water basins
with thick limestone developments, and this was when the suture began to re-assert itself. It coincided with the edge of some
basins, including the Dublin Basin, and the associated faults increased the permeability of the deep crust, allowing seawater to
penetrate to greater depths. In doing so it became hot, acidic and
metal-enriched and, when convected back to the seabed, it was
spewed out in the form of "black smokers", superheated jets that
immediately precipitated their metals on and within the seafloor
sediments. This process was sustained long enough to ensure that
more than 100 million tonnes of rich ore were formed beneath
the Navan area, sufficient to sustain a world-class zinc-lead mine
for half a century and more. Those ores became buried beneath
thick sequences of barren limestone, posing a major challenge for
prospectors. It was fortuitous that, as a result of its subsequent
tectonic history, the ore came to the surface at the River Blackwater, where it was discovered. But there could be other such deposits entirely buried beneath the limestone terrain of Ireland and

we need a better understanding of how they formed in order to discover them.[3]

Navan is midway between the archaeological landscapes of Loughcrew in the west and Slane in the east and I have chosen a poet from each to represent the poetic landscape of County Meath. Peter Fallon (b. 1951) and Francis Ledwidge (1887–1917) share some significant similarities, for they both look to their landscape to provide important needs – Ledwidge seeking the beauty and diversity of nature and Peter Fallon desiring its solace and healing. However Fallon is more of an insider than Ledwidge, being a publisher of poetry, so that he is prominent in the world of poetry. In contrast, Ledwidge, prior to his friendship with Lord Dunsany (1878–1957), relied upon the pages of *The Drogheda Independent* to supply the vital oxygen of acknowledgement. Furthermore Ledwidge, the landless labourer, would have sought out nature in accessible areas of the Boyne River valley, whereas Fallon the farmer would be free to explore the many links between farming and nature starting from the psychological security of his own Loughcrew landholding. There is also an historical (if tenuous!) link between their two localities in that Lord Dunsany belonged to the Plunkett family and his martyred ancestor, St Oliver Plunkett, is buried at Loughcrew.[4]

It is towards the close of summer that rock music fans in large numbers visit Slane, the home of Ledwidge, but its own residents consider Easter a more important occasion for this Georgian village. The Hill of Slane rises to the north of the village and it was here in 433 that the newly-arrived St Patrick heralded the advent of Christianity with his illegal Paschal fire. But however prominent that hill may be physically, it does not dominate the life of the village as thoroughly as does the River Boyne. The northern bank of this river is graced by Slane Castle, the annual host to rock concerts, and a large mill, now disused, which was an important mid-eighteenth century industry, producing flour for downstream Drogheda as well as for export. Slane village itself, built at a safe height above the Boyne's floodplain, is overtly proud of its most famous son and the tasteful Ledwidge Museum, just east of the village, is based in the poet's family cottage.

Ledwidge, a labourer's son, left school at age 13. He worked at a variety of labouring jobs, including in the local Beauparc mine, where copper ore was extracted from a narrow quartz vein within Carboniferous limestones. The mine was shallow, prone to flooding, and its working conditions were hazardous.[5] Francis, as the mine's shop steward, organised a short-lived protest strike during 1910 following which he was fired. Having initially opposed calls to enlist in the British Army, he then inexplicably joined himself and saw extensive war service before being killed in 1917 at Ypres in Belgium.

Lord Dunsany ensured Ledwidge's output was published after his death and praised his pastoral lyrics extolling rural Meath. Writing while war was still in progress, Dunsany felt Ledwidge's poems conveyed a much-needed peacefulness and he baptised Ledwidge as the Poet of Blackbirds.[6] Killed just days short of his thirtieth birthday, Francis Ledwidge's celebration of the Meath countryside can be deeply satisfying and is much cherished. In "By Faughan",[6] he opens:

> For hills and woods and streams unsung
> I pipe above a rippled cove.

He goes on to describe the wind along the Faughan River and finishes with the:

> Faughan flows,
> In music broken over rocks,
> …
> And here this song for you I find
> Between the silence and the wind.

During military service, he is desperate to return to his beloved environment ("The Hills"):

Meath

The hills are crying from the fields to me,
And calling me with music from a choir
Of waters in their woods where I can see
The bloom unfolded on the whins like fire.

He really enjoys darkness when he will:

wander thro' the moon-pal solitude
That calls across the intervening night
With river voices at their utmost height,
Sweet as rain-water in the blackbird's flute
That strikes the world in admiration mute.

The Ramparts Walk follows the Boyne Navigation on the river's southern side and passes through Slane village. I walked part of it in company with a birdwatcher, just as Francis, the Blackbird of the Boyne, might have done with his naturalist friend. Within a short time we had spotted stonechat, goldfinch, crow, heron and cormorant – Ledwidge would have been pleased. We also saw a bit of geology. The Boyne valley marks the border between the southerly limestones and older rocks to the north. The intermittent cliffs on its south side feature beds of cherty limestone while the north bank rises steeply and relentlessly to the elevation of the village and beyond. It is solidly composed of brown and grey volcanic rock, which is exposed around the ruined 500-year-old Franciscan monastery that marks Slane's summit.

St. Patrick may have been an outsider on the Hill of Slane but so too are its rocks. They resulted from eruptions of volcanic ashes, but Meath's atmosphere was not darkened by them. This volcano formed an oceanic island some thousands of kilometres away from Meath and over a long period of time (maybe 30 million years!) it was gradually shunted into its present position. We all realise that despite the passage of such substantial time, those rocks will never be considered native to County Meath! It was, of course, plate tectonics that supplied the motive force. During the closure of Iapetus Ocean, these volcanic rocks, along with a chaotic mix of ocean floor debris, were swept inexorably along by the Earth's all-powerful conveyor belt before being finally halted by the sealing of the ocean's suture.

Ledwidge's love of Meath was only heightened when he went to war ("In France"):

> The hills of home are in my mind,
> And there I wander as I will.

And in "An Invitation" he says:

> Come where the hills are heaped together
> For the winds are glistening with wings,
> And Autumn's dull flowers droop and wither ...

His fascination with "hills" interests me, for Meath's prominences are hardly of significant elevation, but we will find later that elevation is also a concern of Peter Fallon. Meath's hills may be special but so are its flowers. "Spring" finishes:

> And when the blue and grey entwine
> The daisy shuts her golden eye,
> And peace wraps all those hills of mine
> Safe in my dearest memory.

He addresses all seasons and excludes neither day nor night any more than he ignores any weather changes. Nature features in other ways also: "the spider-peopled wells" ("June"), "the mossy weirs" ("Summer at Home"), "the fiery meteor's slanting lance" ("A Memory"), and of course the night sky is important –whether or not it is raining.

We do fleetingly get to rocks! "Sonnet on some stones Lord Dunsany brought me from Sahara", written in March 1914, shows a touching deference to his mentor by including his name in the title. Dunsany brought neither stuffed bird nor dried plants, so he must have had confidence that Ledwidge's interest extended beyond biota to the geological foundation.

Meath

There is a melody I cannot hear
But mem'ry takes me down a flight of days,
Across green paths and bending waterways
Where one made music in a mountain's ear.

I imagine Ledwidge is thinking of the spreads of cobbles that fringe stretches of the River Boyne – and he seems to have been thinking also of their mountainous origins. Equally, "those coloured gifts" fired his imagination to muse on the sights and history of exotic Egypt (not anticipating he would be hospitalised in Cairo just two years later). Shortly before his death, he wrote to Katherine Tynan (1861–1931), the poet:

> But, more particularly, I want to see again my wonderful mother, and to walk by the Boyne to Crewbawn and up through the brown and grey rocks of Crocknaharna. You have no idea of how I suffer with this longing for the swish of the reeds at Slane and the voices I used to hear coming over the low hills of Currabwee.[7]

That brown and grey rock is of course Slane's outsider rock.

Loughcrew, home of Peter Fallon, occurs near Oldcastle in County Meath. The summit of the nearby ridge, underlain by greywackes, contains the Loughcrew megalithic tomb. It was fun striving to reach it before dawn on the March equinox and fascinating to see the light illuminating images on the chamber's backstone, mainly circular and radial patterns representing the sun itself. Both this cairn and its more famous cousin at Newgrange are passage tombs which also charted the changing seasons in an agricultural community 5,000 years ago. They pay homage to the solar energy that drives nature's annual cycle.

The hills at Loughcrew were shaped by a major ice sheet, over 400 metres thick, which moved southeastwards across them and left an indelible impression. Incorporated rock fragments in the ice scored the underlying bedrock, leaving linear marks, or striae. As the ice crunched its way forward it sometimes sheared off bedrock fragments so that some prominent outcrops have a smooth gentle slope at the northwest end and a sharp steep termination at the other; these are called *roches moutonees*. The melting ice left a blanket of boulder clay which is thin on uplands but can exceed 50 metres in depth on lower ground. Glacial erratics may be dumped in unexpected and even prominent positions. At Loughcrew, there are many of local greywacke, but there are also some carried from the region to the northwest. These are mostly of Old Red Sandstone and were used to construct the Loughcrew cairn.[8]

Peter Fallon farms at Loughcrew and a recurring theme in his poetry is an exploration of nature and its relationship with farming life. He is content, especially in his early collections, to view both nature and weather from the relative comfort of his own farm. In "Legend",[9] he describes water that flows uphill in a way that is eye-catching without being fanciful. Many of us know places where this happens without defying the law of gravity. It just requires a landscape where the surface contours conspire to produce an optical illusion. "The Speaking Stones"[9] occurred in rich farmland near Oldcastle. Despite their reputed mystical powers, they were a tempting source of convenient rock for farmers, so now only one out of four remains. But one man who interfered with them found to his horror that his child had drowned at the same time.

Fallon does observe landscape beyond the limits of his own farm. He eloquently notes the contradiction where lowlanders call the gentlest incline a mountain, while mountain residents might call even Everest a hill! ("Home"). When does a hill become a mountain? Is it, for example, through increased height or alternatively the presence of a rocky summit? There seems to be no widely accepted or consistent answer!

When staying in Massachusetts, Fallon appreciates its landscape with a simple clarity. His rivers adopt attributes that are almost human and we can imagine him pausing in sympathy while strolling their banks ("Stillwater") or admiring the glancing sunshine ("Beaver Ridge").[10] His easy relationship with nature gathers some pace in "The Heart's Home", which expresses joy in nature – flowers and wildlife – that is untouched by any hint of farming. Here we see, as elsewhere, his regular search for healing and peace in the outdoors. In another poem, "Go", Fallon prescribes a walk in the quiet wilderness to cope with illness and the sorrows of life. There is the wonderful metaphor of a rock pool "convalescing" after rain – there is healing in nature, that's his message. Rivers are important to Fallon and they have the power, in his view, to wash away our sorrows, just like weirs can calm troubled water ("A Visiting"). But then his mood changes rapidly and the poet delights in Connemara's landscape for its beauty alone, the top of Ben Lettery gleaming and glowing.

He recognises the potentially global impact of local events in the poem "One World", citing the worldwide coastal ripples experienced after the Indian Ocean tsunami of 2004. We know that at the same time, for example, Irish wells experienced sudden changes in their water levels. Meanwhile as life in Clifden settles down once more, we sense the poet extends the globalisation concept to our environment as he observes a passing fleet of supertankers.[11]

In "Geography" the poet states:

> When I looked
> at the mountain
> long enough
> I grew to know
> all manner of mountains.

Living in Connemara can do this to you! Peter Fallon is fascinated sufficiently by one particular mountain that his reflections opened his mind to new insights about the nature of mountains. But he still did not lose his sense of humour ("Daylight Robbery"):

> You think you'll dander out
> to look at the mountain
> and find yourself venturing out
> to look for the mountain.

While life in Connemara had brought him into unaccustomed contact with mountains, he still kept a last word for rivers ("Devotions"), stating that he must take the time to learn from them.[12]

Peter Fallon has a distinctive relationship with his landscapes. He looks to them for peace and rest and healing, not just for himself but for those around him. Healing as a theme forms an enduring thread through much of his work – rivers, holy wells and plants all have powers and qualities that we can tap into either for ourselves or on behalf of others. There is likely to be a chemical basis for the healing power of many plants and waters, but in the case of some healing may rely largely on faith. Yes, Fallon assures us, landscape has powerful impacts, especially when we are open to a suitable blend of reason and faith.

Notes

1. From "Home" in Peter Fallon (1983) *Winter Work*. Dublin: The Gallery Press, page 11.

2. Book of Job, chapter 28, verses 1-2, of *The Jerusalem Bible* (1968). London: Eyre & Spottiswoode, page 656.

3. Ashton, J. H. and others (2003) "The Navan orebody – discovery and geology of the South West Extension". In: Kelly, J.G. and others (Eds.) *Europe's Major Base Metal Deposits*. Dublin: Irish Association for Economic Geology, pages 405-436.

4. For biographical and critical information on the two poets see Alica Curtayne (1972) *Francis Ledwidge: A Life of the Poet*. London: Martin Brian and O'Keeffe. Russell, R.R. (2014) *Peter Fallon: Poet, Publisher, Editor and Translator*. Sallins, County Kildare: Irish Academic Press.

5. See page 28 of G.A.J. Cole (1922) *Memoir of Localities of Minerals of Economic Importance and Metalliferous Mines in Ireland*. Dublin: Geological Survey of Ireland.

6. Alice Curtayne (Ed.) (1974) *The Complete Poems of Francis Ledwidge*. Dublin: Poolbeg. I quoted from the following poems: "By Faughan" (page 22), "The Hills" (page 28), "In France" (page 31), "Spring" (page 39), "June" (page 47), "Summer at Home" (page 49), "An Invitation" (page 52), "Sonnet on Some Stones Lord Dunsany Brought Me from Sahara" (page 67) and "A Memory" (pages 76-77). Prefaces by Lord Dunsany are on pages 197-202.

7. Quoted on a poster display in the Ledwidge Museum, Slane (viewed in December 2013).

8. Meehan, Robert T., and Warren, William P. (1999) *The Boyne Valley in the Ice Age: A Field Guide to Some of the Valley's Most Important Glacial Geological features*. Meath County Council and the Geological Survey of Ireland.

9. Peter Fallon (1978) *The Speaking Stones*. Dublin: The Gallery Press. The text refers to "Legend" (page 38) and "The Speaking Stones" (page 39).

10. Peter Fallon (1998) *News of the World: Selected and New Poems*. Oldcastle, County Meath: The Gallery Press. The text refers to "Beaver Ridge" (pages 85-89), "Stillwater" (page 90) and "The Heart's Home" (pages 133-134).

11. Peter Fallon (2007) *The Company of Horses*. Oldcastle, County Meath: The Gallery Press. The text refers to "Go" (pages 11-12), "A Visiting" (pages 31-34) and "One World" (pages 34-35).

12. Peter Fallon (2007) *Ballynahinch Postcards*. "Aghabullogue", County Cork: Occasional Press. Limited signed edition. No pagination. The text has quotations from "Geography" and "Daylight Robbery". It also refers to "Devotions".

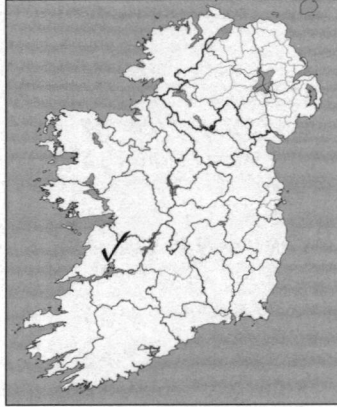

19

At Peace with Myself
in the First Sunshine
(Clare)

a livid wilderness of limestone
striated with the ogham of ages
– Desmond Egan[1]

East Clare is countryside I know from my first geological work as a young student – a whole summer wandering places with wonderful names like Bodyke, Ogonelloe and Feakle, places full of character and characters! East Clare embraces the hilly areas of Slieve Aughty and Slieve Bernagh, founded on relatively old slates and volcanic rocks, as well as their slopes which sweep down to limestone-floored low ground around Lough Derg and the Shannon River. Its landscape is best appreciated from hills such as Moylussa, Clare's highest point and the summit of the Slieve Bernagh mountains. The bedrock here consists of greywackes, siltstones and mudstones which formed on the floor of Iapetus Ocean long before its opposing margins merged along Iapetus Suture to form Ireland as we now recognise it.[2] Deposited about 420 million years ago, these rocks were deformed some 20 million years later when the Iapetus margins finally collided. This deformation imparted a cleavage to the rock, which splits easily into thin slates that were commercially worked nearby in the nineteenth century. A good base from which to explore this area is the nearby cathedral town of Killaloe on the River Shannon, birthplace of Brian Ború (c.940–1014), one-time High King of Ireland, and starting point on the East Clare Way.

East Clare may expose quite a range of sediments but it also records episodes of volcanic activity and over a considerable time span. During the Ordovician, while the Iapetus Ocean was still a major global feature, some lava flows were spewed out on its floor and remnants are still preserved in the slaty rock sequence at the south end of Lough Graney. Much later, when the formation of Carboniferous limestone was in full swing in shallow seas, some ashes and lavas formed near Tulla. However there is no evidence that either volcano lit up the Clare sky, for they were both submarine and may have been but whimpers. Nevertheless there is no denying Clare's volcanic past!

Writers from east Clare have always been proud of their home place, none more so than its most famous, the acclaimed novelist, Edna O'Brien (b. 1930).[3] Commentators have pointed out that her thoughts are never far from the lovely fields and drab villages around Tuamgraney.[4] In her recent memoir O'Brien left readers in no doubt that famous west Clare could hold no torch to her oriental portion of that county. The west might have awesome sea cliffs, but they were nothing compared to the loveliness of her home place.[5] O'Brien opens *House of Splendid Isolation* by seeing the land as having layers of history, contained in its people and buildings, but also in the soil and subsoil. History is everywhere and extends back in time to the geological.[6] She is also taken with wild countryside and, for example, the Prologue to *Wild Decembers* describes her local bogs. These contain much history also, ranging from relics of ancient battles to bog bodies and pottery remains. Here again, it is human history, or prehistory, that fascinates O'Brien. Her observations on the field patterns bring us closer to modern times and the traditional Irish obsession with land ownership, for fields can mean much more than simply agricultural land.[7]

The distance from Tuamgraney to Lough Graney is only about 10km, yet it takes us inexorably back almost two centuries, for this is Merriman country. "The Midnight Court" by Brian Merriman (1749?–1803), is considered one of the outstanding Irish folk poems of the late eighteenth century. This is how Thomas Kinsella (b. 1928) translated its opening lines, with their simple delight in the pleasures of the early morning countryside:

> By the brink of the river I'd often walk,
> on a meadow fresh, in the heavy dew,
> along the woods, in the mountain's heart,
> happy and brisk in the brightening dawn.
> My heart would lighten to see Loch Gréine,
> the land, the view, the sky horizon,
> the sweet and delightful set of the mountains
> looming their heads up over each other.[8]

The poem was written in 1780, when Merriman was teaching and farming near Feakle, and he knew the countryside intimately:

> The description of the landscape is exact and we can follow his route through the narrowing of the hills to the point where the lake appears shining to the north, just as he describes it. River and meadow are still there. The countryside is still a delight to see …[9]

Of course the hapless narrator then fell asleep and was accused by a "vision-woman" of being a poor lover. The explicit account of his subsequent trial ensured that Frank O'Connor's 1945 translation was censored. Merriman himself commented:

> The translation of his long poem is doubly banned in Ireland, and I believe the best authorities hold that it is almost entirely my own work, the one compliment Ireland ever has paid me.[10]

East Clare is separated from the county's more famous western region by a tract of limestone-based country comprising the Burren uplands and extending southwards to the lowlands karst country around Gort and Ennis. The hillside exposures of karst limestone beds in the Burren are splendid and environmentally unique. Desmond Egan's epigraph at the head of this chapter captures their essence. They comprise indeed "a livid wilderness" that is packed with a great biodiversity and their plant life is particularly celebrated. The quotation also succinctly captures both the glacial ("striated") and archaeological ("ogham") dimensions of this landscape. The glaciated surface of the Burren is remarkable, with its bare striated rock and common erratic boulders, but there is still controversy as to whether humans helped the erosion process through their farming practices.

People familiar with the Burren will recall the iconic image of Mullaghmore mountain, its limestone bedrock forming a gentle synclinal fold that can be clearly seen from a distance, but only because it is special limestone. Of course it is special, its *Burren* limestone, I hear you say! But not all Burren limestone occurs as thick beds which form distinctive steps along the side of Mullaghmore. Without them the effects of end-Carboniferous stresses would not be so elegantly displayed. Each of these beds consists of a cycle of sedimentation. The limestone at the base formed in a sub-tidal environment which was subsequently flooded by rising sea levels so that the succeeding limestone, containing debris of sea lily stems, formed in deeper water. The marine environment then gradually became very shallow once more, giving rise to limestone with plentiful brachiopod and coral fossils. The cycle was completed when the sediment was exposed above sea level so that the upper surface of the bed is usually karstified or may even have a soil horizon. The cyclical variations in sea level that gave rise to these limestones were caused by multiple pulses of glaciation, spanning several million years, that took place about 330 million years ago. As ice sheets expanded they absorbed very significant quantities of seawater, causing the sea level to drop and the reverse happened when the ice melted, an elegant mechanism with such a profound impact on the slopes of Mullaghmore!

The writer Robert Macfarlane (b. 1976) envisaged a different cyclicity in the Burren. The fact that its limestone is composed of the skeletons of once-living creatures reminds him that physical matter is simultaneously indestructible and entirely transmutable. It can undergo remarkable transformations. Yet he says that this inherent contradiction of permanence and mutability can be useful, making us feel both valuable and superfluous. We become aware of ourselves as being constituted of matter that is endlessly convertible while at the same time we are continuously perpetuated in some form. Such knowledge grants us the cold comfort of realising that our bodies belong to a limitless cycle of dispersal and reconstitution.[11]

The lowland limestone country is no less special and W. B. Yeats experienced this amid the woods and turloughs of Coole Park and Thoor Ballylee. If this landscape inspired him to pen some of his most admired poems, the same cannot be said of a famous son for whom it comprised his childhood countryside. I am referring to the poet Michael D. Higgins (b. 1941), academic, politician and President of Ireland. He is most closely associated with Galway, but spent his formative years on a small farm between Newmarket-on-Fergus and Sixmilebridge. The landscape here, complete with forests and lakes, is established on those same limestones that stretch northwards more than 30 kilometres to Coole Park. At one time I felt that I might gently chide the President for a lack of generosity in overlooking his lovely karst scenery, but then the district I visited one cold sodden morning displayed damp woods and wet fields, darkened farms and misty hills, a bleakness unrelieved by villages that seemed quite dreary.

Higgins' poetry describes his childhood as an emotionally unsatisfactory time when the pace of farm activities was such that he had no time to savour nature or enjoy the sunset ("Too Close to the Ground").[12] For Higgins, nature at best became interminably intermixed with farming and often represented simply a distraction from that activity ("The Ass"). But he generously acknowledges a home and a teacher that encouraged him to explore literature, a habit he brought with him as he transited from the cold limestone of rural Clare to the warm granite of urban Galway. He would continue to love certain aspects of rural life, especially animals, but he had effectively turned his back on Clare's raw landscape.

Now he was energised by the teeming city, often writing of human relationships and referring to countryside with an unexpected harshness. For example, in setting a Connemara scene, the black bog is reduced to soup, the hillside is bare and he senses a violence against nature ("Meeting"). Back in Galway his mischievous sense of humour ensures that any hint of pretentiousness is quickly banished from his work, which now displays a re-discovered marvel at nature, especially wild flowers ("Of Little Flowers"). He gives them real personality! But his muse never really reverts to Clare and in one of his later poems ("The Ebbing Tide") he reveals that in turbulent times it is to the sea, more typical of west Galway, that he will turn for wisdom, rather than the countryside he might have found on Clare's lowlying limestones.

In the case of Rosita Boland (b. 1965), journalist, travel writer and poet, the lowland karst of Clare sparked her creativity so fully that she went on to celebrate not only the landscape of her county but also of more distant destinations. Born in Ennis and raised on its limestone lowlands, she was familiar with its unreliable turlough lakes just as much as with the water-sculpted karst of the Burren uplands ("Birthright").[13] Her County Clare childhood certainly opened up new possibilities for Boland and, when she travelled in the Australian outback, it sensitised her to the subtleties of landscape there. She traversed 3,000 kilometres across the bare Nullarbor plain, where even a petrol station might feature on the maps ("Crossing the Nullarbor"). Her poem "Map-reading" is simply an alphabetical listing of place names, not an immediately appealing prospect. Yet we can sense her love and understanding of that landscape through the names she chooses. None start with upper case letters and this sense of fun might suggest that the odd one was plucked mischievously from Rosita's head! The names include physical features – great sandy desert, red rock, glasshouse mountain – as well as mining areas – broken hill (actually a major mining community), diggers rest (golden thoughts!) and andamooka opal fields. There are further interesting names, the lyrical "come-by-chance", the Irish-sounding "coolangatta", the unexpected "useless loop", the resigned "walkaway" and the honest "tin can bay". Elsewhere ("Camping on the Coburg Peninsula"), proximity to some crocodiles stimulated memories of her father's much-loved if fearsome bedtime stories, thus catapulting (or can boomeranging be a valid verb?) the poet back to her Clare home place.

West Clare for me comprises the region south of the Burren and west of the Gort limestone lowlands, a special district that in geological terms is called the Shannon Basin. This basin is different from the earlier Munster Basin which was composed of riverborne sediments derived from the north. The Shannon Basin was actively subsiding along marginal faults which were sufficiently active to ensure its surface remained at or below sea level. Indeed it had already accommodated a substantial thickness of Carboniferous limestones. Now the district lay close to the shoreline of that time and a major delta expanded across it to encompass the basin. This was a truly significant feature which might have been on the same scale as the modern Mississippi delta. It is easy to envisage it, rivers flowing westwards from the hills of east Clare, right? Not so! The evidence in the rock sequence indicates that river flow was actually eastwards from a hilly source that we can no longer see – it should be somewhere out there in the modern Atlantic Ocean! Thanks to the vagaries of plate tectonics, the land source is now buried somewhere on our continental shelf, or else it lies on the North American shelf. Less than half of the basin itself is exposed onshore, but the rest of it does exist off the coast of County Clare and indeed it has been explored unsuccessfully for petroleum: A deep borehole penetrated through the delta sediments and the underlying marine shales to reach the familiar limestones. Although the borehole was unsuccessful in finding any oil or gas, the area remains very popular with exploration geologists because the 3D architecture of its sediments could in other circumstances be very capable of holding large petroleum reserves. That architecture is so spectacularly exposed in the West Clare cliffs that they attract geologists on field courses from all over the world.

A good place to start your own study of these sediments is at the Bridges of Ross.[14] Here we see the basin's earliest sandstones, sandy turbidites which built up a submarine fan from turbulent clouds of sediment. When seabed slopes became too steep, this sediment would slump down the delta and form a jumbled mess at its base. This in turn often excessively pressurised water trapped in underlying sediment which was released as small jets of water that formed distinctive "sand volcanoes" on the seabed. The examples here are among the earliest ever described and are excellently exposed. No doubt you have sensibly chosen a calm day for your excursion but those volcanoes are likely to have been the result of a more turbulent day: one that may have witnessed seismic movement along one of the basin's many faults and dislodged any finely balanced sediments. If strong enough it might even have triggered a tsunami that would threaten coastal habitats in this entire region and beyond. Or alternatively that day may have seen the climax of a major storm that dispatched large quantities of sediment to the base of the delta, through a combination of an additional surge of river-delivered sediment and the ferociously agitated sea state.

As the delta built outwards the proportion of mud and silt increased, but sediment still periodically slumped down along its slopes, with quakes and storms recurring regularly on a geological timescale. The products that resulted can be inspected in cliffs at Gull Island and you can see how the strata were faulted and folded in the slumping process. As the delta reached a mature profile, sediment accumulated in shallow water as a series of coarsening-upwards cycles, each initiated by fault-controlled subsidence and completed by sedimentation. Often the cycle ends when sediments are exposed in the inter-tidal zone, giving wave-rippled surfaces with worm burrows and grazing trails. The latter are best seen, not on the coast itself, but in the flagstones around Liscannor that have been quarried extensively to floor buildings and pavements throughout Ireland. If you do not have time to track these features along the full length of this coastline, do allow yourself the exhilaration of visiting the Cliffs of Moher (200 metres), the highest viewing point and now part of a UNESCO-supported Global Geopark. There you can join some of the 750,000 visitors who each year gaze in wonderment at the surrounding cliffs and Atlantic Ocean, and explore their formation, environment and history from the Cliffs of Moher Visitor Experience.[15] You will notice I have featured no poet from the Clare Basin, but then I think you will agree that its rocks tell a sufficiently exciting story.

Notes

1. From "Clare: The Burren" on pages 26-27 of Desmond Egan (1992) *Selected Poems*. Omaha, Nebraska: Creighton University Press and Newbridge, County Kildare: The Goldsmith Press.

2. For the geology of Clare see Sleeman, A.G. and Pracht, M. (1999) *Geology of the Shannon Estuary*. Geological Survey of Ireland. Archer, J.B., Sleeman, A.G. and Smith, D.C. (1996) *Geology of Tipperary*. Geological Survey of Ireland.

3. See Kathryn Laing, Sinéad Mooney and Maureen O'Connor (Eds.) (2006) *Edna O'Brien: New Critical Perspectives*. Dublin: Carysfort Press.

4. John Banville (2013) Article on Edna O'Brien. *The Irish Times*, Arts and Books Section, page 9, Saturday, 23 November 2013.

5. See page 38 of Edna O'Brien (2012) *Country Girl: A Memoir*. London: Faber and Faber.

6. See page 3 of Edna O'Brien (1994) *House of Splendid Isolation*. London: Weidenfeld & Nicolson

7. See pages 1-2 of Edna O'Brien (1999) *Wild Decembers*. London: Weidenfeld & Nicolson.

8. Extract from "The Midnight Court". Translated by Thomas Kinsella. From Seán O Tuama (Ed.) (1981) *An Duanaire – An Irish Anthology. 1600-1900: Poems of the Dispossessed*. Philadelphia: University of Pennsylvania Press, page 221.

9. Liam de Paor (1998) "The World of Brian Merriman: County Clare in 1780". Chapter in his *Landscapes with Figures*. Dublin: Four Courts Press, pages 37-64. Quotation is from page 46.

10. Quotation comes from page xii of the Preface to Frank O'Connor (1962) *Kings, Lords & Commons: An Anthology from the Irish Translated by Frank O'Connor*. London: Macmillan & Co.

11. Robert Macfarlane (2007) *The Wild Places*. London: Granta Books. See pages 172-174 for his account of the Burren.

12. Michael D. Higgins (2011) *New and Selected Poems*. Dublin: Liberties Press. I have referred to the following poems: "The Ass", pages 62-63; "Too Close to the Ground", pages 66-67; "Meeting", pages 101-102; "Of Little Flowers", pages 174-175; "The Ebbing Tide", pages 176-177).

13. Rosita Boland (1991) *Muscle Creek*. Dublin: The Raven Arts Press. I have referred to the following poems: "Map-reading", page 43; "Crossing the Nullarbor", pages 44-45; "Camping on the Coburg Peninsula", page 46; "Birthright", page 63.

14. See Field Trip 6 (pages 154-180) of Pat Meere, Ivor MacCarthy, John Reavy, Alistair Allen and Ken Higgs (2013) *Geology of Ireland: A Field Guide*. Cork: The Collins Press.

15. See www.cliffsofmoher.ie (accessed 19 January 2014).

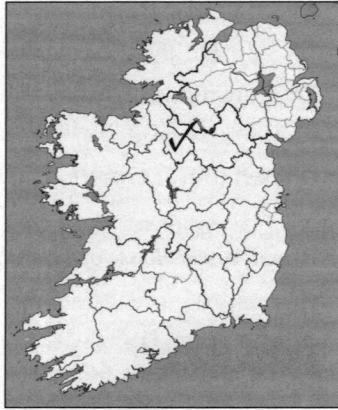

20

Timber!
(Leitrim)

Man makes an end of darkness
when he pierces to the uttermost depths
the black and lightless rock.
Mines the lamp-folk dig
in places where there is no foothold,
and hang suspended far from mankind.
– The Book of Job[1]

The heart of Leitrim, for me, comprises Lough Allen and its surrounding mountains. This reflects my personal links with this coalfield district just as much as the physical fact that the area lies at the rather constricted centre of this oblong-shaped county. Extending southeastwards from this heart is drumlin country of smooth hills and intervening lakes, all based on a foundation of limestone. Northwest of its heart, Leitrim's bedrock is also mainly limestone but it is crossed by a fault-bounded line of low hills composed of older rocks, a continuation of the Ox Mountains. This was a significant source of seismic disturbance through much of Leitrim's history. The limestone forms mountainous landscape here, a reminder that it represents the eastern part of the Yeats Country that is more usually associated with County Sligo.

Although she was reared on the limestone in the southeastern part of Leitrim, around Carrick-on-Shannon, Nora Murray's (1888–1955) geographically-based poems tend to deal with the more rugged limestone terrain at its northwestern end. Her poetry is a joyful celebration of rural nature and she particularly delights in birds and flowers. Feeling nostalgic in her grey urban life, she pines for glorious "Glencar", its lake and waterfall, with birds and flowers aplenty, and much more besides. She would find joy and peace here, sensing the hand of God at work in creating its nature. My only surprise with this verse is that a Carrick-bred woman would concede all of Glencar valley to her neighbouring county of Sligo! Particularly as its gem, Glencar Falls, is entirely within Leitrim. Granted she does knowingly stray across the county boundary to Sligo when she describes "Knocknarea", in Yeats' own country, its noble head overseeing the harvest in the surrounding fertile valleys with "silent majesty." Lough Gill and Ben Bulben, also familiar to Yeats' readers, make guest appearances. Then "Wind of the West" might equally apply to either Leitrim or Sligo and broadens the focus to deal with upland bogs, an energy source that forms a useful link back to Leitrim's heart.[2]

Arigna names both a district and a valley that is bounded on one side by Altagowlan Hill and by the Kilronan–Geevagh ridge on the other, both coal-bearing hills. I have chosen to stroll up Altagowlan Hill. Its lower slopes are underlain by dark grey mudstones, the product of a shallow coastal lagoon, and some exposures show strings of ovoid-shaped bodies that are made of siderite. The value of this as an iron ore was recognised in the sixteenth century and Arigna enjoyed prosperous iron extraction over the period 1600–1770. Key to this success was the ready availability of local timber and indeed the industry only waned when this supply was exhausted around 1770. But while it lasted, ironmasters produced pig iron that was relatively free of sulphur and that was used to manufacture durable and popular products.

The need for timber would be no less when extraction switched from iron to coal, for now it was required to make pit props to support the underground coal workings (more timber recycling!). This switch happened soon after 1765, just as timber supplies were exhausted, when coal was discovered on Altagowlan. By 1800 pits on both sides of Arigna valley were operating successfully and were considered to contain the country's most promising coal resources. Continuous coal output was sustained for almost two centuries until 1990, with its main source lying to the west of Lough Allen. Nevertheless, a combination of high transport costs and unattractive seams of low height and poor quality ensured few operations remained profitable in the long term. From 1958 until the 1990 closedown, Arigna supplied coal feedstock for a 15-megawatt power station on the shores of Lough Allen.

The upper Altagowlan slopes are formed of sandstone, composed of river-borne sediment transported from mountains further north. This sedimentation led to the development of a delta with a cyclical pattern of deposition. Each cycle starts with fine muds which give way upwards to sands that become progressively coarse-grained and culminate in vegetation-rich soils that in time give rise to coal seams. There are several such cycles, all controlled by periodic changes in sea level.

Plant life during coal formation was luxurious, perhaps more so than at any other time before or since, and trees were every bit as dense and high as in modern tropical swamps. The outcrops remaining from open cast mining on Geevagh preserve carbonised plants in 2D impressions. The most distinctive were the fern trees with lozenge-patterned bark. I recall one farmer remarking to me on the peculiar "tyre marks" left in these rocks – I cannot think of a better description! Their most enduring remains are in the form of 3D moulds, now an inherent part of the very durable sandstone that is the floor of the Main Coal. Such fossilised timber logs, complete with growth rings, can be inspected on an interior wall at the Arigna Mining Experience.[3] This is a worthwhile visitor destination and not just to put an age on its fossilised tree!

Coal will form from vegetation where it is preserved in stagnant water-logged conditions. The coalification process can then begin, initially forming peat and, according as the material is buried deeper, turning to lignite and finally coal. While this process continues, the amount of moisture and volatiles is reduced and the carbon content and calorific value increase proportionately. The final outcome depends on the ambient temperature in the Earth's crust. In the Late Carboniferous it increased southwards across Ireland so that bituminous coal formed at Arigna but anthracite resulted in the warmer crust at Castlecomer and elsewhere. Later dolerite dykes did intrude into the rock sequence and had no impact on the coal seams – but demonstrate that volcanism, however quiet, was part of Leitrim's history.

More than 200 miners were employed for many decades at Arigna and mining was an important economic activity for its community. Trim and sprightly, our guide at the Arigna Mining Experience had left school sixty years previously to push coal-filled tubs from underground coal faces along rail tracks to surface. At sixteen he earned a man's wages and started working the coal face itself, which was back-achingly low. An engaging storyteller, he concluded by inviting us to denotate a simulated blast intended to extend a tunnel, re-creating the sharp sound and dense dust of mine operations. It was a vivid reminder that the same dust had impacted badly on the lungs of many miners. Coal dust covered the miners entirely, apart from the whites of their eyes, as they emerged at end of shift to make their way home still unwashed.

The environmental impact of open cast mining is evident in the late-twentieth century workings on top of Altagowlan plateau. But the presence of the Miners' and Historical Way here, which links with the Arigna Mining Experience, reflects the strong awareness in the community of the heritage value of this defunct industry. This is just one element of the spirit of enterprise which is very strong here. Another is the cluster of modern windmills atop Altagowlan whirring industriously and generating electricity in the very place where once coal was hard-won for a similar purpose. Named Spion Kop Wind Farm, just as the older mine workings were also called Spion Kop, this recalls a rock-strewn and steep-sloped hill of the same name close to Ladysmith in South Africa. This locality was on everyone's lips in the early months of the twentieth century.[4]

The Boer War pitted the imperial ambitions of Britain against the fierce independence of the Boers, Britain mistakenly thinking it could easily subdue these apparently simple and disorganised farmers. One night in late January 1900 a large column of British troops seemed to attain the relative security of the summit of Boer-occupied Spion Kop. Alas, dawn revealed the British troops had made a tragic mistake and, in the ensuing brutal engagement, the Boers inflicted heavy casualties on them. Nevertheless, by the following nightfall, both sides– unbeknown to each other – made tactical retreats. The wily Boers were the first to spot the resulting opportunity and quickly re-occupied Spion Kop without a single additional casualty. It was Winston Churchill himself, as a young journalist, who brought this bewildering news to a disbelieving public.

Why would Leitrim take any notice of events in far-off South Africa? I think the answer lies in the politics of the day because, while many Irishmen saw distinguished service with British forces in the Boer War, a minority – including the future 1916 leader Major John MacBride – had served in the Boer ranks. For them Spion Kop was no defeat, but represented a remarkable victory! Maybe as they trudged up Altagowlan in those wintry days after the Spion Kop debacle, the miners took some gleeful pleasure in Britain's embarrassment and christened the hill accordingly!

The trees may be re-asserting themselves on the low ground around Arigna, but the ground is not soggy enough to hope the timber might end up as feedstock for future coal seams! The naturalist R. L. Praeger felt that this boggy mountain rather let down the attractiveness of Lough Allen. In a querulous frame of mind, he clearly saw the underlying coal-bearing bedrock as the culprit and indeed he regretted the history of coal and iron mining here, despite recent government investment. He was wrongly of the view that prodigious investment in exploration had taken place in every county of Ireland for any number of mineral commodities and never to any benefit.[5]

Given these views, it is very likely that Praeger had been disheartened by the events of July 1921. On the very day that the impending Truce was announced, newspapers carried accounts of recent studies asserting that Ireland's coalfields contained 2.4 billion tons of coal.[6] On the basis of its recent coal consumption, it seemed that Ireland would be self-sufficient in coal supplies for at least another five centuries! For long there had been a feeling that Britain had played down the extent of Irish natural resources, so maybe the truth was at last emerging? Yet looking back today, the aggregate annual coal output of Irish mines since 1921 has seldom exceeded 200,000 tons and virtually no coal has been mined for more than 20 years – so where have all our resources gone? In truth the 1921 assessment had been wildly optimistic and indeed misleading.

Ireland lacks the enormous coal resources that drove Britain's Industrial Revolution. We may once have had valuable coal seams but if so they were subsequently removed by erosion so that now only the oldest and least attractive seams are preserved in a series of isolated upland areas, with little potential for additional onshore resources. The unwarranted enthusiasm of the authors of the 1921 evaluation probably persuaded Praeger to adopt a pessimistic view! Of course, thick coal seams have since been discovered in our offshore territory and may one day prove profitable to work.

The modest drumlin landscape southeast of Lough Allen has managed to inspire a remarkable group of writers, perhaps the most celebrated being John McGahern (1934–2006). Based in his small farm at Foxfield, County Leitrim, he achieved international success with work that often evoked the landscape and rural life of his home place. McGahern would not claim to be a naturalist but he did lend weight to the importance of his environment. In an interview late in life, he disdained any claim of a strong spiritual link with nature, saying: "we are all part of that passing world we learn to love and leave ..." He simply tried to describe it accurately and attentively.[7]

Born outside Carrick-on-Shannon, Mary Guckian (b. 1942), poet and photographer, may be a long-term Dublin resident, but her work inevitably harks back to life in rural Leitrim.[8] Whenever Guckian visits hilly summits she reflects on the depth of history which is stored there, remembering the burial places of her ancestors ("Standing Stones"). Guckian also looks northwards in Leitrim to the Arigna miners, recounting a visit she made to the Arigna Mining Experience. She celebrates their way of life, many having lain on their sides in wet and dusty tunnels to earn an unhealthy living. The title of this poem, "The Miners' Way", points not only to their lifestyle but also to the way-marked trail of the same name.

Speaking of Leitrim miners, William Henry Drummond (1854–1907) does not deserve to be forgotten. Born near Mohill, he became a medical doctor in Montreal and spent his last few years serving the mining community of Cobalt, northern Ontario, where he died unexpectedly. He achieved huge popularity as a poet both within and beyond Canada, sometimes using a French-Canadian dialect that did not meet with universal approval. He developed a strong love of nature which he indulged as much as possible in northern Ontario and is reflected in his poetry. He was proud of his Irish heritage although he never wrote about his native Leitrim.[9]

My interest lies in Drummond's life and experience in Cobalt district. "Silver Lake Camp" gives an atmospheric description of the simple camp life of prospectors working out in the forest as autumn turns to winter. Here was a cheerful work crew who managed to banish the forest's loneliness through nightly fireside singsongs:

> The bleak wind sighs thro' the leafless trees
> Like a spirit's wail, and the white snow-flake
> Drifts silently down with the fitful breeze,
> On the lonely camp at Silver Lake.
> …
>
> Yet the ruddy glow of our camp-fire bright,
> Not long ago, when the fall was young,
> Illumined the gathering shades of night,
> And the forest rang with the songs we sung.

The reason for Drummond's isolated sojourn was the silver mining boom of 1905–1906, when Cobalt became known as the Silver Capital of Canada. He and his brothers had invested in a small silver prospect, Drummond Silver Mine. His poem "The Calcite Vein (A Tale of Cobalt)" is a wry and humorous commentary on prospecting a silver and cobalt lode which has the mineral calcite as its matrix. If the miners are to make their fortune from it, then they must excavate sufficiently to establish that it persists at depth. They must also be confident of how much silver and cobalt it contains should they wish to sell it to another company. Otherwise they risk underpricing their cherished and hard-won prospect. Drummond's widow, in introducing "Bloom (A Song of Cobalt)", explains that the soft, flower-like pink patina of a cobalt vein, known as cobalt bloom, promises riches to the prospector:

But to-day I'm weary, weary, and the bloom I long to see,
Is the bloom upon the cobalt – that's the only bloom for
me.

While Drummond Silver Mine and other mines around Cobalt
were primarily silver mines, an important by-product was cobalt
and this area was a major global source of this metal in the early
decades of the twentieth century. Cobalt bloom is the mineral ery-
thrite and it forms from the near-surface weathering of primary
cobalt-arsenic minerals. Nowadays cobalt is mainly used in spe-
cialised alloys and is sourced as a by-product of copper mining on
the African Copper Belt of Zambia and the Democratic Republic
of the Congo. So here we have managed to unite imaginatively
mining camps that are thousands of kilometres distant from each
other through the good offices of a son of south Leitrim, William
Henry Drummond. We could also assert a variety of connections
between the south Leitrim writers we have spotlighted here. One
pair wrote poetry, another pair made their living in Ireland and at
least two were keenly aware of mining. But all three certainly share
one common link – that they each drew early inspiration from the
countryside of their birth, established on that diverse limestone
landscape with drumlins and lakes.

Notes

1. The Book of Job, chapter 28, verses 3-4 of *The Jerusalem Bible* (1968).
London: Eyre & Spottiswoode (Publishers), page 656.

2. Nora J. Murray (1918) *A Wind upon the Heath*. Dublin: Maunsel &
Company. The specific poems referred to are "Knocknarea" (pages 4-5),
"Glencar" (page 21) and "Wind of the West" (page 23).

3. See http://arignaminingexperience.ie. (Accessed 5 February 2014).

4. See http://en.wikipedia.org/wiki/Battle_of_Spion_Kop. (Accessed 21
February 2014).

5. See pages 134-135 of Praeger, R.L. (1937) *The Way that I Went: An
Irishman in Ireland*. Dublin: Hodges, Figgis & Co and London: Methuen
& Co.

6. Reported on page 4 of *The Irish Independent* of Saturday 9 July 1921 ("The Coalfields of Ireland: Remarkable Researches").

7. The quotation comes from "An Interview with John McGahern", pages 143-161. In Eamon Maher (2003) *John McGahern: From the Local to the Universal*. Dublin: The Liffey Press.

8. Mary Guckian (2010) *Walking on Snow*. Dublin: Swan Press. I have referred to "The Miners' Way" (page 51). I have also referred to "Standing Stones" (page 52) in Mary Guckian (1999) *Perfume of the Soil*. Dublin: Swan Press.

9. William Henry Drummond (1911) *The Great Fight: Poems and Sketches by William Henry Drummond*. New York: G. P. Putnam's Sons. I have quoted from the following poems: "Bloom (A Song of Cobalt)" on pages 87-88 and "Silver Lake Camp" on pages 101-102. I also referred to "The Calcite Vein (A Tale of Cobalt)" on pages 91-95.

21

LIFE CAN BE SO WONDERFUL!
(Kilkenny)

The ground itself is kind, black butter

Melting and opening underfoot,
Missing its last definition
By millions of years. They'll never dig coal here,

Only the waterlogged trunks
Of great firs, soft as pulp.
– Seamus Heaney[1]

D id you realise that County Kilkenny played an active role in the nineteenth century debate regarding the evolution of life, the theory we commonly invoke to explain the Earth's enormous biodiversity? For long, scientists had argued over whether species might evolve one to another, rather than being spontaneously generated, but without the support of a credible mechanism. Accordingly, the 1859 publication of *On the Origin of Species* by Charles Darwin (1809–1882) became a galvanising event because it proposed natural selection, whose effectiveness would subsequently be verified by molecular genetics, as a scientific explanation of how creation works.[2] This held that those individual animals or plants which were best suited to their environment were more likely to survive, reproduce and so pass on their attributes to offspring. Thus, over a sufficiently large number of generations, a species might assume significantly different attributes. Darwin was a retiring person, content to allow others to debate the merits of his conclusions. He did come to Ireland and on his last visit he went to Killarney and the Giants Causeway, but not Kilkenny. What a shame!

Kilkenny possessed two fossil localities where important biological evidence was gathered in the mid-nineteenth century and these are respectively 20 kilometres north and south of Kilkenny city. We will visit the southern locality later in the chapter. The first locality is situated on the Castlecomer Plateau, which stands about 200 metres above the surrounding limestone lowlands, between the Nore and Barrow Rivers. The plateau contains narrow seams of anthracite coal in Upper Carboniferous sediments which were mined on a significant scale up to 40 years ago. This is the Castlecomer Coalfield and its Jarrow Colliery was the scene of remarkable fossil discoveries back in the 1860s.[3]

The seam here marked the site of an oxbow lake, or abandoned river meander, in a coastal swamp where plant and vertebrate remains accumulated over a long time period about 315 million years ago. The coastal swamps not only had luxurious vegetation and a rich fish fauna, but also very favourable conditions for their preservation. But the discovery of reptile fossils caused great excitement, because reptiles were the first animals to emerge from water and fully live their lives on dry land. They were accordingly very important in the evolutionary chain that led ultimately to the emergence of humans. The Castlecomer examples were regarded as among the earliest known and they ranged up to several metres long, with well developed limbs, sophisticated teeth and scaly skin. Seven new genera were eventually named among the beasts here, which included a horseshoe crab, a sharp-toothed carnivore, salamander-like creatures, and (this was a considerable time before St Patrick's arrival!) a snake-like reptile. But which geologist would gain the scientific glory associated with describing these special animals?

The best qualified person was undoubtedly Thomas Henry Huxley (1825–1895), known as Darwin's Bulldog, and a key figure in the evolution debate.[2] Indeed, his contributions were informed by his research on reptilian fossils. While probably excited to hear of the new reptile finds in Ireland, he must have wondered how, as a London-based scientist, he might gain access to these splendid fossils. He was never going to crouch along confined mine tunnels in search of his own fossils, no more than he would bargain with crafty miners in Castlecomer's pubs to buy their treasured finds. So imagine his delight when the holder of these precious remains, Dublin zoologist E. Perceval Wright (1834–1910), actually approached him![4]

Nevertheless Huxley was wary of Wright who wanted to restrict his access to the fossils. Huxley would have none of this and had the precious loot transported to his London laboratory. But he was acutely aware that an enthusiastic fossil collector, W. B. Brownrigg, owned these fossils and had published a note in 1865 to that effect. When Huxley contacted him, Brownrigg recognised that a taxonomic description of these magnificent fossils was beyond him and Huxley was satisfied that Brownrigg's response authorised him to do the job. This meant that the field was now clear for Huxley, he could satisfy Wright's modest scientific ambitions while ignoring the potential counter claims of other Dublin-based experts. An 1866 paper co-authored with Wright had the latter as first author which must have been gratifying to him. Huxley knew that the next more rigorous paper was key, so the 1871 paper had Huxley as first author and set out explicitly the leading role that he took in the research. No doubt both authors were reasonably satisfied with the result although the generous man who made it possible, Brownrigg, was so disgusted by his own exclusion that he abandoned the study of geology altogether. E. Perceval Wright would not go on to a glittering career in the study of fossils, but he would be a successful ophthalmic surgeon and professor of botany (not zoology, despite his earlier position) at Trinity College Dublin.[5]

Huxley did not sustain his interest in those Castlecomer reptiles and this was at least partly because he was diverted by another fossil find. This was the wonderfully preserved vertebrate, *Archaeopteryx*, and it was Huxley who realised that it shared the characteristics of both birds and dinosaurs, a so-called missing link. He assembled compelling evidence indicating that birds had evolved from dinosaurs and, although it was not fully accepted for more than a century, this firmly established Huxley's scientific reputation and lent more support to the theory of evolution.

Not everyone identifies coalfield areas as poetical country, but Austin Clarke (1896–1974) did. In his 1963 poem, "Beyond the Pale", which he described as an old-fashioned descriptive one, he ranged widely over localities and incidents throughout the midlands and southeast of Ireland. But when he came to the Castlecomer Plateau it was of mining he spoke, employing an authentic if curious blend of religious and commercial images.[6] Clarke focused on the story of a praiseworthy Irish mineowner, based at The Swan in the north of the coalfield, who had fought for Ireland's independence, remained devoutly religious and established an industry based on efficient use of natural resources and fair treatment of his workers. Joseph Fleming in 1935 established Fleming's Fireclays, now Lagan Bricks, for brick manufacture. Fireclay formed the fossilised soil horizon on which coal-forming vegetation grew.

As an employer, Fleming stands in contrast to his contemporary at Castlecomer, Capt. Richard H. Prior Wandesforde (1870–1956). The latter's unyielding management style at his Deerpark Colliery, 5 kilometres from the Jarrow workings, pitted him against the union activist Nixie Boran (1903–1972). These two strong personalities each attracted both admiration and hostility from their community. Prior Wandesforde was a vigorous and innovative mine manager who introduced modern mining methods and led a successful campaign to extend the railway system as far as Castlecomer. He employed several hundred men when the operation was at its peak in the 1950s. This made a considerable difference in those economically depressed days. But he was regarded as a harsh employer who did not easily grant concessions to his workforce. Nixie Boran, on the other hand, was a committed socialist who led a trenchant and prolonged campaign to seek better pay and more healthy working conditions for miners, thereby drawing the hostility of both Church and State. It was only following some bitter strikes that he was ultimately successful, only to find that his victory was pyrrhic because coal resources were inadequate to sustain production beyond 1969.[7]

To reach the second celebrated Kilkenny fossil locality we must travel to Kiltorcan Hill near the village of Ballyhale. Here the youngest beds of the Old Red Sandstone are exposed. Actually they are not red, but green and yellow and quite coarse grained. They are overlain by flaggy siltstones which in turn pass up to massive red mudstones. In the mid nineteenth century, beautiful plant fossils – associated with fish, arthropods and large freshwater mussels – were uncovered in the siltstone, which is dated at 360 million years. So they are actually earliest Carboniferous despite being part of the normally Devonian Old Red Sandstones. The evidence suggests that the various organic remains had been washed along with stream sediment into a quiet part of the river system where they accumulated over time. James Flanagan was the most successful fossil collector in the Geological Survey of Ireland at that time and it was he who in 1851 made these remarkable discoveries. Kiltorcan specimens of *Archaeopteris hibernica*, the beautiful fern-like plant, are internationally renowned, their fronds extending to an impressive metre in width. This plant should not be confused with the aforementioned vertebrate, *Archaeopteryx* –

palaeontologists do seem to run short of distinctive new names at times! *Archaeopteris* is among the earliest land plants and marks the start of the process of greening our planet. No wonder this locality became part of the contemporary debate on evolution. Sadly, it was while re-visiting this locality in the summer of 1859 that Flanagan became gravely ill and died.[8]

Natural selection is not a quick process and time is essential to allow evolution to operate. Our two Kilkenny localities give us interesting snapshots in time and therefore allow us to view the progress of biodiversity over a critical period in Earth history. The time gap between the snapshots, 45 million years, seems enormous yet it is only 1 per cent of Earth history – and quite a lot happened in that interval! The Kiltorcan plants grew in a relatively barren landscape with little vegetation to stabilise soil or control erosion. When we fast-forward to the Castlecomer swamps, we are skipping over the greatest marine incursion that Ireland has witnessed and during which our very extensive limestones accumulated (they cover large areas of Kilkenny!). The Castlecomer climate, about 315 million years ago, was still tropical but the environment was quite different – abundant vegetation decayed in swamps, leading in time to coal formation. The trees ranged up to a majestic 50 metres in height. They tended to snap off at their base so the roots were usually preserved separately from the trunks. Accordingly, in the 1 per cent of Earth time between the Kiltorcan and Castlecomer events, we see a huge development in greening Kilkenny's land, with a significant increase in biodiversity.

I am not aware that any serving U.S. President has claimed strong links to, or even visited, Kilkenny. But American Presidents do seem to like Irish poetry – they have such good taste! President Bill Clinton, who played a key role in the negotiations leading to peace in Northern Ireland, developed a great fondness for the poetry of Seamus Heaney, while President Kennedy quoted Gerald Griffin before his departure from Ireland. But for sheer sentiment it would be hard to trump President Ronald Reagan who turned to

Kilkenny poet, John Locke (1847–1889). in choosing "Dawn on the Irish Coast".[9] Many readers of a certain age will already be familiar with these verses, learned by rote at an early stage of schooling by the Christian Brothers and which I remember as "The Emigrant's Return". Locke was raised in Callan, birthplace of the founder and first Superior General of the Irish Christian Brothers, Blessed Edmund Ignatius Rice (1762–1844). Known in the United States as "the poet of Ireland-in-exile", Locke became a successful journalist who was regarded as patriotic and comforting by homesick emigrants. A friend of the poet, on a voyage back to Ireland, witnessed some passengers assisting an elderly man onto the deck for a first glimpse of the Kerry coast. This was the inspiration for "Dawn on the Irish Coast", with the aged individual, an exile in Texas for 30 years, witnessing landfall at dawn. Seeing "the hallowed shore", he savours its headlands, birds and waves, and feels repaid "lavishly" for his deprivation over many years. He expresses the universal feeling of exiles:

> The alien home may have gems and gold,
> Shadows may never have gloomed it;
> But the heart will sigh for the absent land
> Where the love-light first illumed it.

Now he is closer to shore, he yearns for the scenes and friends of his youth, ending with the patriotic thought that he might help achieve Ireland's freedom.

While this was undoubtedly Locke's most popular poem, "The Calm Avonree", was the favourite around Callan, which lies on the King's River (its Irish form is anglicised as Avonree). This poem repeats the predictable themes of a longing for his homeplace and winning both his loved one's heart and Ireland's liberty:

> Again would I roam through the green shady bowers,
> Where the boys used to drill e'er I first crossed the sea,
> And I'd weave for my Kathleen a garland of flowers,
> On the green grassy banks of the calm Avonree.

I have a mischievous feeling that some Loyalist marchers in Northern Ireland might feel Locke was stealing their clothes by using that expression, "green grassy banks"!

Callan lies in Kilkenny's limestone country where bedrock aquifers are rendered more productive by karstification, the process whereby limestone is dissolved by percolating rainwater. So Locke gets close to earth with his poem "The Old Abbey Well":

> And oh! how a drink from its depth upward pressing
> Would act on one's frame like a magical spell,
> That methought there was nothing in life so refreshing
> As the water which shone in the old Abbey Well.

Kilkenny did extrude volcanic rock also and if you want to inspect the evidence you must seek out the county's oldest rocks, such as the lavas around Inistioge. Do not leave its vicinity without enjoying the tranquillity of the grounds of Woodstock House. Its one-time owner, William Tighe (1766–1816), completed one of the earliest county geological maps, among the finest of its time. [10] His cousin was the poet, Mary (née Blachford) Tighe (1772–1810), who was much acclaimed during the nineteenth century for her long love poem, "Psyche; or, the Legend of Love". Graced with intelligence, imagination and beauty, she stayed with her cousin at times and yet, despite his acknowledged influence in her life, landscape does not feature prominently in her writing. But she did seek solitude in nature ("Calm Delight"):[11]

> Birds, flowers, soft winds, and waters gently flowing,
> Surround me day and night,
> Still sweetly on my heart bestowing
> Content and calm delight.

Some of Woodstock's tenants, however, might have been surprised by her next stanza where she seeks sleep to restore her work-weary body, but then, as any writer will vouch, pushing the pen or tapping the keyboard can constitute honest toil!

She manages a happier and lighter tone on a visit to Killarney, with none of the ambivalence of other early visitors to this fabled Kerry resort ("Written at Killarney. July 29, 1800"). She clearly enjoyed boating on the lake with its peace and gentle breeze and evening sunshine. But her pleasure was not confined to her lake trip, because before she left she was lyrical about Killarney's entire scenery ("On leaving Killarney. August 5, 1800"):

> Farewell, sweet scenes! pensive once more I turn
> Those pointed hills, and wood-fringed lakes to view
> With fond regret; while in this last adieu
> A silent tear those brilliant hours shall mourn
> For ever past.

Mary Tighe's last journey was to Woodstock House in summer 1809 where she remained until her death from tuberculosis the following March. Already suffering from poor health, she seeks poetic inspiration as a means of lifting her spirits ("Sonnet Written at Woodstock, in the County of Kilkenny, the Seat of William Tighe. June 30, 1809"). She acknowledges that some of the inspiration comes from the wooded hills around Woodstock, those same hills that her caring cousin, William, understood so well.

Notes

1. From "Bogland", by Seamus Heaney. Quoted from: Seamus Heaney (1990) *New Selected Poems 1966-1987*. London: Faber and Faber, pages 17-18.

2. Biographies of Darwin (volume 15, pages 177-202) and Huxley (volume 29, pages 99-111) can be found in: Matthew, H.C.G. and Harrison, B. (Eds.) (2004) *Oxford Dictionary of National Biography*. Oxford: Oxford University Press.

3. Tietzsch-Tyler, D. and others (1994) *Geology of Carlow-Wexford*. Geological Survey of Ireland.

4. A biography of Wright (volume 9, pages 1048-1049) can be found in McGuire, J. and Quinn, J. (Eds.) *Dictionary of Irish Biography*. Royal Irish Academy and Cambridge University Press.

5. The most recent paper concerning the Jarrow reptile fossils is by P. N. Wyse Jackson and others in *Irish Journal of Earth Sciences*, volume 29, pages 19-22.

6. "Beyond the Pale" is on pages 64-68 of Austin Clarke (1976) *Selected Poems*. Edited by Thomas Kinsella. Dublin: The Dolmen Press.

7. For additional information on Deerpark Colliery see Walsh, J. and Walsh, S. (1999) *In the Shadow of the Mines*. Published by Seamus Walsh.

8. For information on James Flanagan and the Kiltorcan discovery see Herries Davies, G.L. (1995) *North from the Hook*. Geological Survey of Ireland.

9. John Locke (1952) *Dawn on the Irish Coast*. Edited with memoir and guide to Callan by James Maher, Mullinahone. Published by Kilkenny Journal. Extracts from the following poems are used here: "Dawn on the Irish Coast" (pages 12-13), "The Calm Avonree" (page 18) and "The Old Abbey Well" (page 19).

10. Herries Davies, G.L. (1983) *Sheets of Many Colours: The Mapping of Ireland's Rocks 1750-1890*. Dublin: Royal Dublin Society.

11. Linkin, Harriet Kramer (Ed.) (2005) *The Collected Poems and Journals of Mary Tighe*. Lexington: The University Press of Kentucky. I have quoted from "Calm Delight" (page 28) and "On Leaving Killarney. August 5, 1800" (page 46). I also refer to "Sonnet Written at Woodstock, in the County of Kilkenny, the Seat of William Tighe. June 30, 1809" (page 203) and "Written at Killarney. July 29, 1800" (page 45).

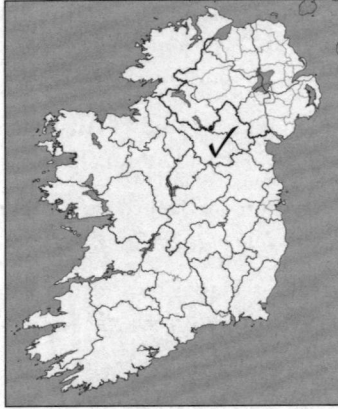

22

SEISMIC SHIFT!
(Cavan)

The Garden of Eden has vanished they say
But I know the lie of it still
Just turn to the left at the bridge of Finea
And stop when halfway to Cootehill.
— Percy French[1]

The Cavan Lakes Country, in the central part of the county, is a great example of flooded drumlin landscape. The drumlins were formed during the movement southeastwards of ice sheets across this region. Those in the wide valley of the River Erne became partially submerged as water levels rose in the post-glacial period. The lakes in turn became foci for bog growth according as the climate became milder so that now we see a dense pattern of drumlin hills interspersed with lakes and bogs. Lake margins underwent a series of vegetation changes on the way to their current treeless state as raised bog dominated by sphagnum moss. Bogs tend to grow at a tediously slow rate, usually only increasing their height at a rate of one millimetre per annum – although when conditions are favourable this annual rate can accelerate to as much as fifteen milimetrers.

Belturbet poet P. J. Kennedy (b. 1950)[2] cherishes his local bogland and would like to see it fully preserved from future turf extraction. A damaged bog bank, he argues in "Wound", will take seven years to recover. However if turf must be harvested, then traditional methods are preferable. Mechanised extraction causes greater environmental damage and he uses stark, graphic language to emphasise this. Kennedy also has a poignant poem, set on a drumlin hillside ("Buried Unknownst"), dealing with a burial ground for infants who should have been afforded greater dignity in death. Encountering some stones which mark their resting places, he imagines these coming alive and transforming into thriving and even boisterous children. There is even a stone "with a crown of fossils" – we are in limestone country here. But this is a poem which can be read only with a heavy heart.

County Cavan has a pan-shaped outline, with the narrow handle extending northwestwards towards Sligo Bay, and the Lakes Country occurs immediately west of Cavan town in the area where the pan meets its handle. Heather Brett (b. 1956) lives in Cavan and writes about relationships and the swings of contemporary life. Indeed she uses the quiet anticipation of a couple's relationship to capture Cavan's lakeside mood ("Under the Rhododendron").[3] Feelings and landscape come into harmony with each other in a curiously satisfying way as she describes their walk in drumlin countryside. But then, just like Kennedy, she acknowledges that landscape may not always have blissful associations, for she pictures desperate people who have suffered greatly and her references to wet earth and darkness leave little doubt as to where this narrative will take them ("Landscapes for Suicide").

There is more to Cavan, of course, than the Lakes Country. The extensive area east and southeast of Cavan town is composed of low hills underlain by slates and greywackes that were deformed during the closing stages of Iapetus Ocean. Those greywackes, essentially sandstones with a clay matrix, make great aggregates and the quarries here are largely based on them. The main supply of sediment came from the continent away to the northwest, but some enriched in volcanic debris also came from volcanic islands elsewhere in the ocean. These were oceanic volcanoes whose products were basaltic in composition and largely erupted in the form of lavas. There was also much seismic activity throughout the region's history, but none as traumatic as during the climax of ocean closure and plate collision. We can see the result on Slieve Glah, a hill south of Cavan town, which does not seem exceptional among the many drumlins but is actually cored by distinctive bedrock. Here the rocks were deformed to such an extent that their original sedimentary nature is obliterated and a new rock type produced. Called phyllonite, it has a very pronounced cleavage and records the prolonged devastation wreaked by those colliding plates.[4]

Tom Conaty (b. 1957) of Ballyhaise describes a satisfying walk one misty morning along his local stream ("River Annalee").[5] The images and repetition of language slow me down and remind me of Brian Merriman, I want to walk with Tom along that river bank! But his collection title, *An Exaltation of Starlings*, troubles me for I have never experienced exaltation of any kind in the urban company of my local screeching and polluting starlings! Faraway landscapes come to his mind when the wind carries dust from the Sahara ("Mission Sunday") and when he compares his personal challenges with a Himalayan ascent ("Altitude Sickness"). One poet in no danger of forgetting his Cavan environment is Eamon Cooke (b. 1944), who observes the course of his daily life through the rhythms of seasons, nature and especially rivers ("Forest, Music, Stream"). This is the landscape of the southeast part of Cavan. He is out walking with his son in "Summer Walk" and they "sing up" water from a roadside pump. That lovely expression might refer to their own rhythm as they swing the pump handle, or to the music of water as it gushes from the spout, or perhaps even to father and son accompanying the pumping process in song.[6]

The songwriter and raconteur Percy French (1854–1920) was a popular performer, who celebrated personalities and events in many different parts of the country, his humour and humanity raising his songs above the ordinary.[7] "The Mountains of Mourne" may be the most evocative of these, partly because of its appeal to Irish emigrants and partly because of the haunting rendition recorded many years ago by the popular US singer Don McLean. But remember that it was in County Cavan that Percy French first saw service, in the honourable role of County Surveyor of Drains. His time in this job is captured in the parody, "The Effusion of William, Inspector of Drains", a typical verse of which goes:

> He plunges through marshes long haunted by cranes,
> Quite heedless of how the dark bog-water stains;
> Traducers assert that this ardour he feigns:
> They little know William, Inspector of Drains.

He composed some of his best songs during his seven happy years in Cavan town, where he was made welcome despite coming from a landowning family armed with a university degree in civil engineering. Twenty years later, with fond memories still of his youthful sojourn, it is not surprising that he chose a Cavan town, Ballyjamesduff, as the backdrop for another successful song. "Come back, Paddy Reilly" tells the story of a "toil-worn and tough" emigrant who feels strongly drawn back to his native place, largely because he is forlorn without his girlfriend. He is actually quite a quarrelsome character, stoutly defending her honour against imaginary detractors and offering violence to any who might verbally abuse her! Ballyjamesduff to him is the Garden of Eden, Heaven, Nirvana ... a place where eternally "the grass it is green" and "the blue sky is over it all"! No doubt the town was chosen for the comic effect that its unwieldy and awkward name might have. He did not linger over the beauty of its landscape as he might justifiably have done, for nearby Nadreegeel Loughs is a pretty lake surrounded by drumlins, the sort of delightful locality where one might seek refuge on a balmy summer evening. Perhaps French had already experienced too many lakes and waterways in his daily task of drains' inspection to be tempted out there after dinner!

Actually, in 1919, the year before he died, a remarkable hoard of Bronze Age gold ornaments was discovered at depth in a bog at that very place. Although by this time Percy French was suffering ill-health, he was still performing regularly and must have been aware of these remarkable objects, which are now displayed in Dublin's National Museum. He might have mused fondly on their discovery while introducing his ballad on Paddy Reilly. As far as his audiences were concerned, there was no doubt that the fame of this Ballyjamesduff resident quickly overshadowed that of any older treasure, however golden or hallowed it might be.[8] As a result, it is Percy French that is commemorated in the town's centre with a statue, a seated figure on a public bench where the passer-by might join him for a rest. If so his companion would notice that the singer is dressed ready to perform and the sheet music he is holding is for that same Ballyjamesduff ballad – surely he was not in danger of forgetting the words!

The poet Noel Monahan spent his teaching career in the southeastern part of County Cavan.[9] I cannot say for sure that he was reminded of Cavan with its evidence of ancient volcanic activity when he visited Mount Etna, Sicily's active volcano ("Etna"). Cavan's volcano would have been hidden beneath sea level and a bit shy, but not Etna's:

> Smoke plumes rise above her head. She throws
> Tantrums, wriggling red-hot spaghetti through
> Her teeth, sending rocks flying down to sea.

Monahan finds her irresistible and he is reminded of the Sicilian philosopher, Empedocles, the first to recognise our planet's four elements – fire, air, earth and water – and how they are kept in balance. He was well placed in Sicily to observe the behaviour of all four elements, which was probably not fundamentally different to how they have presented themselves even in droll Cavan!

Away to the northwest of the Lakes Country, along Cavan's panhandle, the varied Carboniferous rocks underpin rugged and hilly countryside that is quite distinctive from elsewhere in Cavan. A low dense cloud canopied the hills around Bellavally Gap during my visit, giving it a gloomy atmosphere. There was little sign it would lift for any length in advance of a threatened storm later that day. Cuilcagh Mountain (666 metres) itself is composed of pale coloured sandstones whose outcrop forms cliffed steps on the horizon. This gives way downwards to open boggy hillside underlain by black fissile shales which split as thinly as newspaper. Watch out for exposures along forest tracks where you may find delicate fossil impressions of gastropods and bivalves. Northwest of Cuilcagh lies the limestone pavement of the Burren Forest and the Shannon Pot, source of the Shannon River, which extends across to County Fermanagh as part of the Marble Arch Caves and Geopark. Water is constantly trickling down through the limestone, creating a caving wonder-world that is best seen at the Geopark. But the poet by-passes this and takes us to an Adriatic cave ("Postojina Cave, Slovenia") for a tourist train ride "Past drapery of rock, lichen grey candles" and "Eternal dripping, metronome of drops" to introduce us to a fascinating animal. *Proteus anguinus*, called "human fish" because of its skin colour, has a life expectancy approaching 100 years and is so cherished that it features on Slovenia's currency.[10]

Now let us imagine Cuilcagh Mountain ("Cuilcagh") as a deathly woman through the words of Noel Monahan. She scents of moss and asphodel, the latter wild flower associated with death and the afterlife. He sees her as squatting in the wilderness and powerless against the intrusions of humans and nature alike. It is a ghastly and wintry picture, with a blanket of bog around her shoulders, her breasts held in place by whins and heather, and bog water flowing down her legs. Hardly a glamorous impression of this sturdy woman of the mountains! When he reaches the lower ground near Glangevlin ("Glangevlin Prayer"), the poet wishes for a time when Cuilcagh could raise her head free of its surrounding stones so he could identify the lost child in the hard rock of her face.

Eighteenth century Irish-language poetry may display a warm feeling for nature and even an occasional awareness of environmental change, although it is rare for it to consider anything amounting to catastrophe. But this is precisely what "Róisín Dubh" contemplates, extending even as far as widespread seismic disaster. The poem, translated here by Thomas Kinsella,[11] is a passionate assertion that Ireland's nationhood would prevail against British aggression so long as it was not overwhelmed by powerful natural forces:

> The Erne will be strong in flood, the hills be torn,
> the ocean be all red waves, the sky all blood,
> every mountain valley and bog in Ireland will shake
> one day, before she shall perish, my Róisín Dubh.

The spectre of strong earthquakes is unequivocal here and the spotlight is falling on the Erne catchment, including Cavan Lakes Country. Is there any scientific basis for raising fears among Cavan residents?

I'm not sure that this chapter's title is helpful: Seismic shift! This phrase commonly indicates some unprecedented change. Irish radio news recently referred to Silicon Valley as the epicentre of the IT industry. It is certainly an international hub for IT innovation and enterprise but, living as they do close to splays of the San Andreas Fault, I wonder how comfortable their staff would be to learn of this quaking news? Indeed it was California, if not Silicon Valley itself, that had a key influence on earthquake research in Ireland, because it was in the wake of the 1906 San Francisco earthquake that the country's first seismograph was established at Rathfarnham Castle.

It served as Ireland's seismology centre until 1967, when Met Eire-ann, Ireland's meteorological service, assumed responsibility for seismic monitoring. Since 1978, the Dublin Institute for Advanced Studies has been recording systematic seismic data for Ireland, based on a network of five stations around the country.[12]

Seismic research confirms what we all sense – that Ireland lies in a low-risk seismic area. The area of Great Britain and Ireland together experiences no more than a few earthquakes of magnitude five each century. This is a log scale so the San Francisco earthquake at magnitude eight was 1,000 times stronger than any of these. The area of Ireland with most persistent seismic activity is the upraised landscape around river valleys in the southeast, such as the Barrow and Nore. But in historical times even that region has experienced only mild earthquakes that might cause limited structural damage at worst. There is also a seismic outlier in Donegal, probably controlled by a local fault, where occasional quakes are similarly mild but do attract some publicity. Although the Erne catchment does not feature in this seismic action, bear in mind that Frank Mitchell, the noted naturalist, speculated that it might owe its origin to sagging of the Earth's crust during the formation of the Atlantic Ocean.[13] If so, then that sagging would have been caused by seismic activity. So that eighteenth century Gaelic poet may have been more knowledgeable than we give him credit for and Cavan's seismicity may not be limited to some far-off event that resulted in the Slieve Glah fault zone!

Stresses build up unevenly in the Earth's crust according as tectonic plates move and adjust relative to each other. Earthquakes occur when stress is released, usually suddenly and along pre-existing fault planes. The resulting energy is dissipated through seismic waves some of which pass through the Earth's interior, giving us valuable information on its structure and composition. However other waves move along the Earth's surface and these can cause devastation by toppling buildings and other structures such as bridges. They also cause landslides and even tsunamis that can be potentially catastrophic. As many as 200,000 quakes are recorded annually around the world, the vast majority of which are barely noticed even by local residents. Areas with high seismic risk tend to experience a cyclic pattern where major quakes are separated by extended periods of seismic calm. In the case of San Francisco, the cycle duration is estimated at perhaps 300 years, so hopefully the next major quake may still be at least a century in the future.

Notes

1. From "Come back, Paddy Reilly", which appears on pages 24-26 of: James N. Healy (1966) *Percy French and His Songs*. Cork: Mercier Press.

2. P. J. Kennedy (2007) *Shadows on Our Doorstep: A Collection of Poetry*. Original Writing Limited. I have referred to the following poems: "Buried Unknownst" (page 16) and "Wound" (page 28).

3. I have referred to two poems from Heather Brett, as follows: "Under the Rhododendron" is from page 4 of Heather Brett (1991) *Abigail Brown*. Galway: Salmon Publishing. "Landscapes for Suicides" is from page 25 of Heather Brett (1994) *The Touch-maker*. Cavan: Alternative Publishing Co.

4. Geraghty, M. (1997) *Geology of Monaghan-Carlingford*. Geological Survey of Ireland.

5. Tom Conaty (2010) *An Exaltation of Starlings*. Tralee: Doghouse. I have referred to "River Annalee" (page 10), "Mission Sunday" (page 43) and "Altitude Sickness" (page 50).

6. Eamon Cooke (2002) *Berry Time*. Dublin: Dedalus Press. I have referred to "Forest, Music, Stream" (page 9) and "Summer Walk" (page 38).

7. James N. Healy (1966) *Percy French and His Songs*. Cork: Mercier Press. 172 pages. I have quoted from "Come Back, Paddy Reilly" (pages 24-26) and "The Effusion of William, Inspector of Drains" (pages 16-19); I referred to "The Mountains of Mourne" (pages 65-66).

8. For information on the Lattoon (Nadreegeel Loughs) gold hoard see www.museum.ie/en/list/artefacts.aspx?article=85ce2f72-0ffc-47f2-a84e-cbc9573b5e57 (Accessed 12 February 2014).

9. I have referred to "Glangevlin Prayer" on page 22 of Noel Monahan (2004) *The Funeral Game*. County Clare: Salmon Publishing. I have quoted from "Postojina Cave, Slovenia" (page 53) and "Etna" (page 57) in Noel Monahan (2010) *Curve of the Moon*. County Clare: Salmon Poetry. I also refer to "Cuilcagh" (page 56).

10. For information on Postojna Cave visit en.wikipedia.org/wiki/Postojna_Cave (Accessed 11 February 2014).

11. This translation by Thomas Kinsella appears on pages 310-311 of Seán O'Tuama (1981) *An Duanaire: An Irish Anthology. 1600-1900: Poems of the Dispossessed*. Philadelphia: University of Pennsylvania Press.

12. For more information on Ireland's seismicity see: www.dias.ie/index.php?option=com_content&view=category&layout=blog&id=30&Itemid=42&lang=en Accessed 28 October 2014.

13. See page 23 of Frank Mitchell and Michael Ryan (2007) *Reading the Irish Landscape*. Dublin: Town House.

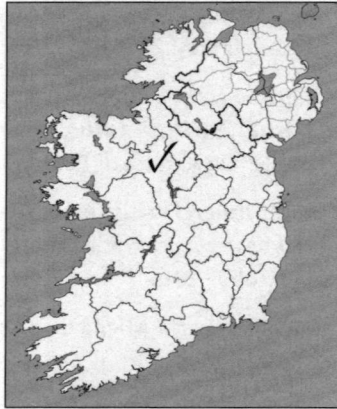

23

WHAT! NO DINOSAURS?
(ROSCOMMON)

Then the wet, winding roads,
Brown bogs with black water,
And my thoughts on white ships
And the King o' Spain's daughter.
— Padraic Colum.[1]

I am standing in the imposing atrium of the American Museum of Natural History, on the edge of New York's Central Park, and I find it amazing, if endearing, that the re-assembled skeleton of *Barosaurus* should take centre stage. This dinosaur mother is fiercely protecting her brood from attack by a flesh-eating preda-tor. Arriving visitors congregate here in large numbers to plan their day and, however casually they may initially glance, inevitably they become drawn into its saga, overcome by its scale and starkness. And yet, they are not staring at models or reconstructions of these extinct animals, only their skeletons. The power of imagination![2]

Of course we are used to displays of fully-fleshed and properly preserved animals. Many have received the attention of taxidermists, whether the fisherman's proud catch, the dog lover's fond pet or the museum's display of wild animals. But this list cannot easily extend to extinct animals, where we are often obliged to rely on randomly fossilised remains that may convey little of the demeanour or personality of the living creature. While a mammal may well have its robust backbone fossilised, it is less common to find traces of its fleshy parts preserved in rocks. In the case of soft-bodied creatures such as the jellyfish nothing may remain except in the most exceptional burial circumstances. If dinosaurs were quickly entombed in muddy sediment after death, there is the prospect of finding reasonably complete skeletons, perhaps with even remnants of skin and muscles. On the other hand, where a dinosaur died after being attacked and dismembered by ferocious predators then its resulting fossilised remains are likely to comprise only bone fragments.

Nevertheless it would not tax the technical resources of New York's distinguished museum to erect life-like models of dinosaurs, but I applaud its decision to use these skeletons. In fact, *Barosaurus* skeletons have become one of our most familiar dinosaur images, every bit as popular as realistic models of the fearsome carnivore, *Tyrannosaurus rex*, because they feature prominently in prestigious museums. In life, these magnificent herbivores were among the most gigantic that ever strolled across our landscapes, well capable of extensive travel in search of nourishment and safe habitats. To view a cousin of our Central Park specimen, you must take a transatlantic flight to Heathrow, from where it is just a short Tube trip to the Natural History Museum in South Kensington. Although its cousin is called *Diplodocus*, recent taxonomic research has shown it to belong to the very same genus as *Barosaurus*, but has bestowed on both a less pronounceable name!

Dinosaurs must rank among the most successful and enduring of all animal groups, and they thrived over a lengthy period amounting to about 150 million years. The very first dinosaurs were neither large nor domineering but they were opportunists and, when an environmental catastrophe wiped out much other animal life, they propagated quickly to occupy the vacated ecosystems, eventually embracing the seas and even taking to the air. Innovative, adaptable and determined are adjectives that come to mind although, surprisingly, management consultants still stubbornly invoke the name of dinosaurs when describing the contrary of these qualities! Indeed it would take another global catastrophe to herald their demise 65 million years ago. That catastrophe is generally regarded as the result of a comet striking the Yucatan Peninsula in Mexico, although an alternative view is gaining traction that extreme volcanic eruptions contributed.

Recent research has recognised birds as the present-day descendants of dinosaurs, which are widely seen as having bird-like rather than lizard-like links. Just like birds, many were covered not in scales but in colourful feathers of orange, red, russet brown and white, plumage that may have provided insulation or attracted mates rather than primarily facilitating flight. We also now recognise these animals could be graceful and swift, bearing their tails aloft and running like elephants. As we look increasingly to birds to explain dinosaur biology and behaviour, it seems our image of them as drab and growling creatures is destined to grow more colourful – and perhaps more tuneful! I wonder what they smelt like?[3]

Returning to New York's Central Park, it was constructed with love and creativity from an unpromising jumble of quarries and wasteland, so that now it abounds in lush hills, elegant parkland, sparkling lakes and profuse tree and shrub coverage. This same area may well have been equally fertile 140 million years ago when

Barosaurus stood her ground in defence of her brood. However its bedrock of granite gneiss, well exposed throughout Central Park, formed 500 million years ago, long before the arrival of the earliest dinosaurs. Any younger rocks containing dinosaur fossils, if they ever existed, have long ago been removed by erosion. Thus arises what might be called the Dinosaur Gap, the absence of any sediments formed during the dinosaur era.

This Dinosaur Gap should be a familiar concept on the island of Ireland, because so much of its surface comprises Carboniferous or older rocks, overlain only by very recent unconsolidated materials remaining from the Ice Age. Sediments of suitable age to potentially contain dinosaur remains are confined to the northeast, the hinterland of Belfast's Ulster Museum. This museum does not disappoint us for it exhibits some small bone fragments from Island Magee, on the County Antrim coast, which it describes as Ireland's only dinosaur fossils. Those remains are insufficient to say much more about this unique animal. Could it fly or swim or run? What kind of diet did it enjoy? How big was it? What kind of lurid plumage did it sport – it could have ranged from simply gaudy to truly meretricious! And, with only bone fragments preserved, the poignant question remains as to how painfully it met its end. Maybe the discovery of new evidence in the future will provide answers.

Roscommon is typical of Ireland's Dinosaur Gap territory, with widespread unconsolidated glacial deposits overlying Carboniferous or older bedrock. We cannot say that dinosaurs never frolicked across this landscape, only that we have no evidence of their presence. I decided to explore the area around Boyle and Lough Gara with its karstified limestone. The Old Red Sandstone ridge of the Curlew Mountains sheltered Boyle on its northern side as I headed westwards under a broken cloud cover. These sandstones accumulated on an alluvial plain while active faulting, on a splay of the Highland Boundary Fault, was uplifting the older mountains further north. There was also some contemporary volcanism in the Curlews, giving rise to some distinctive lava flows and volcanic conglomerates. So volcanic and seismic events played no small part in shaping Roscommon's landscape.[4]

South of the road, the hummocky and poorly drained limestone countryside had considerable marsh and bog. The irregular field pattern and small field size gave rise to a profusion of boundary-forming trees that was particularly pleasing. Beyond tidy Cloonloo the road crossed the now-muted Curlew hills and the walls of red sandstone became quite abundant in places, showing layers rich in either silt flakes or quartz cobbles, both evidence of severe storms during its deposition. Turning south, I remained in sandstone country all the way to Monasteraden but then encountered the indented limestone shore of Lough Gara, which spread its tentacles to the very fringes of the Curlews. All the well-known features of karst can be discovered around Lough Gara: water-worn fractures and conduits, caves and – Ireland's contribution to international karstic terminology – turloughs (small impersistent lakes). It is essential to understand karst in order to manage water supply – aquifers provide 90 per cent of drinking water here. A knowledge of karst is also needed to control river flow, conserve the associated habitats and support agriculture.[5]

Entering Monasteraden, I felt the first few raindrops and looked wistfully eastwards across the lake to the plains of Boyle where the horizon still had an attractive blue fringe. I walked eastwards along the south shore of Lough Gara, passing through flat-lying cattle pastures along the Roscommon-Sligo border. A low misty cloud settled in for the afternoon and was quite capricious as to when and where it shed its moisture. At Clooncunny Bridge, where the Upper Lough Gara drains into the main Lough Gara, a solitary angler was resolutely trying to tempt fish onto his line. Soon I took the road northwards back to the hummocky limestone terrain I had experienced that morning. The road then followed a broad clockwise arc to the Boyle River, which flows from Lough Gara into Lough Key, reaching the Curlews before entering Boyle, where I boarded my train home. Samuel Lewis in the mid-nineteenth century preferred the lake country around Boyle to any other part of Roscommon, describing mournfully the rivers as sluggish and prone to flood the surrounding countryside. The largest lake was Lough Key, whose main water supply was from Lough Gara, and he considered the scenery throughout this chain of lakes was highly picturesque.[6] I agreed.

Another reason for my Lough Gara odyssey was to visit Monasteraden Church where a small burial plot is reserved for the Mac Dermots, Princes of nearby Coolavin. There, comfortable among the princes, lay the mortal remains of the geologist Conor Victor Mac Dermot, who died in 2001 at the early age of 56 years. Conor was a career-long member of staff at the Geological Survey of Ireland who was an expert on every limestone county in the country. Given his inquisitive nature, he got to appreciate far more than just the limestone itself. Along the way he learned much of the history, archaeology and habitats of these limestone districts. He liked nothing better than talking to people about all of these, so that he inspired many young geologists and forged strong links with several communities across the country.

If we were to lift the carpet of overburden and expose the underlying limestone bedrock across Ireland we would reveal a few surprises. For example, bedrock depressions conceal some rare vestiges of sediment formed during the heyday of the dinosaurs. At Cloyne, County Cork, there are clays of Jurassic age and at Ballydeenlea, near Killarney, is chalk of Cretaceous age. Ireland was under seawater for much of this time but its land emerged above sea level at various times, when pre-existing sediments were subject to removal by erosion. Of course this process continued after dinosaurs died out 65 million years ago, with karst still forming in a sub-tropical climate. Our exotic flora, with profuse tree and shrub coverage, was perhaps akin to that seen in swampy areas of Florida today. Subsequently the global climate gradually cooled and culminated, about 2.6 million years ago, in our entry into the Ice Age.[7]

Pollnahallia, east of Lough Corrib in neighbouring County Galway, provides evidence of the climate and environment at this time. The area would have had dramatic limestone pinnacles and upstanding boulder stacks, possibly comparable with the spectacular Stone Forest of the Kunming region of China, before they were largely dispersed by advancing ice sheets. But at Pollnahallia, some deep fractures and cave passages in bedrock have been preserved, and spores in lignite from one fracture have indicated the abundance of redwood and swamp cypress in contemporary forest throughout western Ireland. Lignite originated from vegetation which accumulated in the quiet waters fringing Lough Corrib. Finally before the first ice front approached, thick deposits of very pure silica sand accumulated at Pollnahallia and indeed were quarried in the past. This was wind-blown sand and similar to that of coastal sand dunes.[8]

So Roscommon region may have had a major Dinosaur Gap but it also had a most interesting landscape history. Enter Robert Lloyd Praeger with some cold water! He was one of Ireland's most dedicated naturalists in the first half of the twentieth century but he spared little of his enthusiasm for Roscommon.[9] The county was very dull in his view, just widespread sheep pastures with the usual midlands mixture of bog and marsh. He advised the visitor to stick to the lake district around Boyle or else the Shannon along Roscommon's eastern margins, both distinctly attractive. We have already endorsed his view of the lakes so let's take his other advice and head towards the Shannon.

The River Shannon is immensely important to Roscommon, forming its entire eastern border and influencing the nature of its nearby limestone landscape. It defines the rhythm of life for Roscommon-born poet, Mary Turley-McGrath (b. 1948), in the landscape of her childhood. She sets the scene ("River"):[10]

There are no mountains where I grew up.
Only the miracle of McGann's Hill
sloped towards the sky.
...
No drumlins ruffled the flat fields
that forced themselves to the horizon.
...
The river broke the flatness,
wound like a tired snake
across the farms, dividing and joining.

These are "calla" lands for her, the well-known Shannon callows which are subject to regular flooding ("Waterlines"). She observes the seasons through its changes. Its flow swells during autumn, then it spreads across fields in winter creating its own empire. But when spring arrives, floods recede and growth begins. The river's force delivers new alluvium and renewed growth to farmland. The poet feels an integral part of this vibrant system – she is the river bed over which the river water flows. Her concerns remain modern and even geological in "April", as she becomes aware of spring. The earth pumps new life into nature and she rejoices at its success even in extreme circumstances.

This chapter seems to be book-marked between the American Museum of Natural History and the lake country around Boyle – and there is actually a link between the two. That link comprises two contemporary Presidents, one American and one Irish, who had a strong regard for each other. Theodore Roosevelt (1858–1919),[11] a hero of the Spanish-American War, was a vigorous and exciting American president in the first decade of the twentieth century who went on to gain the Nobel Peace Prize for his active role in foreign affairs. He was familiar with Irish political developments and deeply interested in the Irish Literary Revival, indeed he published an essay on ancient Irish sagas. As both Governor of New York and US President, he had a remarkably holistic view of conservation and anticipated many modern concepts of sus-

tainability. Having overcome personal ill-health, he became an
advocate of the outdoor life and sought to convince the American public of its benefits. It is fitting that his philosophy should
be summarised on the walls of the entrance hall at the American
Museum of Natural History:

> There is a delight in the hardy life of the open. There are
> no words that can tell the hidden spirit of the wilderness
> that can reveal its mystery, its melancholy and its charm.
> The nation behaves well if it treats the natural resources
> as assets which it must turn over to the next genera-
> tion increased and not impaired in value. Conservation
> means development as much as it does protection.

This is remarkable in foreseeing issues that society only seri-
ously engaged with many decades later.

President Douglas Hyde (1860–1949)[12] was an unusual man of
unusual achievements. Son of a Protestant rector at Frenchpark,
County Roscommon, he was an ardent nationalist and president
of Conradh na Gaeilge (1893–1915) at a time of great national
sentiment towards the Irish language. He served as Professor of
Modern Irish at UCD (1909–1932), making a great impact on Irish
scholarship, and later as President of Ireland (1938–1945), when
he was considered a genial public figure and was held in very high
regard. He devoted his adult life to the noble ideal of promoting
Irish as an everyday language and no one since has been more successful. Although the outdoors did not feature prominently in this,
both his youth and retirement were spent on the shores of Lough
Gara where he enjoyed hunting, fishing, boating and swimming.
In practice he shared with Roosevelt a great love of the countryside and the latter in turn was most interested in Irish affairs. I am
not aware that Roosevelt ever visited Ireland but had he done I am
convinced the two presidents would have discovered many shared
interests, being both natural story tellers. I like to picture them in
deep conversation strolling the hallowed shores of Hyde's Lough
Gara before dinner!

Notes

1. Quoted from "Drover" on pages 41-42 of Padraic Colum (1981) *The Poet's Circuits: Collected Poems of Ireland*. Mountrath, Ireland: Dolmen Press.

2. See www.amnh.org (Accessed 29 October 2014).

3. A wide variety of dinosaur books are available, including Scott, C. (2011) *Planet Dinosaur: The Next Generation of Giant Killers*. London: BBC Books.

4. See J.H. Morris, I.D. Sommerville and C.V. MacDermot (2003) *Geology of Longford-Roscommon*. Geological Survey of Ireland.

5. Daly, D., Drew, D., Deakin, J. and Ball, D. (Eds.) (2000) *The Karst of Ireland: Limestone Landscapes, Caves and Groundwater Drainage Systems*. Geological Survey of Ireland.

6. See pages 519-525, volume 2 of Lewis, S. (1837) *A Topographical Dictionary of Ireland*. Reissued 1970 at Port Washington NY: Kennikat Press.

7. C. H. Holland and I. S. Sanders (2009) *The Geology of Ireland*. Second edition. Edinburgh: Dunedin Academic Press.

8. Coxon, P. and Flegg, A. M. (1987) A Late Pliocene/Early Pleistocene deposit at Pollnahallia, near Headford, County Galway. *Proceedings of the Royal Irish Academy*, volume 87B, pages 15-42.

9. See page 246 of Praeger, R.L. (1937) *The Way that I Went: An Irishman in Ireland*. Dublin: Hodges, Figgis & Co and London: Methuen & Co.

10. Mary Turley-McGrath (2003) *New Grass under Snow*. Kilcar, County Donegal: Summer Palace Press. I have quoted from "River" (pages 13-14) and referred to "April" (page 45) and "Waterlines" (pages 57-59).

11. Harbaugh, W.H. (1999) "Theodore Roosevelt". In Garraty, J.A. and Carnes, M.C. (Eds.) American National Biography. New York: Oxford University Press, volume 18, pages 829-835.

12. Dunleavy, J.E. and Dunleavy, G.W. (1991) *Douglas Hyde: A Maker of Modern Ireland*. Berkeley: University of California Press.

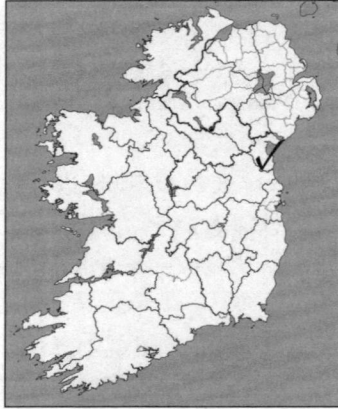

24

Epic Landscapes
(Louth)

Away, away, from men and towns,
To the wild wood and the downs –
To the silent wilderness
Where the soul need not repress
Its music lest it should not find
An echo in another's mind.
– P. B. Shelley.[1]

When the Norwegian explorer Roald Amundsen (1872–
1928) successfully navigated the Northwest Passage, he
solved a puzzle whose solution had eluded many previous expedi-
tions, often tragically. His achievement was considerable because
he had successfully traversed the ice-packed seas of the Arctic Ar-
chipelago north of Canada, a distance of 3,500 miles. So it would

be curmudgeonly of me to mention that fewer than a dozen teams bothered to re-trace his steps in the succeeding century, each taking an inordinate three years on average to complete it. But that is hindsight, for the Northwest Passage, with its promise of efficient trading, was a glittering target in the minds of explorers over the previous four hundred years.[2] And in that history, two Irishmen played notable roles, one of them coming from County Louth. Dundalk-born Sir Francis Leopold McClintock (1819–1907) is remembered as the person who discovered the dismal fate of an earlier expedition, that of the other and more illustrious Irishman, Sir John Franklin (1786–1847). Sir John had in 1845 set out to explore the Northwest Passage but neither he nor his team would ever return and for ten long years there was no reliable information on what happened to all 140 of them. It was McClintock who discovered their grim fate, finding debris of the expedition and a note from one of its members. This was indeed a considerable achievement which earned him a knighthood, he would retire with the rank of Admiral, and he would remain a much-consulted authority on polar exploration. But maybe his most cherished acclamation was that accorded him by his home town, Dundalk, where his family lived.[3]

Franklin is still recalled in song and story, much more than the man who followed him, but I am pleased that their memorials in Westminster Abbey are located together, one above the other. For McClintock had more strings to his bow than being an explorer: he was also an enthusiastic amateur geologist who collaborated with Professor Samuel Haughton of Trinity College Dublin. McClintock encountered granite, gneiss and fossil-bearing sediments ranging in age from Silurian to Tertiary and Haughton prepared an early Arctic geological map based on these observations. McClintock's work received widespread notice because it suggested for the first time that the Arctic had a warm climate in earlier times, untroubled by the precarious pack-ice that clogged modern explorers.[4]

Under a clear winter sky the waters of Dundalk Bay are a crisp blue colour, an unusual sight in itself. From its southern shores the low coastline swerves in a large curve around to the cluster of gleaming buildings that is Dundalk town, backed by the jagged hills of Carlingford. Sweeping further to the right, extending way beyond the limits of Dundalk Bay itself, are the majestic Mountains of Mourne, with a few of their highest summits tinged snowy white. The southern shore of this great bay is visually less spectacular and yet it contains a boundary worthy of bugle calls. Because it is here, somewhere between Annagassan and Dunany Point, that the trace of the Iapetus Suture comes ashore and starts its journey across Ireland. We might be forgiven for expecting marked differences in bedrock across this most fundamental geological boundary, which once separated two quite distinctive continents. But the bedrock on both sides comprises very similar grey sandstones and mudstones and are, after all, the products of very similar environments. So it is not possible to straddle the two ancient continents no matter how large your stride! Nevertheless the bedrock bears the marks of the brutal stresses associated with the final closure of Iapetus Ocean, with its beds folded, faulted and traversed by white quartz veins.

If Louth was responsible for burying the last vestiges of that ancient ocean, it also provided some compensation in the evidence for the later opening of another ocean, our more familiar Atlantic. And we will find that story, as played out on the Cooley Peninsula, intertwined with legendary events of heroic dimension. For the mythical landscape there is nothing short of volcanic!

Louth's legendary heroes do not come more celebrated than Cuchulainn, the Ulster warrior who, by himself, repelled an assault on his province by Queen Maeve's Connaught army. She resolved to capture Ulster's Brown Bull of Cooley, the only bull in Ireland superior to her husband's White-Horned Bull. She set out with an army from her Roscommon headquarters for the Carlingford Peninsula, at that time the southern frontier of Ulster. But Cuchulainn, the superhero and accomplished warrior, stood between her and her ambition. He blocked her army's progress, having chained himself to a tree so he could fight to the death, and thereby gave his fellow warriors sufficient time to muster and prevail over Maeve's army. Subsequently, the Brown Bull attacked and killed the White-Horned Bull but itself died as a result of the struggle. The net outcome – ignoring a bewildering range of lesser plots and subterfuges – was that peace was restored between Ulster and Connaught, a happy development even if the parties had between them destroyed Ireland's most prized bulls![5]

Embarking on my Louth odyssey from Dundalk, I crossed the Castletown estuary and took the road to Cooley peninsula. I was pondering the fact that Eleanor Hull (1860–1935), one of the early Celtic scholars, was none other than the daughter of Edward Hull (1829–1917), Director of the Geological Survey of Ireland and (simultaneously) Professor of Geology at the Royal College of Science in Ireland.[6] Born to a Church of Ireland curate in Antrim town, his early career was in Great Britain and he returned to Dublin in 1869 to take charge of a very active mapping campaign at the Geological Survey. He was sufficiently successful in his task to aspire to a knighthood, but that honour eluded him. A vain man of outspoken and conservative political views who sought fulfilment in occasional overseas assignments, his daughter's Celtic interests seem unexpected. But then I recall that he became proficient in Irish while studying at Trinity College Dublin, so I am less surprised at Eleanor's blossoming involvement in Irish language literature. She moved with her family to London in 1891 after her father's retirement and became very influential in Irish literary circles there, as much for her popularising of Irish literature as for her scholarly work on it. A copy of one of her books in the National Library of Ireland was donated by the Christian Brothers in Youghal while another was formerly in the possession of playwright Sean O'Casey (1880–1964): this is not the kind of company in which her father would have been comfortable. He did have an interest in volcanoes, however, whatever about the heroic struggle between Cuchulainn and Maeve's army, and this would have been whetted by the countryside I was entering. I imagined that the Hulls, father and daughter, passed close by on many an occasion, while using the main road between Dublin and Belfast, and I wondered whether they shared many conversations based on their different perceptions of this fine district! Its geology is radically different from that around Dundalk and to properly appreciate it, we must fast-forward from the closing of Iapetus Ocean to the opening of the North Atlantic. This was accompanied by a surge of magma into the crust, giving rise to widespread basaltic lavas in Antrim and elsewhere, swarms of doleritic dykes and several volcanoes, including one at Carlingford.

The root of Carlingford's volcano forms an oval mountainous area comprising a central granitic area surrounded by gabbro. This latter is chemically identical to basalt but is as coarse-grained as granite due to its crystallisation at depth. So its large rectangular pyroxene and rusty-surfaced olivine grains can be seen with the naked eye. The gabbro exposed on Slieve Foye (588 metres) is layered because it formed from magma that was fed in successive pulses from deeper down. This magma was hot enough to melt considerable volumes of enclosing rock, forming a relatively fine-grained variety of granite called granophyre. This created smoothly-contoured hills, such as Clermont Cairn (508 metres), in contrast to the rugged outlines of the gabbro hills around Slieve Foye. The granite is considered to take the form of a ring-dyke and its upward intrusion was facilitated by the subsidence of a central block of ground. Fluid gabbro and granite magmas did mingle and react together. Also, the very hot gabbro had a further impact on its surroundings, metamorphosing the Silurian siltstone to hornfels and Carboniferous limestone to marble.

The first expression of this impending volcanic event was the eruption of magma which reached the surface in the form of basalt lava. Somewhat coarser-grained dolerite forms narrow sheets in several areas, including at Carlingford Castle. These sheets are oriented tangentially around the gabbro-granite complex and they slope inwards towards its centre. They collectively form a downward-pointing cone and owe this distinctive geometry to the pressure of magma rising from the underlying magma chamber. In fact dolerite and granite were molten at the same time, giving rise to curved mutual contacts (a tell-tale sign) as well as an array of veins and breccias.[7]

Carlingford is an attractive and prosperous peninsula, with the Cooley Mountains forming its core and surrounded by fertile coastal plains. I gained height gently along the wooded banks of the Flurry River, passing by small rolling pastures, and joined the Táin Way that traverses much of the Cooley Mountains. I turned northwards and climbed up to the rounded granophyre outlines of Slievestucan. Then the Way dropped down into the valley of the Big River, a great name for a river occupying such a confined valley, before rising again towards the shoulder between Slieve Foye and Barnavave (350 metres). This shoulder is a faulted gully in the gabbro of Slieve Foye and reputed to be where Maeve attempted an incursion into Ulster. If you have sufficient wind and time, it is worth looking (with care) at its excellent gabbro exposures. Slieve Foye is a jagged rocky dome which sits uncomfortably atop the smoother grassy slopes lower down. This country always seems to have an extra ridge beyond what I anticipated – ideal landscape in which to hide valuable cattle from one's enemies. Away to the northwest is Windy Gap, where Maeve's army may once have passed. It owes its existence to a major northwest-southeast-trending fault zone which offsets the contact with Silurian mudstones by as much as 1km. More importantly, if you have felt that the differences in granite and gabbro landscape were at all vague, then this is the place to visit. The contrast in both landscape and bedrock on either side of this Gap is very striking.

Relics of that old Iapetus Ocean re-appeared, in the form of Silurian mudstones, as I headed down to the coastline near Carlingford. These have some elaborate bedding folds, so splendid that they inevitably spark the query as to whether they might have formed by slumping chaotically along the seabed rather than being squeezed later by tectonic stresses between two gigantic plates. Generally sedimentary folds can be recognised where they are confined to specific beds with no folding in the beds above and below, whereas tectonic folds can be diagnosed if the fold axes have a consistent orientation. But sometimes geologists have a reluctance to finally terminate an entertaining debate!

Typical effects of glaciation are evident throughout this district, but its aftermath has also left its mark. At Templetown, the beach is raised 10m above present sea-level. This is because the Earth's surface has relaxed as the enormous weight of ice melted away and it has gradually been uplifted as a result. This is a feature common throughout northeast Ireland and the surface readjustment has yet to be completed. In fact recently a minor earthquake (merely of 2.2 magnitude) was ascribed by the Dublin Institute for Advanced Studies to the same influence.[8] This learned institute (and it has a School of Celtic Studies!) never even considered the possibility that the seismic legends of this district might have been a contributory factor!

So two interwoven and complex narratives can be discerned in the landscape of the Cooley Mountains and they can enhance our appreciation of their scenery. Despite the intrigue underlying the Cattle Raid, it bears a simple message of the power of one determined man against many. And behind the deep complexity of the landscape lies the uncomplicated power of magma to shape and influence our environment. Both stories, however real or imagined, have an equally compelling grip on our imagination as we visualise the past of this landscape, so do draw strength from them as you traverse the steeper slopes of Cooley!

But when in County Louth my ancestral roots will inevitably draw me back to the Boyne valley (and isn't it worth it?) and a poet of that historic river. Director of Dublin's Abbey Theatre and friend of W. B. Yeats, his was widely acknowledged as an attractive poetic light that was snuffed out all too early. F. R. Higgins (1896–1941) grew up at Ballivor, County Meath, within the Boyne Valley. On a sweltering summer's walk along the Boyne ("The Boyne Walk"),[9] Higgins struggled to keep pace with his vigorous and unrelenting companion, probably the writer Brinsley Macnamara (1890–1963). The poet found the heat overpowering and "each rock blazed like a drunken face". This is lyricism with attitude! But it is a welcome counterpoint to the Wordsworthian bliss of so many poets in similar circumstances! He found little pleasure in watching fish leaping, but he certainly savoured the moment he spotted a sign boasting that the establishment was 'Licensed for Liquor!' He quaffed thirstily and, despite painful exhaustion, he nonchalantly completed a poem.

In "Meath Men" he urges his fellow-writer, the same Brinsley Macnamara:

> This is our land; and here no summer mocks
> The stony crops we've known in Aran Islands,
> Where seas break silence and strip the yellow rocks
> Of rich top-dressing for lean highlands.

There is a sharp contrast in landscape style here but it is the Boyne's waters that give him June delight above Galway's countryside:

> Yet by the weirs that shiver with dark eels,
> Dusk breaks in leaps of light; and salmon-snarers
> Are nightly sharing fish in salley creels
> That merely seem a dream to Clare-men.

Then, lest he get too pretentious, he rounds on Macnamara, a childhood neighbour and mere novelist, telling him to

> not forget
> The poets and their privileges in Tara.

Macnamara was, after all, raised across the border in Delvin, County Westmeath!

Higgins' intense interest in the Irish folk tradition opened up to him the possibility of poetry based on his natural surroundings and the everyday.[10] For in truth Higgins, despite his Republican sympathies, was something of an outsider, coming from a family where his father was a staunch Unionist and comfortable farmer. This caused a temporary estrangement between father and son and it is interesting that it was the landscape of the upper Boyne that facilitated his final reconciliation with his now-deceased parent. In one of his most popular poems, "Father and Son", he walks the river's bank recalling his father's more acceptable qualities and how they both spent a happy day there. Nearby Laracor, where Jonathon Swift (1667–1745) once ministered, was now his father's final resting place and it would soon receive his own remains. Fittingly it is winter – "hushed fields ... thinned by November" – for it seems that it was only in his father's own bleak winter that the two came back together. "For that proud, wayward man now my heart breaks" – a father who increasingly loved him. Gradually, he recognises parallels in both their lives:

> And yet I am pleased that even my reckless ways
> Are living shades of his rich calms and passions.

He would not be the first offspring to assume those very attributes he once found unwelcome in a parent!

Notes

1. Extract from "The Invitation" by P. B. Shelley on page 289 of Palgrave, F.T. (Ed.) (1954) *The Golden Treasury*. London: Collins.

2. For an interesting account of polar exploration, including of the Northwest Passage, read Ranulph Fiennes (2013) *Cold: Extreme Adventures at the Lowest Temperatures on Earth*. London: Simon & Schuster.

3. See David Murphy (2004) *The Arctic Fox: Francis Leopold McClintock, Discoverer of the Fate of Franklin*. Cork: Collins Press.

4. N. T. Monaghan (2009) "Leopold McClintock – 'Arctic Fox' and his natural science collections". *The Geological Curator* volume 9, pages 85-92.

5. Daithí OhOgáin (2006) *The Lore of Ireland: An Encyclopaedia of Myth, Legend and Romance*. Cork: Collins Press.

6. See entries on Edward and Eleanor Hull on pages 840-841 of volume 4 of James McGuire and James Quinn (Eds.) (2009) *Dictionary of Irish Biography*. Royal Irish Academy and Cambridge University Press.

7. Sadhbh Baxter (2008) *A Geological Field Guide to Cooley, Gullion, Mourne and Slieve Croob*. Louth County Council.

8. Tom Blake, Director of the Irish National Seismic Network, Dublin Institute for Advanced Studies, was quoted to this effect on page 8 of *The Irish Times*, 20 March 2014.

9. F. R. Higgins (1940) *The Gap of Brightness: Lyrical Poems*. London: Macmillan & Co. I quoted from "Father and Son" (pages 1-2), "The Boyne Walk" (pages 4-7) and "Meath Men" (pages 56-57).

10. W. R. Rogers (Ed.) (1973) "F. R. Higgins". In *Irish Literary Portraits*. New York: Taplinger Publishing, pages 169-184.

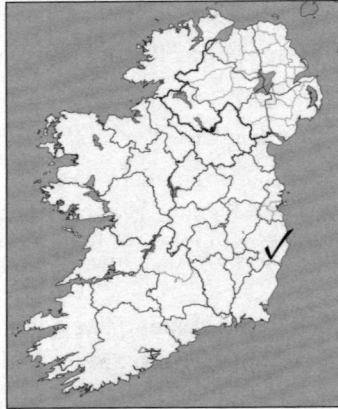

25

MOUNTAIN-BUILDING IN SEVEN EASY STAGES (Wicklow)

Still south I went and west and south again,
Through Wicklow from the morning till the night,
And far from cities, and the sites of men,
Lived with the sunshine, and the moon's delight.
– J .M. Synge.[1]

We take our mountains for granted. They may be important places of adventure and leisure, but sure they have always been there. Of course we turn to them when we need solace or contact with nature. But we can also be indifferent to them, like when we dismiss unfashionable items by saying they are "as old as the hills". So have those mountains always been there, are they really as old as their oldest bedrock? Or could their history be more intriguing? We may have looked at various components of mountain-building already, but now I want to integrate them all for one specific district, the Wicklow Mountains, and I will do this in seven stages.

Stage 1.

In any construction job, whether mountains or buildings, good preparations are essential to success. We need reliable foundations to ensure our structure will be robust and long-lasting. We also require comprehensive plans, in this case geological maps, in order to guide our way, but let's start with the foundations.

The Earth is over 4.5 billion years old, formed from dust clouds in a very hazardous environment. The cratered surface of the Moon suggests just how dangerous it was – and our own planet must have been bombarded just as intensively by meteors and comets. However, much of the evidence has been removed through the growth of new ocean floor and the burial of old continental crust within the mantle. While still a very young planet, Earth suffered a collision with a Mars-sized body and that impact gave birth to our Moon. Earth in time did stabilise as a planet and developed a life–supporting atmosphere and hydrosphere, long before any of Ireland's currently exposed rocks were formed. Our oldest rocks, at about 2 billion years, reflect only the more recent 40 per cent of our planet's history – and Wicklow's bedrock is much younger. Its rocks range back in age only to 550 million years but what they lack in longevity they compensate for in their diversity, which is the basis of its splendid (and secure!) scenery.

Maps are to me what airline timetables were to former Taoiseach Garret FitzGerald (1926–2011). Evidently even in his most fraught moments he could revive his spirits by immersing himself in the detail of those apparently turgid manuals, and I have occasionally experienced a similar sense of renewal by engaging with maps. Geological maps, more flamboyant than airline timetables, can tell us not only about the present state of our environment but can allow us imagine the past. Where drumlins are abundant we may be sure that ice sheets once prevailed and where moraine ridges are obvious we can guess they resulted from the melting of those glacial masses. Delving back further, inland outcrops of marine sedimentary rock give us a hint that the ground was once submerged beneath seawater. And of course the evidence for eruptions and earthquakes is commonplace as volcanic rock formations and faults, respectively. There is a sense in which maps can become the landscape itself! Nothing is static and significant changes are apparent in many places. Coastal erosion is significant along many stretches of coast, while inland the changing course of rivers can be detected in ox-bow lakes and abandoned meanders. We as humans are adding to the pace of change, through activities such as construction, waste disposal and atmospheric emissions. If we monitor all these changes rigorously we could eventually build a model of how mountain-building will operate into the future!

Stage 2.

The bulk of the rocks, both volcanic and sedimentary, surrounding the mountainous Leinster Granite was formed in this stage, prior to 420 million years ago. The area of Wicklow was part of Iapetus Ocean and impersistent volcanoes would have formed the only visible land. Sediment came from two sources, firstly fine pelagic mud which rained down at an excruciatingly slow rate to form mudstone. Secondly, turbidity currents hugged the seafloor and delivered a mix of sediment which spread across large areas of the ocean to form greywackes, siltstones and quartzites. When Iapetus Ocean finally closed, the ensuing plate collision crumpled and faulted these beds and those with significant clay content developed a slaty cleavage.

George Francis Savage-Armstrong (1845–1906), a Dubliner who became Professor of English and History at Queen's College Cork, was called the Poet of Wicklow, he admired its scenery so intensively.[2] Sometimes he savoured it on his own ("An Apology"):[3]

In this delicious land of hills
Some dear and hallowed spots there be
With which a thousand joyous things
Are blended in my memory.

The poet remembered glens where he roamed as a boy and which greatly influenced his subsequent life ("Glens of Wicklow"):

Through your woodland—hollows wild,
Hear your plunging cataracts cry,
Watch the wild—hawks in the sky,
Climb the fraughan—tufted steep,
Down the dizzy gorges peep.

The Devil's Glen is one of the most visited and it is carved in those sedimentary rocks we have just discussed. The overlooking hill has a Seamus Heaney Walk to commemorate where this eminent poet began his full-time writing career. The forestry roads here have variety of trees, rock outcrops and wooden sculptures. The Glen's wooden benches invoke the words of both Heaney and J. M. Synge and surely they have sufficient space to also remember the dedicated Savage-Armstrong?

Stage 3.

This stage spotlights the rocks surrounding the Vale of Avoca which developed as part of a chain of volcanic islands on the Iapetus Ocean floor. Imagine an explosive eruption where the ashes fall into the surrounding sea and are then disturbed by storms or seismic activity. The ashes would move down slope as turbidity currents and then spread out over considerable areas of the deeper seafloor. The eruptions on Montserrat in the Caribbean during the 1990s were probably similar in scale and impact.[4] Hot circulating seawater beneath Avoca's seafloor dissolved metals from its surroundings and, when convected back to the seafloor, precipitated its metals in those ashes. The Avoca copper deposits formed from such seafloor emissions.

The Vale of Avoca became a popular visitor destination following publication in the early nineteenth century of Thomas Moore's (1779–1852) familiar ballad, "The Meeting of the Waters":

> Sweet vale of Avoca! How calm could I rest
> In thy bosom of shade, with the friends I love best.[5]

The blend of lost friendship and scenic beauty became irresistible in Moore's sentimental rendition:

> the best charms of nature improve,
> When we see them reflected from looks that we love.

This was not the first time, however, that this district came to public attention, because little more than a decade earlier, a remarkable gold rush took place in the valley southwest of Woodenbridge. Between diggers and spectators, perhaps thousands were present some days. But talk of national good fortune was premature and the most lucrative deposits were exhausted without a valuable bedrock source being discovered. Nevertheless, its fame was such that the popular Irish playwright, John O'Keeffe (1747–1833) produced a successful play on the West London stage, *The Lad o' the Hills*, based on events surrounding it.[6]

Stage 4.

This stage concerns that familiar rock, granite, whose mica flakes sparkle at us in sunshine from city pavements and public buildings. Their creamy feldspar crystals are larger and better shaped than the smaller translucent spheres of grey quartz.

The granite originated in the plate collision following Iapetus Ocean closure, when sediments descended deep in the Earth's interior and melted to form magma. This relatively light fluid gradually cooled as it ascended to finally solidify at a depth of 5 to 10 kilometres below surface. It metamorphosed its enclosing rocks, giving new minerals, such as biotite, garnet and andalusite. The Wicklow Way between Lough Tay and Djouce Mountain has elaborately folded quartzite beds that are textured with abundant red garnets which are just visible to the unaided eye. Larger oblong crystals of grey andalusite can be seen in pavement slabs at many localities including Glendalough. The granite formed a comparatively thin, flat-lying sheet which was fed from nearby steeply-dipping faults and its roof is exposed on the summit of Lugnaquillia (925 metres). Its emplacement was one of the final acts in the development of the major Caledonian Mountains, whose eroded roots can be traced across eastern North America and northwestern Europe.

The grandiloquent Savage-Armstrong recalled his youthful adventures on "Lugnaquillia":

> Yon long hill
> Seems but a slope of velvet. Let us take
> The rougher path, and scale the wall of crag
> That breaks and cleaves the Mountain's grassy top.

This is an authentic picture of Lugnaquillia, which has both velvet slopes and sheer rocky faces. Its summit is indeed a grassy plateau generated by flat-lying schists. Lug was unshaven by ice sheets, but its flanks have been gouged out by rapacious local glaciers, leaving some dangerous corrie cliffs. Savage-Armstrong followed my own preferred route of ascent to Lugnaquillia from Glenmalure, a route that traverses a district associated with playwright J. M. Synge (1871–1909). This hilly country flanks the Leinster Granite between Aughrim and Rathdrum, and Synge passionately proclaims his love of its environment in stanzas such as:

> I knew the stars, the flowers, and the birds,
> The grey and wintry sides of many glens,
> And did but half remember human words,
> In converse with the mountains, moors, and fens.[1]

Stage 5.

Glendalough is a serene and glaciated valley which combines attractive scenery with an important monastic history, so it is no surprise that both of Ireland's Nobel-winning poets wrote about it. Belfast-born Joseph Campbell (1879–1944), author of such well-liked ballads as "The Gartan Mother's Lullaby" and "The Spanish Lady", wrote of many Wicklow places, but never with the same intensity as he did about Glendalough. He succinctly captures in "A Vision of Glendalough" the monastic and tranquil mood of the place, recreating the world of St. Kevin and the many powerful and saintly worthies that followed him.[7] In less spiritual mood, Thomas Moore recites the initially playful flirtation of Kathleen with the saint which tragically leads to his killing her and subsequently repenting of his action ("By that Lake, Whose Gloomy Shore").[5]

Glendalough has another context beyond the peaceful allure of its monastic site. Prior to 1960 Wicklow was the mining capital of Ireland and Glendalough was one of its most productive lead mining centres. Copper and sulphur mines at Avoca had opened around 1720 and later that century lead ore extraction started from a series of granite-hosted veins, including Glendalough. The copper ore was exported for smelting while the lead ore was transported by horse-and-cart to the smelter at Ballycorus, County Dublin, and the lead subsequently used in Dublin's plumbing system. Dublin also benefited from the produce of Wicklow's granite stone cutters, such as paving slabs, lintels and even water troughs. In "Music in Stone", Maureen Perkins describes their industry based on quarries around Ballyknockan that have lost the battle with Chinese competitors. She records the rhythm of workmen's tools as they split the grey-white granite, taking careful account of its grain, and re-creates the steady and contented pace of work.[8]

Stage 6.

In this stage the Wicklow Mountains as we now know them will once more raise their proud peaks above the surrounding plains.

The story is not straightforward. The original mountain range containing the newly-formed granite was subject to intense erosion as soon as it formed so that by about 350 million years ago the granite itself was exposed. Ireland was then inundated leading to the formation of thick limestone deposits and even coal seams across the country. About 75 million years ago something very distinctive happened. Chalk seas spread right across Ireland and whitewashed every part of it, probably including Wicklow, which was now largely low-lying. Chalk is a limestone composed of microscopic algae, familiar from the Cliffs of Dover and the Antrim Coast Road. Wicklow can no longer boast of its chalk because alas it has been subsequently removed by erosion.

The renewed growth of Wicklow's mountains can be tracked using two mutually independent lines of evidence. Firstly granite contains tiny crystals of apatite, a phosphorous mineral, and its isotopic composition can be used to track the progress of its erosional history. In the case of Wicklow, its granite mountains began overlooking their surroundings some time after 36 million years ago. This major landscape transformation was driven by seismic activity and we have already seen that this part of Ireland had a noticeably more extended and intensive seismic history than elsewhere in the country. This is the second line of evidence. Although individual quakes are very mild these days, nevertheless earthquakes were once more prominent here – and they can make mountains![9]

Change is a constant feature of landscape and the poet Sheila Wingfield (1906–1992), Viscountess Powerscourt, addressed its impact on the coast of her native England ("Remote Matters").[10] Severe coastal erosion over many centuries had caused the town and harbour of Dunwich in Suffolk to largely disappear and Wingfield's poem acknowledges the inevitability of such change and the futility of attempting to arrest it. Her poem particularly caught my eye because her younger relative, the late Robin Wingfield, was a geologist whose career was partly devoted to charting the same marine and coastal changes in England, but from a scientific perspective.

Stage 7.

In this final step, all of the Wicklow Mountains, except around Lugnaquillia and Djouce, were covered by ice, perhaps 400m thick. This was during the Ice Age, whose impacts were felt most strongly between 15,000 to 70,000 years ago. Glaciers surged down valleys carving out their distinctive U-shape and creating waterfalls such as at Powerscourt. On a broader scale, Wicklow was surrounded by two large ice sheets, one stretching down from Scotland along the east coast. This would have created an awesome sight from the summit of Djouce Mountain and no less impressive than many modern Antarctic scenes. The other regional ice sheet approached eastwards from the Midlands. Its melting generated a large lake between itself and the Wicklow foothills in which a substantial delta of sand and gravel accumulated. It has been a source of Dublin's aggregates for many decades.

The poet Joseph Campbell imagined how Glendalough valley was sculpted and shaped by an Ice Age glacier ("A Vision of Glendalough"):[7]

> Then upon my ear
> Suddenly crashes a dreadful roar
> Of rending rocks, and on my eye
> Looms imminent a wall of earth
> Slow-sliding from dark Tethra's cave.

I am confused by the appearance of Tethra, Goddess of the sea, but Campbell continues:

> Huge icebergs, free of primal cold,
> Thrusting before them with vast strength
> The stuff that filled this ancient glen
> Ere Time began.

This is indeed graphic language, "Time" referring to historical rather than geological time, and there is more:

> Steep granite cliffs are sheared like cheese;
> And as the dinosaurian plough
> Drives on its seaward-plunging course
> Erratics lone are lifted high,
> And perch on level shelves.

This artfully encompasses many of the valley's physical features and the poet only falters when recounting how the valley's two lakes formed:

> Forlorn,
> In coupled pits under their cirques,
> Piast-harbouring lochs are formed …

The lakes were not formed from individual corries (or cirques), but rather by a delta, fed from overhanging streams, which built a barrier across an originally large lake. But "piast-harbouring lochs" might do the valley's tourism no harm, "piast" being derived presumably from the Irish word for monster!

In Savage-Armstrong's day he set off with companions across Djouce to reach Luggala, a lodge on the shore of Lough Tay ("To Luggala"):[3]

> Rain and rough storm the mountains swept that day.
> They had
> a thirst for new delights,
> In search of thy long-sighed-for solitude.

Later that day, after much exertion:

> And lo, in light and glory at our feet
> Lay in their leafy hollow, like a dream,
> Thy smooth bright lake, grey crags, and winding stream!

The landscaped gardens of Luggala stand in marked contrast to the wilderness of Wicklow's surrounding mountains. Robert O'Byrne suggests Tomas Moore was referring to Luggala rather than Glendalough when he penned "By that Lake Whose Gloomy Shore":

> By that lake, whose gloomy shore,
> Sky-lark never warbles o'er,
> Where the cliff hangs high and steep,
> Young Kevin stole to sleep.[5,11]

I think the residents of that valley of the Two Lakes just might have a contrary view!

When the ice melted away many valleys had extensive new deposits of clay and gravel so that drainage patterns were modified, most notably along the Liffey. At the same time woodland and grassland began to re-establish themselves as the climate grew milder and humans were soon evident. Around the same time, blanket bog began to spread across the mountainside, although never to the same intensity as the raised bogs on the low ground to the northwest of the mountains. However, we can now announce that the mountains are completed and ready to accept all visitors!

Notes

1. From "Prelude", on page 29 of J. M. Synge (1909) *Poems and Translations*. Churchtown, County Dublin: Cuala Press.

2. For biographical information on Savage-Armstrong see www. countywicklowheritage.org/page_id_74_path_0p3p.aspx (accessed 9 March 2014).

3. I have quoted from two collections of G.F. Savage-Armstrong's poetry, as follows: G.F. Savage-Armstrong (1892) *Poems: Lyrical and Damatic*. Third edition. London: Longmans, Green and Co. Extracts of the following poems were used: "Glens of Wicklow" (pages 283–286), "Home–longings" (page 289) and "An Apology" (pages 296–297). G.F. Armstrong (1886) *Stories of Wicklow*. London: Longmans, Green and Co. 431 pages. Extracts of the following poems were used: "Lugnaquillia" (pages 158–180) and "To Luggala" (page 420).

4. For more information on Montserrat volcano see www.bgs.ac.uk/discoveringGeology/hazards/volcanoes/montserrat/home.html (Accessed 8 March 2014).

5. I have quoted from "The Meeting of the Waters" (pages 11–12) and "By that Lake, Whose Gloomy Shore" (pages 24–25), both by Thomas Moore and taken from C.L. Falkiner (1903) *Poetry of Thomas Moore*. London: Macmillan and Co.

6. For more information on the Wicklow Gold Rush see Peadar McArdle (2011) *Gold Frenzy: The Story of Wicklow's Gold*. Albertine Kennedy Publishing, Ireland.

7. Austin Clarke (Ed.) (1963) *The Poems of Joseph Campbell*. Dublin: Allen Figgis. I quoted from "A Vision of Glendalough" (pages 209–227) and referred to "The Gartan Mother's Lullaby" (page 55) and "The Spanish Lady" (page 183).

8. "Music in Stone" by Maureen Perkins is on page 4 of Shed Poets (2005) *High Tide*. Wicklow: C. Boland.

9. For background on landscape evolution in this part of Europe see, for example, Dore, A. G., Cartwright, J. A., Stoker, M.S., Turner, J. P. and White, N. J. (Eds.) (2002) *Exhumation of the North Atlantic Margin: Timing, Mechanisms and Implications for Petroleum Exploration*. Geological Society, London, Special Publications, number 196.

10. Sheila Wingfield (2013) *Poems*. Dublin: Liberties Press. "Remote Matters" is on page 121.

11. Robert O'Byrne (2012) *Luggala Days: The Story of a Guinness House*. London & NewYork: CICO Books.

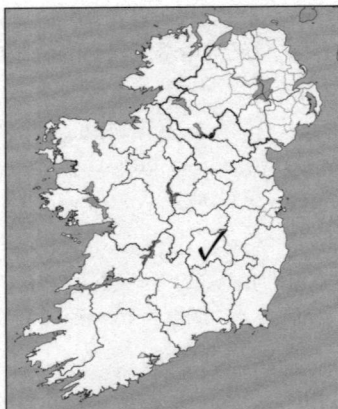

26

COSMETIC SURGERY
(Laois)

What would the world be, once bereft
Of wet and of wildness? Let them be left,
O let them be left, wildness and wet;
Long live the weeds and the wilderness yet.
— Gerard Manley Hopkins[1]

I better start with a confession. I ignored the Slieve Blooms for far too long! Low mysterious hills away to the west, they were so often shrouded in mournful cloud as I drove the old N7 between my early-career Tipperary job and my Dublin home. The dark silhouettes of late Sunday night became lighter landscapes on longer Friday evenings. But I never approached until many years later and then I discovered their magic. I found a convenient car park and a nearby gap in the roadside forest to gain access to Arderin (527

250

metres). But expect no signpost announcements or trail markers! Its name may mean "Ireland's height", but Arderin, Slieve Bloom's summit, is no Carrauntwohill, just a small hilltop in wild country. It is approached by a track that is mossy and moist, starting in one county and ending in another. The summit view encompasses much of Slieve Bloom's elevated peatlands, but extends to the fertile farmland beyond and, in the far distance, some rugged hills and mountains. In these circumstances it is easy for the significance of a hill to be overstated!

The rocks forming the core of the Slieve Blooms are greenish-grey siltstones with some mudstones and rare conglomerates containing volcanic fragments. We know that these sediments accumulated in an offshore environment from a major delta system. In fact, make that two deltas! For while the dominant sediment source lay to the northwest there was another to the east. It seems that the ancient Iapetus Ocean was in the final stages of closure, no more than 100 to 200 kilometres wide, and was now receiving sediment simultaneously from both opposing continental margins. The sediments intermingled with each other, burying the actual suture and hiding it from view. The nearby Glendine Fault might mark its trace, but who can be sure? The opposing continental margins soon engaged in battle as one margin overrode the other in a titanic power struggle through which was formed the now-familiar Caledonian mountain chain. When eroded to its roots, a new cycle of sedimentation started with river-borne sands spreading across its surface. The resulting rocks, equivalent to Old Red Sandstones, are exposed along the Silver River at Cadamstown on the edge of the Slieve Bloom Mountains. Never mind that it is actually in County Offaly, the people there are very friendly! Trace these reddish-brown sandstones upstream and you will find a sudden change to the greenish-grey rocks that form the core of the Slieve Bloom mountains. The gap between the two, called an unconformity, represents a time interval of as much as 60 million years.[2]

The open bogland above the Gorteenameala valley, high up in the Slieve Bloom Mountains, has a curious circular lake. Once considered as a possible meteorite impact crater, it is now regarded as the result of a bog burst, possibly caused by workers undermining the peat here, and the poet Pat Boran (b. 1963) is curious about it ("Corrie Lake, Gorteenameale, Slieve Bloom Mountains").[3] Calling it a corrie, a feature hollowed out by an expanding glacier, is but a diversion on the poet's part for he rightly gives that potential origin no further consideration. He sees the lake as a window on the past, perhaps embracing bog bodies ancient or recent. Its origin becomes less important. But observing the lake can lead to rebirth, in his view, so we cannot remain as passive bystanders, we become fully involved.

The Slieve Blooms form one landscape domain of County Laois, while another is the elevated Castlecomer Coalfield, but the most widespread is the lowlying limestone region. The poetry of Pat Boran covers all three domains. Born in Portlaoise, County Laois, he is a long-term Dublin resident, broadcaster and editor. For him, the nature poet may be concerned with anything from wild hills to details of a nearby field: for every place has a story and every story has its origin in a place.[4] He is fascinated with Castlecomer's coal ("Coal"):

> asteroid-tough, history and memory compressed
> into one, the darkness brought into the light.

His father's family had a long tradition of mining coal, despite the hazardous conditions underground and the prevalence of lung disease among workers. But they attracted unsympathetic attention from the nineteenth century writer, Samuel Lewis, who focused on the economic benefits of the mines: "Yet, notwithstanding these advantages, the workmen, from their irregular and inconsiderate habits, are miserably poor, and the district is frequently disturbed by broils and tumults, so that police stations are thickly distributed throughout this portion of the county."[5]

Pat Boran will also address poetically, but a little later, the third and most extensive domain in County Laois, the lowlands limestone. But for the moment, Boran takes us beyond the Laois county boundary to Kildare town before it was by-passed by the M7 and a curiosity much-noticed by travellers: a house whose walls were richly studded with sea-shells ("House of Shells"). As an alternative explanation to an obsessive plasterer, Boran invokes geological forces to account for it. He envisages the town gradually asserting itself above sea level to become dry land, only to experience a final and gigantic oceanic wave that washed over it and left the house of shells behind. Back in Dublin, Boran looks to the nearby mountains but argues that we use them merely as mirrors of our own importance and seek elevated viewing points of the urban sprawl only to look smugly across what we have created ("Cities").

Dubliner James Clarence Mangan (1803–1849) was in love with landscape, but it was almost exclusively a mythical one. He may have spent a few years working for the Ordnance Survey of Ireland, but apparently never resided, as sometimes suggested, at Mountmellick in County Laois.[6] After his time at the Ordnance Survey, he worked on cataloguing at the Library of Trinity College Dublin, but his quality of life was diminished by poor health and alcohol dependency, and he succumbed to cholera at the young age of 46.

His only important environmental poem is "A Vision of Connaught in the Thirteenth Century".[7] This describes the death of Cathal Mór, an exemplary king of Connaught, as an environmental disaster for his people. In Cathal Mór's day, poets attributed favourable weather and abundant harvests to the good qualities of the ruler, and so this poem opens in optimistic mood:

> I walked entranced
> Through a land of Morn;
> The sun, with wondrous excess of light,
> Shone down and glanced
> Over seas of corn
> And lustrous gardens aleft and right.

Even in the clime
Of resplendent Spain
Beams no such sun upon such a land;
But it was the time,
'Twas in the reign,
Of Cahal Mór of the Wine-red Hand.

This idyllic environment is designated as being in Connaught although in truth it could have described many parts of Laois's limestone terrain between Portarlington and Borris-in-Ossory. In any event all changed when this good king died, which was most unreasonable of him, and subsequently one disaster after another was visited upon his people. Given his lack of familiarity with rural Ireland, it is not surprising that meaningful landscape references are largely confined to Mangan's translations of poems such as "Cill Chais" and "Róisín Dubh", poems that feature elsewhere in these pages. His own compositions do refer to many localities around the country (although not, I think, from County Laois!) but never with the level of landscape detail to convince us that he had actually visited them.

Jean O'Brien (b. 1952) is a Dublin-born poet living in the Midlands. She evokes the broad horizons of Laois' flat landscape in "Eyescape",[8] where her eye tries to focus on more local undulations. Bog is an essential part of her environment:

Miles of brown bog and scrub stretch out,
bright water glints and a large flock of starlings
fly to and fro...

Bogs can be sinister places and later in "Hidden Things" she considers bog bodies, the dark outcome of so many conflicts:

You have to work hard
to imagine their bleached whiteness
whispering from the dark soil, the waterlogged bog.

When bones are revealed:

> they nudge our conscience
> with their numinous presence
> …
> their shocking clarity and then nervously
> we dance on them …

Ouch! There is no denying her strong feelings about the matter. O'Brien visits an old mine or cave that just possibly could have been (but probably wasn't) somewhere in the Midlands ("My Dark Twin"):

> We walked on rocks red veined
> with ore and here and there
> An adamantine shine.

She captures the underground atmosphere, the hard footsteps and her breath hanging in the air. When I see that uncommon adjective "adamantine" (O'Brien also features it elsewhere) I can recognise a fan of John Milton (1608–1674) for it brings to mind from "Paradise Lost" the "adamantine rock, impenetrable", which was a material of impregnable hardness.

In "Skerries Revisited", Jean O'Brien considers the power of rock as memory, using beach pebbles to conjure up memories of childhood swims with her mother. Her feet crunch on pebbles as the sea's motion pulls her back not just physically but in time:

> … thirty years to the feel
> of her hand. I search the stones for some
> nudge of memory to bring her near.

O'Brien lingered on the seashore, not at Skerries, with a companion, each observing the same rock and seeing something quite different ("Other Ways of Seeing"). Her companion noted its physical characteristics and named it basalt, while she noticed the wet rock's sheen and thought it a beached whale. The combination of the rational and imaginative lends richness to each! She is a poet who is proud of her distinctive voice and expresses this through landscape images:

> He doesn't own the talking stones, and the bog, the forge.
> I write poetry of my own, I too have a doorway in the
>   dark,
> the ringing metal the falling meteoric light.

She is, of course, referring to Seamus Heaney's poetry ("Dear Reader Seamus Heaney Doesn't Own Them"), but this is no rancorous whinge: she properly asserts herself with good humour and without disrespect towards our late Nobel Laureate.

The sometime Poet Laureate to Her Majesty, C. (Cecil) Day Lewis (1904–1972), was born in Ballintubbert, County Laois, where his father was a Church of Ireland clergyman. A writer of detective fiction and father of the three-times Oscar-winning actor Daniel, he regarded himself disdainfully as Anglo-Irish and he had a two-fold relationship with Ireland as revealed in his poetry. Firstly there were his roots in Laois, which were severed after a brief 18 months when his father took up church employment in England. He returned on childhood holidays to his uncle who was rector at Monart, Enniscorthy, of which he retained precious memories ("Golden Age, Monart, Co. Wexford").[9] It was a land of milk and honey, where time stood still. In later life this was seen as his Anglo-Irish past, one he was keen to brush off. The Anglo-Irish were "never of a land rightfully ours" ("The Whispering Roots"). He wondered what a birth-place might mean to a rootless man like himself, yet he felt compelled by its peacefulness. But there is little poetic evidence that "the lonely hills of Laois" made a significant impact on him. Nevertheless, he retained a great fondness for Ireland and was particularly gratified by the acclaim he received here as a poet.

His second relationship with Ireland was based on his adult visits, especially on the holidays he spent with his family in Counties Galway and Mayo. In Mayo ("At Old Head, Co. Mayo"), he describes Croagh Patrick fittingly as uncapped, when a cap of cloud has slipped off the Reek's summit. The colours here are all vivid and reminiscent of jewels – gold, emerald and ultramarine. He also recognises the regal colours of purple and gold in the heather and furze of Connemara ("Near Ballyconneely, Co. Galway"). He may not talk about green Connemara Marble but the troubled sea reminds him of it: "the sea is marbled and veined with foam". He then goes on to capture the unsettled mood of the nearby weather-bound mountains. For the poet, Connemara's human history is an essential part of this environment, but its silence is more eloquent and telling than all the songs of past wrongs. The silence of departed emigrants is what tourists call peace. He concludes:

> The landscape's an heroic
> Skeleton time's beaked agents have picked clean.

Place-names can be treasures of hidden meaning, not only for poets, especially where their derivation has a landscape significance.[10] If that is the case then perhaps names with common roots may enjoy a similar physical environment and even share the same bedrock formations. Borris-in-Ossory has already featured in this narrative so let's examine the distribution of its root, Borris, in the region's place-names. Borris-in-Ossory is not alone, for in the limestone lowlands of Laois and its surroundings are Borrisoleigh and Twomileborris, while on the far side of the Slieve Bloom and Silvermines Mountains lies Borrisokane. They all occur on limestone bedrock, but that is not all, for they are situated on the lower beds of limestone. These are relatively muddy and closer to hilly terrain, which has a significance for those Borris-rooted towns. Borris is the anglicised form of *buiríos*, or borough, the name applied by the Anglo-Normans to the smaller towns which they established. These of course are not the privileged principal towns such as Kilkenny or Carlow – these are marginal centres and, in keeping with this, they are restricted effectively to bedrock areas that have agriculturally less attractive limestone bedrock. Now, of course, there is a glaring exception to this happy outcome and that is the borough town of Borris in County Carlow which is granite-based, but here I will rely on the prerogative that the exception proves the rule!

Much of the county is floored by limestone, formed in a warm, shallow sea. Its best-known exposure is the Rock of Dunamase, prominent among the Stradbally Hills. For Pat Boran ("Forest"),[3] its ruined limestone castle draws his thoughts back to its alleged Cromwellian destruction:

> You'd miss the sound of the cannons
> that destroyed the spot I'm standing on.

Still substantial and impressive, so much effort was devoted to its defence yet apparently it has been repeatedly over-run through-out its long history. The Rock is an example of a hum, a remnant hill fortuitously preserved as the surrounding karstified limestone was gradually dissolved away. The most celebrated hums occur in Southeast Asia where they form dense clusters in many areas.[11] Unlike at Dunamase, they have formidable heights many times greater than their girths and their near-vertical walls form real challenges for rock climbers. Boran calls the Rock "a sleeping hedgehog" and this is an apt description for travellers approach-ing from Portlaoise, as Boran himself would have done. The Rock suddenly comes into view after rounding a bend in the road and, from this perspective, it forms the animal's head, with its prickly body stretching away along a low wooded ridge. It is only when we get closer that Dunamase stands proud and alone, surveying its surroundings from atop strong limestone beds. The steepness of its slopes has been exaggerated by quarrying. The more subdued nature of this hum relative to Asian examples finds an explanation in its thinner limestone beds and the fact that it was subsequently modified by the passage of ice sheets. Its contours are more suited to strolling than climbing, just as befits a hilly hedgehog!

Notes

1. This quotation comes from "Inversnaid", pages 94-95 of W. H. Gardner (Ed.) (1948) *Poems of Gerard Manley Hopkins*. Third edition. London: Oxford University Press.

2. For more on the geology of County Laois see John Feehan (2013) *The Geology of Laois and Offaly*. Published by Offaly County Council.

3. See the following two collections: Pat Boran (2007) *New and Selected Poems*. Dublin: Dedalus Press. I referred to "House of Shells" (pages 5-6) and "Cities" (page 28); I quoted from "Forest" (page 46). Pat Boran (2012) *The Next Life*. Dublin: The Dedalus Press. I referred to "Corrie Lake, Gorteenameale, Slieve Bloom Mountains" (pages 19-20) and quoted from "Coal" (page 22).

4. Boran, Pat (2009) "Nine-and-fifty swans: Glimpses of nature in recent Irish poetry". In Boran, Pat (Ed.) *Flowing, Still: Irish Poets on Irish Poetry*. Dublin: Dedalus Press, pages 146-161.

5. This quotation comes from pages 476-477, volume 2 of Samuel Lewis (1837) *A Topographical Dictionary of Ireland*. Reprinted 2004. Baltimore: Clearfield Company.

6. Sean Ryder (2009) "James Clarence Mangan (1803-1849)". In McGuire, J. and Quinn, J. (Eds.) *Dictionary of Irish Biography*. Royal Irish Academy and Cambridge University Press, volume 6, pages 340-343.

7. Chuto, J., Holzapfel, R. P., van de Kamp, P. and Shannon-Mangan, E. (Eds.) (2003) *Selected Poems of James Clarence Mangan*. Dublin, Ireland, and Portland, Oregon: Irish Academic Press. I have quoted from "A Vision of Connaught in the Thirteenth Century" (pages 241-243).

8. I have quoted poems from Jean O'Brien's collections, as follows. Jean O'Brien (2012) *Merman*. County Clare: Salmon Poetry. I quoted from "Dear Reader Seamus Heaney Doesn't Own Them" (pages 19-20) and "Hidden Things" (page 62). Jean O'Brien (2009) *Lovely Legs*. County Clare: Salmon Poetry. I quoted from "Eyescape" (page 71). Jean O'Brien (2004) Reach. Belfast: Lapwing Publications. I quoted from "My Dark Twin" (page 31). Jean O'Brien (1992) *Working the Flow*. Lapwing Poetry Pamphlet No. 8. Belfast: Lapwing Publications. I referred to the following poem: "Other Ways of Seeing" (page 8). Jean O'Brien (2005) *Dangerous Dresses*. Cork: Bradshaw Books. I quoted from "Skerries Revisited" (page 5).

9. C. Day Lewis (1992) *The Complete Poems of C. Day Lewis*. London: Sinclair-Stevenson Ltd. I have quoted from "Near Ballyconneely, Co. Galway" (pages 658-660) and "The Whispering Roots" (pages 674-676). I have referred to "Golden Age, Monart, Co. Wexford" (pages 656-657) and "At Old Head, Co. Mayo" (page 669).

10. "Borris" is discussed on page 352, volume 1 of Joyce, P.W. (c.1869) *The Origin and History of Irish Names of Places*. Dublin: The Educational Company of Ireland (3 volumes).

11. For images of Vietnam's karst, including spectacular hums, see: www.terragalleria.com/photos/?keyword=vietnam-karstic-hills .

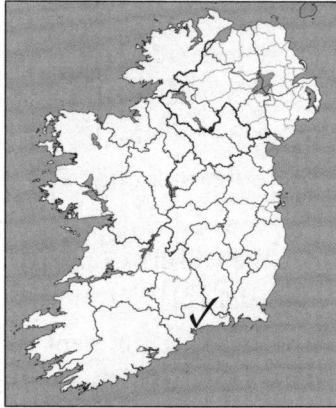

27

THE COPPER COAST
(Waterford)

To see the world in a grain of sand
And a heaven in a wild flower;
Hold infinity in the palm of your hand,
And eternity in an hour.
— William Blake.[1]

The Chester Beatty Library, in the grounds of Dublin Castle, is named after the accumulator of its contents, Sir Alfred Chester Beatty (1875–1968). The fortune he amassed from mining he invested in carefully chosen oriental art and books which he generously donated to Ireland, his adopted country. Born in New York city, Chester Beatty showed an early fascination with mineral collecting that expressed itself in more sophisticated forms in this Library: there are Islamic illustrations employing strongly-coloured minerals such as ochre and malachite, not to mention the fabulous collection of Chinese jade long revered for its religious significance. There is also a medal awarded to him in 1934 by the American premier mining institute for his services to mining. This must have been dear to his heart coming as it did at a critical time in his industrial career.[2]

Known in his day as the world's Copper King, Chester Beatty began his career in the goldfields of Colorado and soon became wealthy as a consultant in many different mining districts. His company, Selection Trust Ltd, catapulted Chester Beatty into the upper ranks of mining industrialists through its role in establishing the Zambian (Northern Rhodesian) Copperbelt as a major copper producer. This is itself a story worth telling, although not here, involving the shrewd geologists who discovered the copper deposits, the enterprising engineers who established a world-class operation in countryside with little infrastructure, and the convincing executives who established markets and financing in the difficult economic climate of the early 1930s. No wonder that prestigious medal came Chester Beatty's way at that time.[3]

In the year of Chester Beatty's birth, 1875, the writing was already on the wall for another copper district, on the Copper Coast of County Waterford, although one on a much smaller scale than Zambia's. Half a century earlier, the Mining Company of Ireland had established operations at Bunmahon, based on significant copper deposits in steeply-dipping quartz veins. This particular mine worked successfully until the early 1850s when operations transferred to nearby Tankardstown where a similar deposit was worked for another 20 years. The operation was significant, employing up to 800 men and extending to 300 metres below surface. Cornwall supplied steam-powered technology to crush ore, drain workings and hoist men, ore and materials. It also provided many skilled engineers and miners, including John Petherick (b. 1804), the accomplished and colourful engineer credited with making Bunmahon a significant commercial success. He managed through difficult times of famine and insurrection. With his departure and the closure of Bunmahon, many workers emigrated to North America.[4] The typical Irish immigrant arriving in the USA at that time was rural and unskilled, so these skilled miners must have received a ready reception in that country's emerging copper mining industry. Many made their way to the Michigan copper mines at Keweenaw, but the copper mines at Butte, Montana, some managed by Irishman Marcus Daly (1841–1900), proved in time to be at least an equally powerful draw. Nevertheless, working conditions were difficult, pay was not attractive and the atmosphere was often charged with tensions between rival unions and groups.

Those who remained behind in Waterford fared no better. They endured poverty and hardship in a demoralised community where the mining landscape and ruined buildings were constant reminders of past failure. It was only around the year 2000 that a revitalised community took renewed interest in its mine heritage and created the Copper Coast Geopark here.[5] The mines were established in volcanic rocks 460 million years old, which dominate the eastern part of the county. They originated as part of a major chain of volcanic islands in the closing Iapetus Ocean.

The remains of two very different volcanoes are exposed along the Copper Coast. The earlier Bunmahon Volcano formed in deeper seawater and its green-coloured andesite lavas fragmented explosively when they were erupted into cold water-saturated sea-floor muds. The second volcano, at Kilfarrasy, was a more spectacular affair dominated by eruptions of glowing ash clouds. This rhyolite ash had a high viscosity and exploded violently as a result. At a late stage in the volcanic activity, but important for our story, superheated metal-bearing fluids percolated through the rock sequence depositing copper minerals along quartz veins and forming the basis of the mining industry here.[6]

When I visit Waterford city I cannot resist a glance at the low cliff behind the main railway station. Now much overgrown and obscured, it consists of flat-lying beds of Old Red Sandstone, a familiar rock better seen in the nearby Comeraghs, and they overlie slates with a steeply disposed cleavage. George Victor Du Noyer (1817–1869), geologist and artist, produced a wonderful watercolour of the scene, showing how science and art can be fused successfully. That fusion would soon have a practical value, for just a few short years later he would die tragically of fever at Christmas time, only a single day after his daughter's death. In a less caring age, his widow had to fend for herself and was obliged to sell as many of his paintings as possible in order to provide for her remaining children. She could not afford to be sentimental about individual paintings and it may have been a quirk of fate that the Waterford scene remained in the possession of his employer, the Geological Survey of Ireland.[7] It must have provoked an amount of discussion down the years, not least about the nature of the contact between slates and sandstones. Although it is difficult to be precise about ages, it is likely that about 35 million years elapsed in the interval represented by that contact surface. In that time, an Earth-crunching collision of plates finally closed off the Iapetus Ocean and in the process deformed the original sediments to form slates. The plate collision led on to the elevation of a major mountain chain which was then actively eroded and the resulting sand formed the younger sandstones.

James Hutton (1726–1797), one of the founders of geology as a science, encountered similar relationships along the Scottish coastline east of Edinburgh and he was the first to recognise their real significance. He and fellow geologists had been aware of extensive exposures of cleaved and folded slates – siltstones and greywackes in today's terminology but then referred to as schistus. They were also familiar with nearby flat-lying sandstone beds that were neither deformed nor metamorphosed. But they had never seen one in contact with the other. So one day in 1788 they set off by boat to seek the contact in the sea cliffs of Siccar Point and were amply rewarded with clear evidence that the sandstones lay flat on top of the vertical schistus beds:

On us who saw these phenomena for the first time, the impression made will not easily be forgotten. ... We often said to ourselves, What clearer evidence could we have had of the different formation of these rocks, and of the long interval which separated their formation, had we actually seen them emerging from the bosom of the deep?

The mind seemed to grow giddy by looking so far into the abyss of time; and while we listened with earnestness and admiration to the philosopher who was now unfolding to us the order and series of these wonderful events, we became sensible how much further reason may sometimes go than imagination can venture to follow. [8]

Siccar Point is recognised as a key milestone in the development of geological science.

The best place to see the Old Red Sandstones which overlie both the volcanic rocks of the Copper Coast and the slates of Waterford city is in the nearby Comeragh Mountains. These form an attractive upland area which is entirely surrounded by fertile agricultural land. The tough sandstones give rise to a mix of moorland and rugged ridges, but the most spectacular scenery of the Comeraghs comprises a set of striking corries etched into their eastern flank.[9] These steep-sided corries are Ice Age features which formed as expanding glaciers gouged out their surroundings. The best known example is Coumshingaun with its lake and 350 metre-high walls. These cliffs tell us a most interesting story of when the Caledonian Mountains further north were being eroded. The earliest sediments are crudely bedded conglomerates with pebbles derived from those older mountains, including a lot composed of distinctively white vein quartz. But as the landscape became more subdued the rivers were more mature and carried finer grained sands to form the well-bedded sediments that can be seen higher in the cliffs. So now we are, like the poet William Blake (1757–1827), envisioning "a world in a grain of sand"[1] – we can track the rise and fall of mighty mountain chains simply by studying the sand grains that rivers (however ancient) carried from them.

Mark Roper (b. 1951) is a nature poet living in the Suir Valley and he is very much in harmony with his local environment. His home place gives him the greatest happiness and even incessant rain does not daunt him ("Out of Water")[10]:

> Rain nags and needles the pond
> but whatever it writes is erased.

The constancy implied by "nags" is given added force by "needles" which suggests that the raindrops are slanting and wind-blown, and that they pester the pond, whose surface cannot retain images such as darting birds or dipping oars. But in "Cry", Roper targets sound as the most distinctive and unvarying aspect of our environment:

> the call, say, of a loon,
> the same over millions of years.

The loon is a duck-like aquatic bird, once considered among the most ancient of birds but now considered to have evolved no more than 50 million years ago. The poet is confident that even were our planet's environment destroyed we might envisage it from such sounds:

> what it was like to live
> in that once green, that once blue world.

Hopefully he is wrong about our ruination!

When you reach the western extremity of the Copper Coast at Dungarvan, you are already standing on Carboniferous limestone and if you follow its synclinal structure along the River Blackwater you will reach Lismore. It is overlooked by the impressive Lismore Castle, which has been in the possession of the Dukes of Devonshire since the mid-eighteenth century. The estate had previously been owned by the Earls of Cork and it was here in Lismore that

Robert Boyle (1627–1691), son of the first earl, was born. He left Ireland aged eight years and, apart from much of 1652–1654, he never returned again.

Sir Robert Boyle became the most eminent scientist of the late seventeenth century, being eclipsed only by Isaac Newton (1642–1727) early the next century, and he was fundamental to the emerging understanding of our natural world and humankind's place in it. He established chemistry as a scientific pursuit based on a rational and experimental approach, and he pointed to the medical benefits of the outcomes. Boyle was among many respected scientists who devoted attention to alchemy, a potentially lucrative, but ultimately impossible, technique that would transmute base metals into gold.

His curiosity extended beyond chemistry, however, and embraced aspects of geology. He was concerned with the nature of the seafloor and its underlying bedrock, while onshore he was fascinated by spas and mineral waters. He investigated the origin and chemical composition of a wide spectrum of minerals, bequeathing his collection to the Royal Society. He harboured few sentimental thoughts of Ireland or the scenic Lismore district. His Irish estates were simply a source of income for him and he was quick to complain that periodic insurrections and social disruption merely had the impact of reducing that income. In fact he looked back on his time in Ireland with disdain, complaining that scientific and intellectual pursuits were at best limited there. He never sought out Lismore's rocks or minerals for analysis, he possessed no desire to stroll around the Castle's gardens nor to explore the wonders of its surrounding Blackwater River valley.[11]

Patrick Barry (1870–1954) was a Cork-born poet and teacher who did love the border area between Cork and Waterford, much of it encompassed by the watersheds of the Bride and Blackwater Rivers. Praising the Blackwater's scenery with its angling and fine meadows, he craves its peacefulness ("The Fair Avondhu")[12]:

How delightful to linger, with heart well at ease,
By this stream as it swells through Lismore's verdant
   leas,
When the wild rose and woodbine o'erhang ev'ry hedge
And glad feet to the flute beat from bank, bower and
   bridge ...

He is in more sentimental mood along the River Bride, recall-ing childhood adventures here and customs long in disuse ("The Banks of the Bride"):

Quiet haunt of the angler and lover true-hearted,
Who blissfully strayed here at eve side by side;
But often, alas, have the fondest been parted
To meet never more by the banks of the Bride.

Another person not immune to Lismore's beauty is Dervla Murphy (b. 1931), the distinguished travel writer. Born in Lismore, where she still lives, she has favoured the less comfortable jour-neys beyond familiar European destinations. Her books take the reader to a dazzling spectrum of places, from the Himalayas to the Limpopo River and from Gaza to the Andes. Somehow I am surprised she hasn't spent much time in North America although I do detect a tendency on her part to avoid the high latitudes! But my interest has been in exploring her attitude towards the land-scape of her own native Lismore. Her memoir on her childhood, concerned with her rather smothering household, is a surprisingly uplifting read and it does deal with her home landscape.[13]

Standing on the nearby wooded ridge of Ballinaspic, with her back to the Knockmealdown Mountains, she can survey the coun-tryside from Youghal eastwards to Dungarvan, feeling as she says an intoxication of joy. She addresses the profound differences in our responses to familiar and unfamiliar landscapes, finding for example that the incomparable grandeur of the Himalayas fills her with a mixture of exaltation and humility. But the beauty of her own Blackwater valley inspires in her an absurd pride, as though she were partly responsible for it herself! She has become an extension of her own landscape, feeling an owner's pride as well as a disciple's homage! She comments on the distinctiveness of each mountain and valley, not least the confluence of the Bride River with the Blackwater River after the latter has abruptly turned south at Cappoquin. She would not be the only writer to note that rapid change in direction!

The sharp swing southwards also fascinated Joseph Beete Jukes (1811–1869), the Birmingham-born geologist, who in early career was a pioneer of surveys along the coasts of Newfoundland and Australia. As Director of the Geological Survey of Ireland in the period 1850–1869, he supervised the efficient mapping of more than half the land area of Ireland, a great achievement in itself. We have already encountered him at Cork Harbour. But his enduring fame and international recognition came through his insight into what caused the puzzling bend in the Blackwater at Cappoquin.

The Blackwater River follows the limestones of the Dungarvan Syncline for most of its extent. But at Cappoquin, instead of continuing its steady progress eastwards, it inexplicably turns south and crosses several sandstone ridges before entering the sea on the south coast. Jukes' insight was to realise that this drainage pattern was initiated at a time when the sandstones and limestones were blanketed by beds of younger sediments forming a planar surface that was tilted southwards. So the older part of the Blackwater River is the south-flowing section from Cappoquin to the sea. It was only when the overlying sediment was eroded away to reveal the sandstones and limestone that the easterly-flowing portion formed. This innovative contribution, which still causes academic discussion, has been significant to our understanding of how landscape evolves. No wonder that Jukes had a mountain feature in the Henry Mountains of Utah named after him or that he influenced some of the most renowned scientists of his day.[7]

Notes

1. "Auguries of Innocence" by William Blake (1757-1827) appears on page 90 of W. B. Yeats (Ed.) (1931) *Poems of William Blake*. New York: Boni and Liveright.

2. The Chester Beatty Library website is www.cbl.ie (accessed 1 November 2014).

3. A. J. Wilson (1985) *The Life and Times of Sir Alfred Chester Beatty*. London: Cadogan Publications.

4. Des Cowman (2006) *The Making and Breaking of a Mining Community: The Copper Coast, County Waterford 1825-1875+*. Published by the Mining Heritage Trust of Ireland.

5. See www.coppercoastgeopark.com (accessed 10 June 2014).

6. A. G. Sleeman and B. McConnell (1995) *Geology of East Cork-Waterford*. Geological Survey of Ireland.

7. Gordon L. Herries Davies (1995) *North from the Hook*. Geological Survey of Ireland.

8. Quoted from pages 93-94 of G. Y. Craig (1960) Grantshouse, Siccar Point, Cove, Catcraig. In G. H. Mitchell, E. K. Walton and Douglas Grant (Eds.) *Edinburgh Geology: An Excursion Guide*. Edinburgh and London: Oliver and Boyd.

9. Declan McGrath (2008) *A Guide to the Comeragh Mountains*. Second edition. Published by the author.

10. Mark Roper (2008) *Even So: New and Selected Poems*. Dublin: Dedalus Press. I have quoted from the following poems: "Out of Water" (page 22) and "Cry" (page 38).

11. Michael Hunter (2009) *Boyle: Between God and Science*. New Haven and London: Yale University Press.

12. Patrick Barry (2003) *By Bride and Blackwater*. Miltown Malbay, County Clare: Donal De Barra. I have quoted from "The Banks of the Bride" (pages 1-2) and "The Fair Avondhu" (pages 175-176).

13. Dervla Murphy (1980) *Wheels within Wheels*. New Haven and New York: Ticknor & Fields.

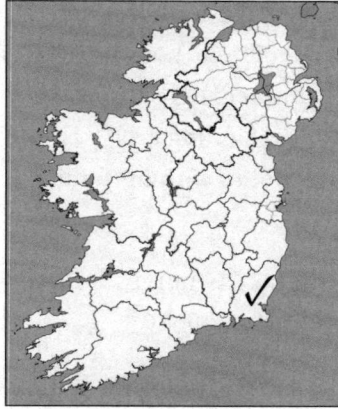

28

FIRE AND BRIMSTONE!
(Wexford)

As land
lies with no answer,
Water
runs
without time.
— Eamonn Wall.[1]

Enniscorthy-born poet and academic, Eamonn Wall (b. 1955), emigrated to America in 1982, eventually settling in the Midwest. His two landscapes, the Midwest prairies and Wexford's Slaney valley, are certainly different from each other, but they crop up repeatedly in his work, representing his present and past. Nebraska's Sandhills remind him of Wexford's Courtown Beach, while the ghost mine towns of Idaho may have reminded him of familiar old mines, such as Avoca, close to Wexford ("Leaving Boise").[2] He stopped in Idaho City, which in 1865 was the largest mining camp in the region, and was immediately absorbed in the equipment and process of mining. But in "Finding a Way Home"[3] he leaves us in no doubt that he is firmly rooted with his family in prairie soil:

> Don't
> you know your place? My home
> is where I am, old wise blue bus.

Wall exults in the landscape of his adopted country and, for example, his fascination with the volcanic features of Yellowstone National Park is evident in his simple name-checking of its interesting places ("Yellowstone Bus Tour")[2] – Twig Geyser, Fumarole, White Dome Geyser, Hot Lake, Hot Dog Pool and more. He is at home equally with the geological "Fumarole" and the less serious (depending on the state of your appetite!) "Hot Dog Pool". Back at home, he reaches a viewing point overlooking the Missouri River and imagines the excitement and difficulty of early explorers such as Lewis and Clark on their 1804 mapping expedition ("Lewis & Clark: Omaha, Nebraska")[2]:

> Where boats fought shallows and snags,
> miners viewed lands under moonlight and
> saw, veiled in mist, islands at dawn.

Wall anchors his Midwest landscape within his relationship with his partner, her hair spread on the pillow like the braided channels of the Platte River ("In Freewheeling by the Platte River: A Song")[3].

Wall's imagination was captured by the enchanting Rockies, yet when he camped there he was sensitive to trespassing in the sacred places of the Lakota nation ("Four Stern Faces/South Dakota")[3]. Quite unlike the understanding he had had from childhood Hollywood films, these native Americans had suffered at least as much in their history as Wall's fellow citizens back in Ireland. He seems conscious of a colonial burden shared by native Americans and the Irish. He had thought that as an outsider he would be untouched by U.S. history, but then he realised that landscapes inevitably draw you into history.[4] Now he sees a universe here much wider than that encompassed by the "four stern faces" of American Presidents chiselled in granite on the side of Mount Rushmore. And that universe, for him, embraces all the nature of:

> these black and holy hills we spend the years
> wandering towards.

We can sense that, despite his confused feelings, Wall will in time grow to love those Black Hills.

Wall gives us occasional reminders of his past Irish landscape. One example is "The Blackbird of Edermine",[3] a poem that takes us on a journey along the Slaney valley, almost from source to sea. Starting at The Nine Stones, beneath Mount Leinster, he descends along the tributary Clody River to join the Slaney at Bunclody. We move downstream through fertile lands to the poet's native Enniscorthy and proceed on to the lagoonal Sloblands at the mouth of the Slaney, as well as Wexford's nearby sandy coastline. Elsewhere ("Land & Water"),[2] he is careful to recognise the influence of the ancient on the recent:

> As land
> lies with no answer,
> Water
> runs
> without time.

In "Mount Leinster and Me"[5] Wall describes his relationship with this mountain in equally human terms to those bestowed on his partner and the River Platte. He sees it as:

> grey-skinned, cracked, older than me
> an ageing slice of a mysterious soul
> in County Wexford.

He may once have enjoyed the view from its summit, but even as his world expands Mount Leinster is still there just as he saw it as a child. There is a sense that the mountain is a living being, older than the poet but perhaps not ageing as quickly as he is!

The landscape of this part of Wexford bears the marks of distinctive conditions during the closing stages of the Ice Age. When the ice sheets started melting here, a number of isolated ice blocks remained and were covered by sediments. When they finally melted they left behind small depressions, called kettle holes, which are now ponds. Superficially similar ponds also developed in other parts of the district that were ice-free. These had permafrost conditions, where the ground did not routinely unfreeze each summer. In these circumstances small domes of ice gradually developed and grew beneath the surface. These are pingos, not kettle holes, and can be recognised because as the ice melted an upraised rampart formed around each one, leaving a central lake. It is worth looking for small ponds in this area and distinguishing between kettle holes, usually in hummocky ground, and the doughnut-shaped pingo. Neither is commonly developed elsewhere in Ireland.[6]

Courtown, County Wexford, and Tramore, County Waterford, are two of the most popular seaside resorts in the sunny southeast of Ireland, both blessed with fine sandy beaches. Enniscorthy, discreetly poised inland on the River Slaney, might not immediately identify itself with them, indeed its more refined residents might eschew the garish excitement associated with those towns. And yet the fact is that all three are linked together by a major development of volcanic bedrock and, to emphasise the point, the important fault that borders one side of it is termed the Courtown-Tramore Fault. But it is Enniscorthy that lies at the heart of this volcanic excitement which shaped nearby hills that witnessed key events in 1798, including Vinegar Hill.

I visited Vinegar Hill (119 metres) on a dark autumnal day when the sky did deliver its threatened rain in copious amounts. Schools had just re-opened and so the number of visitors was reduced to a steady trickle. They scanned the surrounding countryside, read the history of the 1798 Rebellion and explored the hillside itself. But I wanted to stroll across that upstanding volcanic outcrop, conflicted between thoughts of the geological devastation it represented and the cruel military defeat it witnessed more recently. The hill stands apart from the town of Enniscorthy but before you leave make sure you visit the latter's St. Aidan's Cathedral – and for two reasons. Firstly because its tall slender building is worth a visit, its architect being the celebrated A.W. Pugin, designer of Westminster's Houses of Parliament. Secondly the exterior of the cathedral features local volcanic rocks, in green and brown shades, which demonstrate their features with exceptional clarity. You can see sharply angular lava fragments, some of thumbnail size and a few were originally of pumice. It is much tougher to discern any of this on Vinegar's bare summit, especially in dreary rain!

From an environmental viewpoint, Wexford's most dramatic time came, not in 1798, but during the Ordovician, a time interval of 46 million years that ended 443 million years ago. And, boy, was the Ordovician world different! All landmasses were concentrated in the Southern Hemisphere and Wexford was at the southeastern edge of the closing Iapetus Ocean. Land was bare of vegetation and life was largely confined to the sea. For most of the period the world's climate was in a greenhouse phase, which in turn caused ocean circulation to be sluggish. Sea levels were higher than at any time since – and atmospheric oxygen concentrations were only half today's. These factors all combined to nurture a three-fold increase in biodiversity, which collapsed only at the end of the Ordovician when our planet was plunged into a glacial period. This may have lasted no more than a million years, but it caused a mass extinction as it took hold and another as it released its grip.

As if all this was not enough, another contemporary event had a very specific impact on Wexford and surrounding counties. This was the outpouring of volcanic ash on a scale not otherwise ever experienced in Ireland, driven by increased convection of unusually hot material in the underlying mantle. The erupting magma was silica-rich rhyolite, a viscous material that would have hurled huge quantities of ash into the stratosphere, the larger eruptions causing global cooling for up to five years. In southeast Ireland, we see the volcanic products, mainly ashes, which were deposited and preserved close to the erupting vent. Most eruptions were explosive and gave rise to extremely hot glowing ash clouds with molten lava fragments. But some ash eruptions were quite chilled and can be recognised by the angular nature of their lava fragments – remember those cathedral walls![7]

What would the experience be like during one of Wexford's drastic eruptions? Let's look to the 1883 disastrous eruption of Krakatoa in Indonesia as an example.[8] Krakatoa exploded catastrophically on the morning of Monday 27 August 1883 and nobody could say that there hadn't been sufficient warning. The volcano had become active as early as the previous May. Frequent eruptions of ash rained down on the surrounding countryside and were accompanied by earth tremors. All through August, passing ships reported on the increasingly threatening display of fireworks and ash clouds. There were frequent earthquakes and flames issued regularly from the smoke-engulfed island. Matters became frighteningly ominous on the afternoon of Sunday 26 August when coastal residents experienced violent tremors accompanied by tremendous ash eruptions. Showers of rock, pumice and ash rained down from an ash plume that grew taller by the hour and day turned into night as dust and smoke enveloped everything.

And then on Monday morning it really happened! For:

> at 10.02 am, came the culminating, terrifying majesty of it all. … (Then,) according to all the instruments that record it, came the fourth and greatest explosion of them all, a detonation that was heard thousands of miles away and that is still said to be the most violent explosion ever recorded and experienced by modern man. The cloud of gas and white-hot pumice and fire and smoke is believed

to have risen – been hurled, more probably, blasted as though from a gigantic cannon – as many as twenty-four miles into the air.[8]

By the next day, when the quakes had stopped and the dust had settled, it became clear that Krakatoa as an island had ceased to exist: it had apparently been blasted away. The plume of hot ash and superheated gases had been swept along by the prevailing wind, engulfing buildings in its path and, more catastrophically, killing all who chanced to be along its course. As many as 1,000 died in this manner, either asphyxiated by the gases or immolated in the ashy inferno.

Even that is not the full story, for it does not account for the real severity of the eruption as subsequently reported: over 36,000 deaths and 165 villages destroyed. This devastation was caused not by the eruption itself but by the undersea earthquakes that accompanied it. These set off a series of tsunamis on that terrible morning and it was these that swept those tens of thousands to their grim death and totally engulfed their towns and villages. The population over a wider region also suffered, for although their lives were spared their crops were destroyed by the blanketing ash and their herds no longer had sustenance.

It was subsequently realised that, rather than blasting away the island of Krakatoa, the eruption had caused it to founder and collapse into the sea, forming a caldera 350 metres deep. It was not the first volcanic event here, nor is it likely to be the last: within half a century the presence of volcanic islands had reasserted themselves above sea level and its progeny, Anak Krakatoa, has now reached an altitude of 300 metres and regularly performs volcanic feats. The question is how long until the next violent catastrophe? And if its effects match those of 1883, we can be sure that a significant proportion of humanity will hear the explosion – and the rest will hear about it!

We cannot identify the actual volcanic centres which gave rise to the volcanic rocks of Wexford and adjoining counties. So we can only speculate on their appearance. They started in a submarine environment and built cones which rose above sea level. Some could have been mighty features, towering over the surrounding seas. They would have formed over significant magma chambers which would have been the source of material to generate all that ash and lava. The mightier eruptions would have evacuated the chamber at least partially, weakening its roof and leading inevitably to a collapse of the upstanding cone and the creation of a caldera, as happened at Krakatoa.

Krakatoa also had some influence at the global level, because more than 40 cubic kilometres of dust was hurled skywards almost 50 kilometres into the stratosphere. High-altitude winds ensured it was widely dispersed around the globe, and high above any rain clouds that might flush it out. The heavier ash particles did rain down in the succeeding fortnight and were mainly experienced by ships traversing the surrounding seas. But the lighter dust remained aloft for some years to provide vividly coloured sunsets and memorable afterglows that inspired painters and poets alike. And those mighty waves rippled across oceans without faltering, registering their presence in places as distant as India and South Africa, mercifully with very few additional casualties. But tidal gauges did register their passage even in places such as the English Channel.

The prevailing temperature dropped palpably as the concentration of atmospheric dust blocked out the sunlight. This global cooling would persist for a few years, but was appreciated only with some considerable hindsight when records were examined as climatic patterns became a matter of great scientific curiosity. The sound of Krakatoa was, of course, short-lived but it was still felt 3,000 miles away. The islands around Mauritius in the Indian Ocean reported the distant roar of heavy guns or rock blasting operations. This was indeed the sound of the world's greatest detonation.

So how does Earth cope as a planet in the aftermath of such environmental upheaval? We are now recognising (after some decades of disbelief!) that it can heal itself over time. This is the Gaia concept proposed by James Lovelock back in the 1970s. Gaia is a Greek goddess and a powerful metaphor for the living and self-regulating system that is our planet. This system embraces all life forms as well as Earth's surface rocks, oceans and atmosphere. It is of course in a continual state of flux and Gaia seeks to maintain an environment as favourable as possible for the flourishing of contemporary life. No mean task! And let it be said that there are many now who consider we have tested Gaia's patience to breaking point in recent times. As maybe indeed Wexford did in its own time![9]

Meanwhile back in Dublin, news of the calamitous 1883 eruption was received calmly, judging by the coverage in the popular *Freeman's Journal*.[10] No doubt the impact of the unfolding catastrophe was greater on the sympathetic public than might be imagined from the meagre column-inches assigned to it over several days of August and September that year. On Wednesday 29 August it was reported that the dense shower of ashes, mud and pumice stone had almost ruined the crops and orchards. On the Friday it was reported that Krakatoa itself had disappeared and that 16 new volcanic cones were growing in its place. The next day, the total fatalities were estimated at over 30,000. Curiously, the headlines over these reports tended to refer to an earthquake rather than a volcano – which is factually correct, for several severe tremors were felt. Soon the coverage tailed off into concerns about shipping and reports of relief committees. But the enduring impact in far-off Wexford would have been purely visual, with descriptions of those spectacular sunsets being retailed with embellishment by storytellers to succeeding generations!

Notes

1. From "Land & Water" which appears on page 38 of Eamonn Wall (2008) *A Tour of Your Country*. Cliffs of Moher, County Clare: Salmon Poetry.

2. Eamonn Wall (2008) *A Tour of Your Country*. Cliffs of Moher, County Clare: Salmon Poetry. I quoted from "Lewis & Clark: Omaha, Nebraska" (page 27) and "Land & Water" (page 38). I referred to "Yellowstone Bus Tour" (page 10) and "Leaving Boise" (pages 55-57).

3. Eamonn Wall (2000) "Witnessing Two Worlds: Poems". In Charles Fanning (Ed.) *New Perspectives on the Irish Diaspora*. Carbondale and Edwardsville: Southern Illinois University Press, pages 28-39. I have referred to the following poems: "Freewheeling by the Platte River: A Song" (pages 30-31), "The Blackbird of Edermine" (pages 36-37). I quoted from "Finding a Way Home" (pages 37-38) and "Four Stern Faces/South Dakota" (pages 38-39).

4. Eamonn Wall (2013) "The Black Hills, the Gorey Road". In J. S. Rogers (Ed.) *Extended Family: Essays on Being Irish American from New Hibernia Review*. Chester Springs, Pennsylvania: Dufour Editions Inc., pages 203-225.

5. Eamonn Wall (1994) *Dyckman-200th Street*. Galway: Salmon Poetry. I quoted from "Mount Leinster and Me" (page 58).

6. Edward Culleton (1980) *The South Wexford Landscape*. Published by the author.

7. Daniel Tietzsch-Tyler and others (1994) *Geology of Carlow-Wexford*. Dublin: Geological Survey of Ireland.

8. Simon Winchester (2004) *Krakatoa: The Day the World Exploded*. London: Penguin Books. The specific quotation is from pages 234-235.

9. James Lovelock (2000) *Gaia: A New Look at Life on Earth*. Oxford: Oxford University Press.

10. See copies of *The Freeman's Journal* for August and September of 1883.

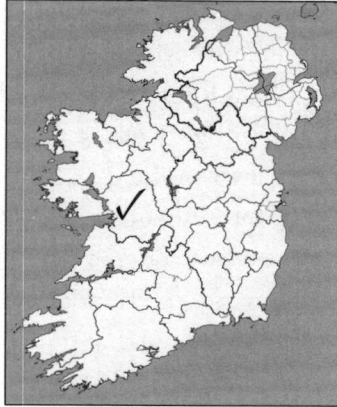

29

TO THE WATERS AND THE WILD
(Galway)

We are all in the gutter, but some of us are
looking at the stars.
– Oscar Wilde[1]

Is was a terrible fall from grace in 1895 and perhaps it was as
well that his father had already died, for his mother would
pass away during his subsequent two-year imprisonment. His
wife, with a view to damage limitation, had renounced his family
name and lived but a few short years more, dying in 1899. This was
the same year in which his only surviving sibling would die and
just a year before the shabby demise of the main man himself. He
was, of course, Oscar Fingal O'Flahertie Wills Wilde (1854–1900),
witty writer and successful playwright. His humour and extrava-
gant lifestyle are attributed to his mother, the virulently national-

281

ist poet, Lady Jane Frances Wilde (*Speranza*) (1821–1896), but his sharp intelligence and unconventional approach to life are credited to his father, Sir William Robert Wills Wilde (1815–1876).[2]

Lough Corrib slices through County Galway unevenly, separating a larger limestone area to the east from the older rocks of Connemara in the west. Sir William was a product of the limestone lowlands, being born in Castlerea, and became an eminent eye and ear surgeon who wrote the standard textbook on his area of expertise. He was also a respected antiquarian and archaeologist whose great love of Lough Corrib was expressed in a much admired book of his, dealing with its topography, history and archaeology. His account of its geology and mineral resources was reproduced *verbatim* from the words of the geologist, G. H. Kinahan (1829–1908). One word is delightfully mis-transcribed: Kinahan is quoted as saying that some sediments lie "uncomfortably", rather than unconformably, on older metamorphic rocks![3] Who says rocks (or geologists) lack emotions!

The widespread and karstic limestone bedrock of Galway was sufficiently mystical to capture the poetic attention of our Lyricist of Limestone, W.B. Yeats. That karst which is spectacularly exposed in the Burren and on the Aran Islands was carved from the same huge block of limestone. The sediment of its upper part was deposited in relatively deep water, while the lower part formed in shallow waters where the sea periodically retreated to give dry land. We have already related the resulting soil horizons in the Burren limestone to the waxing and waning of polar ice sheets. The modern pattern of habitation on all three Aran Islands favours locations some height above sea level and this makes good sense given the prevalence of stormy weather. Tim Robinson's (b. 1935) insightful map[4] suggests that housing on each island is strung out along a specific bed, perhaps corresponding with one of the soil horizons. Several such horizons are visible on the awesome Dún Aonghus cliffs on Inis Mór, the most westerly of the Aran Islands. If we imagine each associated glacial phase lasting 50,000 years and that they recurred every 300,000 years, then the limestones of the Dún Aonghus cliffs might have accumulated in one and a half million years. But that's armchair speculation.

Relatively recent glaciation stripped the islands bare of their soil and, as a poor recompense, left a scattering of granite boulders which the ice sheets carried across the bay from Connemara. Common karst features include grikes (open fractures) and kamenitzas (solution pans with raised rims), both of which can trip the unwary walker. Tourism is important on both Inis Mór and Inis Oirr, being served by ferries from Rossaveal and Doolin respectively. During my recent visit to Inis Mór one visitor, apparently mistrusting of the robust Atlantic breeze, wore a face mask to protect herself against potential pollution! But walking the shoreline of Inis Oirr the next day in company with an island farmer, he predicted that our sighting of several dolphin pods held out excellent long-term weather prospects. And I really wanted to believe him!

Inis Meáin is an island of frugality, with daytime refreshments usually available only at the hospitable and welcoming post office. J. M. Synge once resided in a thatched cottage here and wrote an alarmingly authentic account of island life. Some residents, recognising themselves and their foibles, were said to take exception when the resulting book became successful! Cathaoir Synge, Synge's Chair, is a shelter on the limestone pavement that the writer regularly visited. Having stubbed his toe on a block there, he became conscious of its fossil-rich nature![5]

Most people find it easy to blend in with island life and poets are no different. Belfast-born and Galway resident, Fred Johnston (b. 1951) is no stranger to the Aran Islands ("Poet on an Island"). In fact his identity merges with that of the sea and the island itself:[6]

> I take deep breaths
> as the rocks breathe
> I lean with old men
> against stone walls

That last line captures the easy pace that we as observers ascribe to, and admire in, islanders – rightly or wrongly! It seems compatible with the poet's asserted rhythm of life, from pillow to pen and from dreaming to imagining.

The flat-lying countryside of east Galway has a prairie-like texture that is only partly obscured by the patterns of limestone walls among delicate green pasture shades. The poem, "Keaveney's Well",[7] is set in this country, where karst hidden beneath boulder clay merges eastwards with the callows of the River Shannon basin:

> Land aspired to be water;
> water wanted to be land.

The poet is Patrick Deeley (b. 1953) from Loughrea who is a retired Dublin school principal. His poetry is influenced by his youthful contact with nature around the Shannon callows, a theme he shares with poet Mary Turley McGrath (Chapter 23). Deeley is repulsed by the dank smell of black organic-rich silt, quite unlike the more civilised bog, and he is reminded of childhood excavations in marl ("The Marl Excavations"):

> white, with
> small tell-tale shells remembering a lake
> where the Callows found its first
> foothold ...

This captures the spirit of the callows, the low-lying floodplain which developed on extensive lakelands in the wake of the melting ice sheets. But for Deeley, the callows are really part of his childhood and one becomes synonymous with the other.

Is there any county with greater width than Galway, stretching as it does from Shannon's quiet callows to the turbulent Atlantic waters beyond Clifden? This thought may strike you if you cross the River Corrib by Salmon Weir Bridge to the much older bedrock of Connemara. Padraic Fallon (1905–1974), an east Galway poet who sometimes celebrated its limestone landscape, as a schoolboy used to linger on this bridge, a critical juncture between eastern limestones and western schists. Now, a visit in later years caused him to measure his life's progress. He did not feel triumphant as he compared his own stumbling course in life and inevitable mortality with the throbbing constancy of the River Corrib beneath.[8]

West of the River Corrib, the incomparable Connemara is a scenic land of mountains, lakes and bogs, which embraces at least two different spiritual landscapes, each with its own gateway and personality. Those students seeking Irish-speaking summertime colleges take the southern gateway through Spiddle and onto relatively flat-lying granite terrain. Tourists, on the other hand, tend to head northwest out of Galway through Oughterard in search of the mountains and lakes sustained by the remarkably varied and metamorphic geology of Connemara's northern half. The poet who provides a bridge between the two is Richard Murphy (b. 1927). Born in Mayo, he spent part of his childhood in Sri Lanka, and then more than 20 years in each of Cleggan, County Galway, and Dublin before returning to Sri Lanka.[9]

Although he is actually a child of Wilde's Lough Corrib, he is invariably drawn to Cleggan's granite. For example he records a farmer on the granite island of Omey schooling a tinker in how to scythe ("Scythe").[10] Murphy doesn't need to mention the granite in order to convey the substance of this poem, but it is evidently important for him to do so. On the same island ("Omey Island") he wonders whether some boulders were quarried for a purpose, or just detached from outcrop by sea action. He decides in favour of the sea, noting its power:

> the ocean
> Explodes at the quarry-face of the shore
> ...
> Gathering more and more power
> To rampage over the island ...

Looking at an abandoned granite ball he muses on whether it was a quern, a column top or an archaeologist's oblate spheroid and he marvels at the dedication of the stone cutter ("Granite Globe"). But it is the use of granite in buildings that fascinates Murphy and when he enlarges his Connemara house he indulges a costly passion for building in granite, being prepared to demolish some old cabins and source stone in roofless houses for that purpose.

For him, humankind may acquire "granite" qualities and we should not be surprised that these turn out to be invariably admirable. We realise that his recently-deceased friend's chimney breast may encompass warmth beyond what fossil fuel could produce ("Tony White"). Granite takes on the warm personality of this friend ("Circles"):

> These are rocks he loved when he was alive
> And how alive he was, like the sun this afternoon
> Making mica gleam on the cold face of granite
> And giving walls a long shadow across the grass
> In the dead of winter

Murphy had his very own granite pluton out at Omey, a perfectly circular feature but with over half its area hidden beneath the sea. This is separate from the main Galway Granite further south and is situated within Connemara's metamorphic terrain, an oblong stretch of country extending from Lough Corrib at Oughterard to the Atlantic beyond Clifden. These metamorphic rocks are themselves divided into two halves, a northern half derived from sediments and a southern from magmatic rocks. Those northern rocks, called Dalradian, comprise widespread quartzites which make up mountainous terrain, and schists and marbles which define the lower ground. The original sediments from which they formed had accumulated offshore over a period when Connemara was located close to the South Pole. In any event these rocks collided catastrophically with the northwestern margin of the contracting Iapetus Ocean and became welded onto the zone of

magmatic rocks that now constitutes the southern part of Connemara's metamorphic rocks. Those magmatic rocks are granites
and gabbros that have been highly deformed and metamorphosed
to gneisses and are best seen in the area south of Clifden. During
this collision of ocean and continent, the continent was overridden by a huge segment of up-thrusted ocean floor which altered
the rocks so thoroughly that in some cases their nature can now
only be determined from their chemical composition.

If you wish to examine the effects of deformation in these metamorphic rocks, then seek out an example of Connemara Marble,
derived from bedded limestone, in some convenient building. Its
banded nature highlights the elaborate folds and abrupt faults that
resulted from the stresses endured by all of Connemara's rocks. It
features as a decorative stone in many public buildings because of
its attractive green colour, due to the presence of the mineral ser-
pentine, and its ability to take a high polish. It has been employed
by architects for over 200 years although in recent times its main
use has been in jewellery and souvenirs.

The spectacular beauty of Connemara can hold its own against
any competing region, being based on rocky mountains, dazzling
lakes, open bogland and breathtaking valleys. The parents of Louis
Macneice came from near Clifden and the family much preferred
Connemara to their Ulster home:

> The very name Connemara seemed too rich for any or-
> dinary place. It appeared to be a country of windswept
> open spaces and mountains blazing with whins and seas
> that were never quiet, with drowned palaces beneath
> them, and seals and eagles and turf smoke and cottagers
> who were always laughing and who gave you milk when
> you asked for a glass of water.[11]

Any excursion in Connemara should include the Inagh Valley
for sheer exhileration and Connemara National Park for a stroll
on Diamond Hill, where the diamonds are exclusively spiritual,
but you may be dazzled by the variety of marble, schist, granite

and quartzite rock types. But do not neglect the historically significant area between Clifden and Ballynahinch. Marconi brought ashore his transatlantic telegraph cable at Clifden, while Alcock and Brown completed the first transatlantic flight there. But Ballynahinch remains the historical centre of Connemara, not least because of the colourful history of some of its landlords. "Humanity Dick" Martin (1754–1834), for example, succeeded in changing society's attitude to animal welfare in a very significant way, although he would die in exile and poverty.[12]

Perhaps the best-known poem about Connemara is one written by W. B. Yeats entitled "The Fisherman".[13] Yeats had been contemplating those desirable qualities which he felt were sadly lacking in his fellow citizens. His ideal Irishman would be wise and simple, fishing some stream that crosses those metamorphic rocks. He would have a sun-freckled face, suggesting a lowly outdoor worker, and his grey cloth might point to a relatively poor one. A century later this would scarcely match Connemara's modern reality!

The metamorphic rocks do not stop at the Clifden coastline but are present also on the offshore island of Inishbofin, with which the poet, Seán Dunne (1956–1995) had a close relationship. As his impending and untimely death approached, he sought its healing power on his own ("The Healing Island").[14] Soon he missed his lover and their shared interest in the island's nature. At night the pounding seas woke him and he thought of his partner's spiritual strength, lifting her influence to the majesty of the geological:

> Striations on stones, the worn
> force, of centuries and the sea.
> The thought of you as I work:
> a glacier shifting earth's shape.

He struggled to find meaning through his writing, but expected too much of it, realising that his lover was the real island and source of healing in his life.

The main Galway Granite forms bedrock over the southern half of Connemara and its southern limits extend beyond the highly indented coastline. Its offshore extensions are well constrained in the west and further east its southern contact is concealed by younger limestones and passes between the Aran Islands and the Connemara coastline. The entire pluton has an oval shape and its emplacement was one of the final acts of the collision that finally marked the death of Iapetus Ocean. Its intrusion took time, possibly many million years, and granite magma made its way upwards in small batches along a major fault zone. Its history was far from simple and, for example, additional faults within the granite separate a western part that solidified at a depth of less than 10km from a central part which crystallised at least 6 kilometres further down.[15]

Galway Bay itself is a place of solitude for mainlanders and a sentimental icon for the emigrant. It provides access to Ireland's extensive offshore regions which are much more extensive than its onshore. Although we have only just begun to appreciate the potential value of our seabed's undoubted resources, in fact the first research vessel began exploring it over a century ago. I suspect it may not have helped the public's perception of its work that a vessel of the same name was used subsequently to shell central Dublin during the 1916 Rising. This was the *Helga* and its earlier incarnation served as a fisheries protection and research ship, recovering seabed samples that revealed for the first time that the deeper sea floor was covered by sediments much younger than those onshore. This was the first hint that exciting discoveries might be anticipated – and no doubt the best is yet to come!

Notes

1. Oscar Wilde (1908) *Lady Windermere's Fan*. London: Methuen & Co., Act III, page 110.

2. Gerard Hanberry (2011) *More Lives than One: The Remarkable Wilde Family through the Generations*. Cork: The Collins Press.

3. Colm O'Lochlainn (Ed.) (1936) *Wilde's Loch Coirib, Its Shores and Islands, with Notices of Loch Measga*. Third edition. Dublin: At the Sign of the Three Candles.

4. Tim Robinson (1980) *The Aran Islands: A Map and Guide*. Published by T.D. Robinson, Cill Rónáin, Aran Islands, County Galway.

5. J. M. Synge (2008) *The Aran Islands*. In *The Complete Works of J.M. Synge*. London: Wordsworth Poetry Library, pages 307-373.

6. The poem "Poet on an Island" is on page 35 of Fred Johnston (2001) *Being Anywhere: New & Selected Poems*. Belfast: Lagan Press.

7. Patrick Deeley (2013) *Groundswell: New and Selected Poems*. Dublin: The Dedalus Press. I have quoted from the following poems: "Keaveney's Well" (page 104) and "The Marl Excavations" (page 105).

8. "Weir Bridge" by Padraic Fallon is on page 119 of: Michael Hartnett and Desmond Egan (Eds.) (?1973) *Choice*. The Goldsmith Press.

9. See the chapter entitled "Wings Beating on Stone: Richard Murphy's Ecopoetry" (pages 51-69) in: Eamonn Wall (2011) *Writing the Irish West: Ecologies and traditions*. Notre Dame, Indiana: University of Notre Dame Press.

10. Richard Murphy (2013) *Poems 1952-2012*. Dublin: The Lilliput Press. I have quoted from the following poems: "Omey Island" (page 118) and "Circles" (page 163). I also referred to "Scythe" (page 153), "Granite Globe" (page 139) and "Tony White" (page 160).

11. See pages 216-217 of: MacNeice, L. (1965) *The Strings Are False*. London: Faber and Faber.

12. For a wonderful introduction to Connemara, read Tim Robinson (2006) *Connemara: Listening to the Wind*. London: Penguin Books.

13. "The Fisherman" is on pages 148-149 of : W. B.Yeats (1983) *The Poems, a new edition*. Richard J. Finneran (Ed.). London: Macmillan London.

14. Peter Fallon (Ed.) (2005) *Seán Dunne Collected*. Oldcastle, County Meath: The Gallery Press. "The Healing Island" appears on pages 192-196.

15. J. H. Morris, C. B. Long, B. McConnell and J. B. Archer (1995) *Geology of Connemara*. The Geological Survey of Ireland.

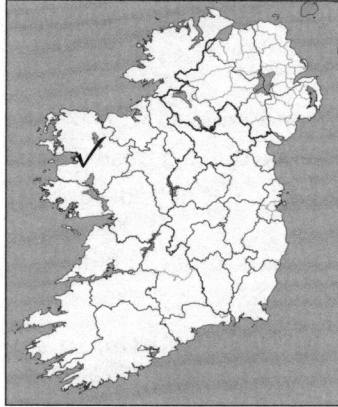

30

CREATING A HABITABLE HOME
(Mayo)

Happy the man whose lot it is to know
The secrets of the earth.
— Euripides[1]

Some poets make direct and fulsome reference to their physical environment, while others provide a more glancing – but no less entertaining – acknowledgement of their surroundings. Take Paul Durcan (b. 1944) for example, one of Ireland's most popular poets and one accomplished to a rare degree in performing his own works.[2] His Mayo credentials are impeccable, both of his parents coming from this scenic county. His themes tend to be of immediate interest and maybe he will help us see landscape in the present tense, not always a strength of geologists! He once unwittingly gave us an insight into his approach, through his assessment of the celebrated geographer, E. Estyn Evans:

> He was an environmentalist who believed with all his heart and conscience that a landscape and a people cannot be understood except in relation to each other.[3]

Let us see how Durcan himself achieves this merger in practice.

Crazy about women[4] is a set of Durcan's poems written in response to paintings from the National Gallery of Ireland, but not specifically landscape paintings. Katherina, for example, is posing against a backdrop of the Danube and the surrounding misty hills but it is "Katherina Knoblauch" herself that largely fills the frame – and why shouldn't she on this her happy day. In Durcan's playful poem, Katherina muses that her intended husband may believe that her Danube landscape is actually Wicklow, after all, both are just mountains and rivers. Only Paul Durcan, as master of everywhere and nowhere, could credibly reduce two such diverse landscapes to simply mountains and rivers! Another young woman is anticipating without pleasure a life of motherhood and she gets no hearing from her preoccupied companions ("Bathers Surprised"). She, just like landscape so often, has receded to become the unwilling and frustrated backdrop. In the painting itself, yellow ochre with dashes of raw sienna commands attention for a rich countryside yet I wonder mischievously if it might, just out of sight, give way to, say, a tumultuous waterfall! Why should only the bathers be surprised? "Dawn, Connemara" is a Paul Henry (1877–1958) landscape, one of the very few with no human figure, but the grey, misty countryside does not hold the poet's attention for long. His thoughts stray to thinking of "Pearse", a poet and political scientist, and I wonder to what extent he may be imagining the executed 1916 leader, P. H. Pearse (1879–1916), who holidayed nearby. But then consider a landscape where Paul feels thoroughly at home ("A Group of Cavalry in the Snow"). With its vivid snow-covered bluff and desolate birches, it is easy to imagine its seductiveness. Yes, Durcan craves snow and actually wants to enjoy it!

He seems less enthusiastic about landscape in his follow-on treatment of paintings in the National Gallery, London.[5] He has a curator there declare that he detests landscape ("Portrait of a Man *with* Susanna Lunden") and he minimises the significance of background landscape by imagining it to be an actual painting ("A Family Group in a Landscape"). I like the Dutch artist Aelbert Cuyp (1620–1691) and his painting "River Landscape with Horseman and Peasants" because in it he has made people subsidiary to a busy landscape. But, to my frustration, Paul chooses to pluck a barely discernible figure from the painting's margins and to focus our attention on him and his hunting gun – providing the poet with echoes of Belfast and Sarajevo. Durcan goes on to fully redeem himself regarding landscape by acknowledging its power in revitalising our spirits. The painting is "A Cornfield, with Cypresses" by Vincent van Gogh (1853–1890), featuring countryside in bright and vivid colours beneath a theatrical sky. The painting itself certainly can do good things for my mental well-being. Curiously, in Paul's poem the artist's mother criticises the art historian who used the painting as evidence of Vincent's unbalanced mind without ever searching the cornfield for its many meanings. Durcan can also incorporate geological themes in an endearing manner and no geologist ever addressed a piece of rock with more reverence than this ("The Mantelpiece"):

> Staring into the marble, I stray into it
> Exploring its pores, its veins, its stains, its moles.
> A block of marble on legs of marble.

Geology also features in Durcan's 2012 collection.[6] The jeweller's matriarchal assistant was Pre-Cambrian and accordingly a solid basis for her employer, Weir's jewellers ("The Lady in Weir's"). He himself wants to fill his pockets with Palaeozoic stones ("Thinking about Suicide"). Interesting that both geological eras, which are old even by geological standards, feature in rather sombre settings. Perhaps Durcan might regard joyful events as being geologically younger, say Mesozoic or Quaternary!

His 2012 collection identifies two recently deceased friends each in their own landscape, revealing the significant influence that landscape has had on Durcan himself. For him, his philosopher friend, John Moriarty, is rooted in Connemara:

> The skull of the mountains the same
> As they were before pre-history began.

The image of a skull may be morbid, but it also suggests mountains washed clean by erosion. Durcan perhaps imagines him influencing events even at a cosmic level ("Post-haste to John Moriarty, Easter Sunday, 2007"):

> The birthpangs of the universe
> Reproduced in your hair ...

His second friend, the postman on Mayo's Achill Island, treasured quartz fragments:

> Quartz – the only metamorphic icon we have for the soul
> And the life of the soul.

Achill is celebrated for its quartz, especially its purple variety, amethyst. This postman placed his quartz on top of the mailbox, surely his most vivid icon, reflecting the value he placed on it. His qualities and those of quartz were both "glittering" against the blackness of their surroundings. The postman becomes not just morphed, but metamorphosed into quartz ("Achill Island Postman").

I would love to read how Durcan might treat that ultimate morphing, the transformation of the rocky wilderness of early Earth into a habitat with air and water, a home fit for humanity! No better place to consider it than in Mayo which harbours some of Ireland's oldest rock. We owe our atmosphere to gases emanating from the Planet's interior and their composition changed over time, the early dominance of methane giving way to nitrogen and oxygen. The oceans represent 97 per cent of our planet's water and probably half of their volume formed through reactions between gases escaping from the Earth's interior. The remainder arrived on Earth through the bombardment of ice-rich comets. Those oceans nurtured early life, which seemingly developed just as soon as our evolving climate would permit it, and life is now considered an integral component of the Earth's system. And yet for 85 per cent of its history, life on our planet was hardly exciting – just some single-celled organisms, such as bacteria and algae. Variety appeared only about 600 million years ago when the so-called "explosion of life" occurred. Even then it was a stop-go affair, with a number of mass extinctions followed by new explosions in life's variety. So our planet may be unique in the solar system with its shades of blue and green but, if so, the latter shades are relative newcomers. [7]

Nevertheless the haphazard result was the emergence of our amazingly rich ecology, such as the Belfast poet Michael Longley (b. 1939) has celebrated as a regular summer visitor to the Mweelrea district of Mayo. His Mayo landscape comprehends the natural world of birds, animals and especially plants. He is at home with mountains and still takes time to notice plants, even on their very summit. I don't know what he sees in them with all those fabulous rocks around! For Mweelrea mountain (814m) has some interesting geology. Overlooking the narrow Killary Harbour on the Galway-Mayo border, its 460 million years old rocks are part (along with Croagh Patrick) of the South Mayo Trough. The rocks accumulated in a basin developed along a linear zone of volcanoes which were swept up and located on the northwestern margin of a contracting Iapetus Ocean. The Mweelrea rocks are sandstones and conglomerates which were deposited in a delta environment and have evidence of five successive volcanic eruptions marked by glowing ash clouds.[8]

In "Carrigskeewaun",[9] an early poem, Longley regards Mweelrea as a place of family picnics supervised by the ravens. He acknowledges how much the weather influences our landscape perceptions and it restricts his view of coast and neighbours ("Landscape"):

> I am clothed, unclothed
> By racing cloud shadows,
> Or else disintegrate
> Like a hillside neighbour
> Erased by sea mist.

By 1979 he is comfortably observing the seasonal rhythms of
farming and nature on the mountain ("On Mweelrea"). Although
then relatively silent about Mayo landscape for many years, he still
derives pleasure from his visits. Consider the delightfully short
poem, "The Meteorite", which describes a night-time walk to count
swans which is enlivened by shooting stars. Longley wants his ashes buried here ("Above Dooaghtry") and the preferred location is
prescribed with Yeatsian precision, a fitting tribute to his love of
this landscape.

In another early poem ("The Hebrides"), Longley refers reasonably to granite as Presbyterian, after all it is commonly used
in constructing places of worship, be they churches, mosques or
synagogues. However the adjective has a Greek root signifying
an elder and he means it to refer to the ancient age of Hebridean
granite. He also describes granite as an orphan stone, but I am
relieved that this is because the Hebrides, as offshore islands, were
orphaned from mainland Scotland.[10]

Croagh Patrick (764 metres) is neither the oldest nor the highest rock in Mayo, but it is familiar to generations of pilgrims as
the Reek, Ireland's most popular pilgrimage mountain overlooking
Clew Bay. St. Patrick is reputed to have done penance on its summit for forty days and nights in 441AD. Pilgrims have been visiting
it for at least a millennium and an oratory was constructed on its

summit at the start of the twentieth century. Tens of thousands now ascend every year, some in bare feet, especially on the last Sunday of July, the traditional Reek Sunday.

One snowy Easter, the poet Paddy Bushe (b. 1948) ascended Croagh Patrick, zigzagging up the pilgrim's path. He welcomed the snow-covered scree higher up, because the frozen snow gave a better grip to his boots. Indeed that white blanket made obvious the footprints of an earlier walker that he found fascinating. At the summit, as a true pilgrim, he circled the chapel pondering the Easter sky and the anonymous footsteps. He may reflect on the climbing difficulties but his mind still soars spiritually and is deflected by neither scenery nor nature ("Footsteps on Croagh Patrick").[11]

Timothy Brownlow, British Columbia-based poet and teacher, recounts a commonplace experience in approaching the mountains of western Ireland: having glimpsed all of Croagh Patrick emerging from mist, he was not quick enough to capture it photographically such was the speed with which it was once more engulfed ("Climbing Croagh Patrick").[12] But it did not deter him from the ascent:

Always toiling up a steep, shingled slope,
A frail, domesticated Sisyphus.

Sisyphus was the classical character destined to continually push uphill a large boulder that invariably rolled back down again. Any weary walker can identify with this. Brownlow pauses, momentarily imagining he is in bare feet, but then proceeds and finishes with exemplary advice: "Just look for the flat stones and take your time."

Uinsin O'Donovan's pilgrim experience ("Croagh Patrick")[13] happens when the Reek is alive with walkers. He gazes at the distant summit and wonders how the builders brought up the materials to construct the small church there. The pilgrims form a weaving line that from a distance seems composed of a million ants. The last stretch of the climb, over scree, is particularly laborious but he persists right to the summit. The view is exhilarating but most pilgrims remain devoutly in prayer and walk around the church. Then prayers over, they descend once more, quite carefully and chatting good-humouredly with others.

Croagh Patrick lies on the margin of the Clew Bay Complex, an aptly named jumble of rocks, still incompletely understood and bound up in a major fault zone that extends from Clew Bay across Ireland to Scotland, where it is called the Highland Boundary Fault. The complex consists of Ordovician rocks of two contrasting types, highly metamorphosed gabbros and serpentinites on the one hand and greywacke and siltstone sediments on the other. This was indeed a fundamental fault zone, for those igneous rocks were portions of the ocean floor itself while the sediments formed in deep seawater resting upon that seafloor. Significant quaking was necessarily involved in shifting this segment of ocean floor up to its present elevated position, but at less than half a billion years ago they were still not the earliest earthquakes that Ireland ever experienced.[14]

There is a vantage point on the approach from Castlebar where the Reek seems to soar Mount Fuji-like above its surroundings, but it is still impressive even when – more commonly – its cone simply sits astride the underlying ridge. The R335 road west out of Westport is part of the National Coastal Route and has a comfortable roadside lane reserved for walkers and cyclists. Clew Bay's celebrated drumlins are not confined offshore, for Westport town is built around them and they are widespread in this hilly country. A rocky ridge parallel to the road gradually gains height and culminates in Croagh Patrick itself. The ascent starts from Murrisk carpark and is marked by outcrops of the Clew Bay Complex, slates and serpentinite. The latter has a distinctly waxy sheen and contrasting shades mainly of green and blue that can sometimes look quite hideous. You can't miss it! But don't linger too long, for I promise that in your forthcoming endeavours you will have more on your mind than a consideration of geological artwork!

Soon you will pass onto quartzite and you will have no doubt when you do so. It is just after the stream, which until now has been a faithful companion, leaves the path. The gravel you are walking on now becomes a bright cream, very different from what you started upon. But the best clue of all is the sound of the quartzite, for it has a very crisp sound underfoot. Well, I should mention that soon afterwards the hill gradient does increase perceptibly, but you were expecting that anyway!

Good-humoured exchanges carry the struggling trickle of walkers upwards to the shoulder of the mountain. Now there is an opportunity to catch our breath before tackling the final ascent along that steep quartzite cone strewn with frost-shattered scree. This unwelcome debris reflects the fact that this was one of just a few Irish mountain-tops that were not overridden by ice sheets in our glacial past. This is where Timothy Brownlow suffers manfully but survives to offer advice to those following. This quartzite formed beneath the marine waters of the South Mayo Trough. When you start the final ascent you may justifiably feel a unifying bond with the mountains beyond the low bogland on your left, for they are also part of the same South Mayo Trough. Mutual encouragement is vital at this stage and comes in many accents – from America, Europe and every part of Ireland. Men patronising women, women encouraging men, and children being praised and coaxed by times. We can sympathise with Paddy Bushe's snowy ascent when he chose to ignore both nature and spirituality! Quiet satisfaction and relief dominate over elation among summiteers, but all savour the scenery – Clew Bay, Mweelrea, Achill and Clare Island. If you have the leisure allow yourself time to admire the summit chapel and, like Uinsin O'Donovan, ponder on its builder's task. From the ridge shoulder downwards the going is more relaxed. A couple pause to admire the receding summit and relish the extent of their day's achievement. We are just grateful to reach the carpark without falls or fractures, happy to indulge sore feet and empty stomachs. My favourite view of the mountain, let me now admit, is a backward glance, content in the knowledge that I have enjoyed its heights again!

Notes

1. Attributed to Euripides (c.480-406 BC), the Greek playwright, and I accessed it on 29 May 2014 at laelaps.wordpress.com/2007/07/17/happy-the-man-whose-lot-it-is-to-know-the-secrets-of-the-earth/

2. Tóibín, C. (Ed.) (1996) *The Kilfenora Teaboy: A Study of Paul Durcan.* Dublin: New Island Books.

3. See page ix of the Foreword by Paul Durcan, dated 16 June 1992, in E. Estyn Evans (1992) *The Personality of Ireland: Habitat, Heritage and History.* Dublin: The Lilliput Press.

4. Durcan, Paul (1991) *Crazy about Women.* Dublin: The National Gallery of Ireland. Poems referred to are as follows: "Katherina Knoblauch" , pages 19-21; "Bathers Surprised", pages 86-87; "A Group of Cavalry in the Snow", pages 96-97 and "Dawn, Connemara", pages 106-107.

5. Durcan, Paul (1994) *Give Me Your Hand.* London: Macmillan, published in association with National Gallery Publications, London. I quoted from "The Mantelpiece" (pages 147-148). Poems referred to are as follows: "Portrait of a Man *with* Susanna Lunden", pages 49-54; "A Family Group in a Landscape", pages 81-83; "River Landscape with Horseman and Peasants", pages 90-91 and "A Cornfield, with Cypresses", pages 134-136.

6. Paul Durcan (2012) *Praise in which I live and move and have my being.* London: Harvill Secker. 157 pages. Poems quoted from are as follows: "Thinking about Suicide", pages 21-22; "Post-haste to John Moriarty, Easter Sunday, 2007", pages 27-31; "The Lady in Weir's", pages 74-76; "Achill Island, Postman", page 94.

7. Charles H. Langmuir and Wally Broecker (2012) *How to Build a Habitable Planet: The Story of Earth from the Big Bang to Humankind.* Revised edition. Princeton, New Jersey: Princeton University Press.

8. For background on Mweelrea geology see J. R. Graham (2009) "Ordovician of the North". In C. H. Holland and I. S. Sanders (Eds.) *The Geology of Ireland.* Second edition. Edinburgh: Dunedin Academic Press, pages 43-67.

9. Michael Longley (2006) *Collected Poems.* London: Jonathan Cape. I have quoted from "Landscape", page 91, and referred to the following poems: "The Hebrides", page 22; "Carrigskeewaun", pages 68-69; "On

Mweelrea", page 142; "The meteorite", page 244; and "Above Dooaghtry", page 289.

10. Personal communication by Michael Longley on the occasion of "Poetry Landscape", comprising readings by varied poets including Longley, held on 1 December 2008 in the Geological Survey of Ireland, Dublin 4, to mark the International Year of Planet Earth.

11. The poem "Footsteps on Croagh Patrick" appears on page 14 of Paddy Bushe (2001) *Hopkins on Skellig Michael*. Dublin: The Dedalus Press.

12. "Climbing Croagh Patrick" is on page 20 of Timothy Brownlow (1998) *Climbing Croagh Patrick*. Lantzville, British Columbia: Oolichan Books.

13. "Croagh Patrick" is on pages 18-19 of: Uinsin O'Donovan (2011) *Hand Me Down the Moon*. Published by the author.

14. For the geology of Croagh Patrick and Clew Bay see D. M. Chew (2009) "Grampian Orogeny". In C. H. Holland and I. S. Sanders (Eds.) *The Geology of Ireland*. Second edition. Edinburgh: Dunedin Academic Press, pages 69-93.

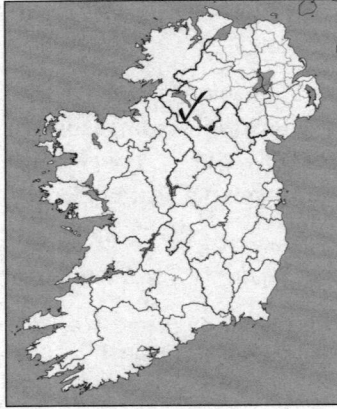

31

GLITTERING FISHES
(Fermanagh)

But for the nature-lover, ... quiet wandering on foot
along brown streams and among the windy hills can
bring a solace and a joy that is akin only to the peace
of God that passeth understanding.
– Robert L. Praeger[1]

Louis Agassiz (1807–1873) was not first attracted to Enniskillen by its glacial landscape of drumlins and lakes, despite the fact that in time his scientific reputation would come to rest substantially on his recognition that ice sheets were once considerably more extensive than at present in northwestern Europe.[2] No, in the mid-1830s Agassiz just came to see fish, but rather special fish. They consisted of the fossil fish collection of William Willoughby Cole (1807–1886), third Earl of Enniskillen. Cole's magnificent collection was tastefully displayed in a specially modified wing of

302

his mansion, Florence Court, 10 kilometres south of Enniskillen. Cole shared an obsession for fossil fish with his friend, Sir Philip de Malpas Grey Egerton (1806–1881), and between them they enthusiastically acquired the finest specimens available. So we can imagine that Egerton would have joined Agassiz on his visit to see Cole and that they spent many satisfying hours poring over the splendid specimens. The Florence Court collection came to number close to 10,000 specimens before the now-blind Earl sold it, shortly before his death, to the Natural History Museum in London. In due course Egerton ensured that his precious fish were united with Cole's in those hallowed halls of South Kensington. The Museum would later proudly assert that it had the world's finest collection of fossil fish.[3]

What could be exciting about Cole's dead fishes? Specimens would trace the progress of fish evolution from the earliest lamprey-types to the highly sophisticated later species with delicately outlined skeletons. Fish are not easily fossilised, so we would need specimens from a great variety of places and from rocks with a substantial age range in order to meet this objective. We can expect to find fish skeletons wherever depositional conditions are calm, but a quick burial would also be essential for the preservation of impressions of soft tissues and scales. The Florence Court collection even included the odd specimen revealing its stomach contents! It seems that few Irish examples were included, although we might have expected some from Irish coalfields, and most came from fine-grained limestones that were much younger than any exposed in Fermanagh.

Cole did take an active interest in the fossil potential of his Fermanagh limestones and collected many fossilised sea lilies, or crinoids, animals that are not capable of moving around. The crinoid is anchored to the sea floor by a stalk so that its "head", containing its main body parts, is poised within seawater. The head is surrounded by elaborately branching arms that sway in the sea current and steer the animal's food supply towards its head. Composed of durable calcite, both arms and stalk are segmented and held together by ligaments that rot away after death. The net result is that the crinoid will leave a legacy on the seabed of a large quantity of disarticulated segments and these are what the fossil collector will typically find. Each crinoid, of course, has only a single head, its most interesting component, and so is rarely encountered as a fossil. However, William Cole was no typical collector and he discovered limestone containing crinoid heads. They were unusual in that during the process of diagenesis, which generates a rock from sediment, these heads had been replaced by silica so that their fine detail was retained and they stood out from the softer limestone in which they were embedded.

But I do not wish to mislead you into thinking that his were the only excellent crinoid fossils ever found in Ireland. To come upon the very best you must travel to the opposite end of Ireland, to Hook Head at the mouth of Waterford Harbour. The extensive limestone beds of this locality have yielded exceptional slabs where crinoids have been fossilised in their entirety, including branching arms, and these now grace the display cabinets of many museums. In some instances the crinoid anchors snapped in some violent storm so that the now-cumbersome individuals keeled over and fell into sea floor sediment where they were quickly buried. So now you can see the entire set of arms, head and stalk – and you may even be able to deduce the direction of the prevailing current![4]

Fermanagh is designed around its lakes, with Lower and Upper Lough Erne stretching northwest-southeast along its entire length and with Enniskillen as a central hub between the two. The discerning naturalist, Robert L. Praeger, passed positive judgement on the region a long time ago, noting that it is more picturesque and interesting than its surroundings. This, he maintained, was due chiefly to the presence of steep hills and great lakes, all carved mainly out of the Carboniferous limestone by the dissolving action of water.[5] The subsequent glacial history has enhanced the landscape, with the development of drowned drumlins that are attractive, not only for cruising but also for angling, a reminder that Cole's fossils are not the only fish in these parts!

The hilly limestone country on the western margins of the Erne catchment has been karstified and as a result has some splendid cave systems. The most famous are the Marble Arch Caves, not far from Florence Court, which were discovered at the end of the nineteenth century and have become the centrepiece of the Geopark of the same name. The caves occur where dissolution of limestone bedrock created spectacular galleries with underground rivers and a dazzling array of white calcite formations – stalactites, stalagmites, veils and cascades – which are the products of calcium carbonate precipitation from percolating rainwater. The caves opened in the 1980s and subsequently the extensive blanket bog of nearby Cuilcagh Mountain Park and the secluded karst area of neighbouring County Cavan were added to create the exciting Geopark that is a prominent visitor destination in this region.[6]

Enniskillen has a proud literary tradition that partly relies upon the fame of former pupils of Portora Royal School, especially the dramatists Oscar Wilde and Samuel Beckett. But the town also has home-grown and more recent poets, including Frank Ormsby (b. 1947). He embraced a teaching career in Belfast, but the Enniskillen environment was important in his early output where he showed himself a shrewd observer of its rural life. In "Caves", he ponders a dark underground world that remains for him both remote and mysterious:[7]

> But here there is a darker underland.
> Moon milk and cave coral sprout below
> In sinks and shakeholes. Quietly they fill.

Sinkholes and shakeholes are funnel-shaped depressions in the ground above a cave and they can give an indication of the extent of its hidden chambers. The calcite formations of those chambers include Ormsby's moon milk and cave coral. In "News from Home", he thinks of Lough Melvin, which straddles Fermanagh's border at its most westerly point. In particular, he recalls nearby caves and their remarkable bats, some reported to be there since the 1880s. In "Stone" Ormsby narrates the life of a local boulder in a homely rather than geological sense. Currently used by horses as a scratching stone, it previously formed part of the bell tower of a ruined church. He muses on whether the enterprising farmer had rolled it or used an ox to drag it when removing it for his own use. In doing so, he was actually returning it back close to its quarry of origin and he finds it heartening to see stone so valued that it is recycled!

Of all the streams flowing into Upper Lough Erne, there is just one that held out glittering prospects two hundred years ago and it occurs on that lake's eastern shore. A young girl found a rough diamond with a reddish tint in the bed of the Colebrooke River in 1816 and gave it to Lady Brooke. It received immediate and serious attention from reputable jewellers, being valued at 20 guineas in 1831, perhaps equivalent to €1,300 today. But that would be just a small fraction of its value when cut and polished – a value that could only be enhanced by the continuing uncertainty concerning its provenance. The treasured specimen, now cut and mounted in Wicklow gold, remains in the careful possession of the Brooke-borough family, owners of the Colebrooke estate. Valentine Ball (1843–1895) was director of the precursor to the National Museum of Ireland and an accomplished veteran of the Geological Survey of India where he had carried out many mineral assessments – including of gold and diamonds. But despite his best endeavours he could not form a definite conclusion regarding the place of origin of Fermanagh's gem.[8] Although Ireland has a proud tradition of manufacturing industrial diamonds, we have no evidence of diamonds occurring naturally here, with the possible exception of Lord Brookeborough's specimen.

Diamond, the most cherished of all gemstones, has its origin at great depths below the Earth's surface. Composed of carbon, no different chemically to soot or graphite, it takes on its sparkling and durable qualities because its atomic structure is modified under conditions of extreme temperature and pressure, the sort found at depths exceeding 100 kilometres and in the Earth's mantle itself. Diamonds typically travel all the way up from mantle to surface along narrow volcanic pipes. These are excavated by very high gas pressure which comminutes an assemblage of rock fragments encountered along the way, including diamonds, and drives them upwards towards the surface. These gems do not originate in the volcanic pipe but simply use it as a very effective transport mechanism! The best-known of these volcanic pipes occurs on the edge of Kimberley city in South Africa where diamonds for long have been extracted from an open pit, called the Big Hole. But many more are now known from around the globe. We have not discovered any such volcanic pipes in Ireland, despite some astute exploration over recent decades. Although they tend to be small features, their unusual mineral constituents can become more widely scattered, especially where the landscape as in Ireland has been scoured by ice sheets, and so much of the initial exploration seeks such indicator minerals in soils and stream sediments.

The interesting question concerning the Brookeborough Diamond is whether it originated locally or was introduced. If it was introduced then perhaps it was lost accidentally by a visitor. In which case it would be extraordinary that someone did not report the loss of such a valuable stone and even offer a reward for its recovery. There is also the possibility that the stone was dropped deliberately by someone who wished an innocent bystander to retrieve and publicise it. In doing so, the diamond prospects of the district would be promoted and the unscrupulous planter of the specimen would have the opportunity for commercial gain. But there has never been any evidence to support that suggestion. That leads us back to the first suggestion – that the stone is of local origin. When diamond exploration became widespread in the 1990s, the existence of the Brookeborough Diamond sparked off renewed interest in the possibility of Irish diamonds, but despite intensive exploration both in Fermanagh-Tyrone and Donegal it yielded no positive results. The story must rest there for the moment![9]

Well actually my personal belief is that somebody in Fermanagh acquired a foreign rough diamond and then realised it would be more interesting and valuable if it were believed to be of local origin. That person gave the gem to a local girl, promising that if she presented it with a credible story to Lady Brooke that she would be amply rewarded. Which is what happened. But then the level of interest shown in the diamond was unexpectedly high, with enormous interest in how and where the gem was actually discovered. This would have caused the now-embarrassed girl and her retiring accomplice to keep their heads down awhile. And just as well – why undermine the lure of a fine mystery!

It may seem that Fermanagh has had a blissfully peaceful geological past and if you have gained that impression then I have misled you! Maybe there is no evidence to indicate that the Brookeborough Diamond was hurled furiously 100 kilometres upwards through Fermanagh's earthly crust, but more gentle magmatic eruptions were definitely a feature here as soon as the Atlantic Ocean began to open. The emplacement of the northwest-trending Kingscourt-Donegal swarm of dolerite dykes was a major component of this process and there are significant examples around Lough Erne, not least the Irvinestown Dyke and the Garrison Sill. But seismic trouble was signalled much earlier in the region's history, the Castle-Archdale Fault being a local splay of the regionally important Highland Boundary Fault. This is in fact the surface trace of a fundamental line which separated the American margin of the ancient Iapetus Ocean from the volcanic islands which collided with that margin as this ocean finally closed. So ferocious Fermanagh has at times both belched and quaked!

Volcanic eruptions in modern times have tended to attract more attention than earthquakes although we noted in an earlier chapter that the latter cumulatively are much more hazardous in terms of loss of life and property. Perhaps the gruesome images of

victims excavated from Pompeii or the publicity attached to explosive eruptions such as that at Krakatoa have unduly prejudiced
us against volcanoes! In reality, it has been estimated that two million people have been killed by quakes since 1900. Their ferocity
still has the power to shock us on a global scale: for example, in
January 2010, a tremor of magnitude seven devastated Port-au-
Prince in Haiti, killing 316,000 people. This was one of the highest
fatalities ever recorded in a seismic catastrophe, exceeding even
the enormity of the 2004 Sumatran Tsunami, where more than
250,000 perished. Many actively seismic areas are densely populated and it is estimated that about 1.5 billion people on our planet
are exposed to significant earthquake risks. This situation can only
deteriorate as the world's growing population becomes more urbanised, simply because cities are often situated in seismic zones.
Researchers are now modelling quakes better and progress has
been made in understanding where the next major seismic event
is likely to occur. There have been new insights into what controls
the frequency of quakes in a given area, but reliable warning signs
of imminent disaster are still not easily identified. Many potential
seismic indicators, such as changes in water table, radon levels
or animal behaviour, have been proposed in different parts of the
world but none has been found to be reliable. Areas of high seismic
risk, where strong earthquakes can be anticipated within a matter
of decades, are well known, however there is as yet no prospect
of being able to pinpoint the time and place of individual events.
But by mapping the state of strain along a fault we can detect areas
where stress is building up and so identify places that are liable to
future shocks.[10]

However we should not regard the huge loss of life involved
in major tremors as an inevitable (even fatalistic) consequence of
our unstable Earth. There is still a shameful contrast between the
impact of a given magnitude earthquake in different parts of the
world. An earthquake that might kill dozens in say California is
likely to cause many hundred times that number of fatalities else-

where. Television footage from catastrophic tremors in the developing world tells its own story of poorly constructed buildings and infrastructure. Countries in seismically active regions need to adopt robust building standards and aid donors like Ireland can insist that such standards are not seen as the preserve of the rich. We have seen that Irish scientists have long played a significant role in seismic studies, going back to Robert Mallet, the founder of seismology as a science. It is a pleasure to note that this is still the case. For example, based on his outstanding research, Professor John McCloskey was able to forecast another major tremor in the region one year after the catastrophic quake-induced Sumatran tsunami. Based at the University of Ulster, a near neighbour of Fermanagh, John and his research group have become passionate advocates of effective cooperation between scientists and humanitarian aid workers in reducing seismic risk in developing countries.[11] This is all a long way from the serendipity of William Cole's fabulous fishes and Brookeborough's glittering diamond, but geology must also address some of the harsher realities of life.

Notes

1. Quotation is from pages 1-2 of Praeger, R.L. (1937) *The Way that I Went: An Irishman in Ireland.* Dublin: Hodges, Figgis & Co and London: Methuen & Co. (Reprinted in 1997. Cork: The Collins Press).

2. E.C. Agassiz (Ed.) (1885) *Louis Agassiz: His Life and Correspondence.* London: Macmillam and Company. Two volumes.

3. Kenneth James (2009) "William Willoughby Cole" (1807-1886). In James McGuire and James Quinn (Eds.) *Dictionary of Irish Biography.* Royal Irish Academy and Cambridge University Press, volume 2, pages 657-658.

4. George D. Sevastopulo (2002) Fossil "Lilies of the Ocean" and other echinoderms from Carboniferous rocks of Ireland. *Occasional papers in Irish science and technology, number 25: John Jackson memorial lecture 2002.* Royal Dublin Society.

5. See pages 102-103 of Praeger, R.L. (1937) *The way that I went: An Irishman in Ireland.* Dublin: Hodges, Figgis & Co and London: Methuen & Co.

6. See www.marblearchcaves.net.

7. Frank Ormsby (1977) *A Store of Candles*. Oxford: Oxford University Press. I quoted from "Caves" (page 6) and referred to "Stone" (page 25). Frank Ormsby (1986) *A Northern Spring*. London: Secker & Warburg and Dublin: The Gallery Press. I referred to "News from Home" (page 41).

8. For more on the Brookeborough Diamond see V. Ball (1886–1887) "On the existing records as to the discovery of a diamond in Ireland in the year 1816". *The Scientific Proceedings of the Royal Dublin Society*, new series, volume 5, pages 332-334.

9. For more information on diamond prospecting in Northern Ireland see www.bgs.ac.uk/gsni/minerals (accessed 10 September 2014)

10. For more information about seismic hazards, see earthquake.usgs.gov/earthquakes (accessed 10 September 2014).

11. Additional information on the research of John McCloskey and his team can be found at "geophysics" on www.science.ulster.ac.uk/esri/John-McCloskey.html#page=background (accessed 10 September 2014).

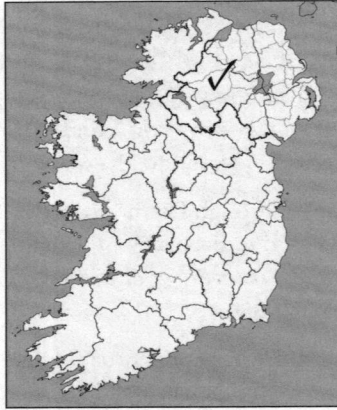

32

So Deep This Landscape Lies in Me
(Tyrone)

Much have I travell'd in the realms of gold
And many goodly states and kingdoms seen;
Round many western islands have I been
Which bards in fealty to Apollo hold.
– John Keats.[1]

So deep this landscape lies
in me; I try to leave it behind
but again and again it returns,
burning with its secret light

Poet John Montague (b. 1929) published "First Landscape, First Death"[2] in his mid-seventies about south Tyrone, his first landscape. Despite living abroad for significant periods, this landscape has been very influential in his writing. He appreciates the influence that glaciation has had on it and I believe this is due to an engaging geography teacher at his Armagh school. He brought his pupils walking in the neighbourhood of Armagh city and described vividly the waxing and waning of ice sheets – which gave rise, respectively, to low, smoothly contoured drumlins and long esker ridges of sand and gravel. Montague would later declare that the only redeeming feature of a bleak town I presume to be Cavan was a small glacial lake which nestled between drumlins ("Border Lake"). He was fascinated by glacial corries, one etched into the hillside near his home ("Home Again-I") and another near the Knockmealdowns summit, in Tipperary, which is backed by a "dreaming cliff" ("Between").[3]

Landscape creates context for Montague's thoughts and topics – it is the stage setting rather than the leading actor. Accordingly he does not always bother with specific locations. "The Black Lake", probably in the Midlands but never explicitly located, is defined fully by the activity taking place around it. "The Hill of Silence" is a low hill probably overlooking the Clogher valley, whose summit spring provided healing for an ancient warrior. He views landscape as a working environment, not simply a place of beauty and tranquillity. Sometimes a landscape is in sympathy with human activity, sometimes not, so it cannot be taken for granted. He is always seeking a deeper meaning, feeling that if you can absorb a landscape you have the potential to glimpse an entire civilisation in a single image ("Slievemore").

The commentator Robert Welch, in discussing the opening lines of "The Hill of Silence", considers Montague is unusually comfortable in binding together human and landscape issues. He calls this activity psycho-geological, a term I am unfamiliar with but find immediately understandable and appealing. When he states elsewhere that Montague's writing displays a capacity to comprehend process in historical, personal, geographical and geological terms, my only disappointment is that he feels the need to insert "even" before "geological"! For in "Process", Welch recognises Montague's insight on the Earth's ever-changing geological processes:

> only the earth and sky
> unchanging in change

and sees the poem's conclusion as a majestic sweep of galactic dimension.[4]

One of the earliest post-glacial developments, overlapping with the onset of human occupation, was the growth of peatlands.[5] The fringes of extensive mud-floored lakes became the focus for fen and marsh development and lakes shrank in size according as peat accumulated and water-tolerant trees were established. Then vigorous growth of sphagnum moss took over, relying on its stored rainwater for nutrients and allowing the bog to thrive well above water level. As the climate became wetter the trees died off, leaving their stumps buried beneath freshly accumulating peat. Montague understands this context at the Bog of Allen ("Bog Royal"), with its

> sea of peat,
> our land's wet matrix

and tree stumps churned up by turf-cutting machinery. The tree stumps recall for him not only the once-flourishing forests but also, as they resemble antlers, the splendid forest hunts of Na Fianna.

Back in his Tyrone childhood, Montague had studied peat extracted from his local bog, where he could recognise three different varieties ("The Long Hangar"). The surface sods were "rough heads" with tufts of heather. Then there were "fúms" – light, dry sods that could readily be lit in the fire-grate. Finally the "boghole-turf" was "tobacco-dark" and would burn with satisfying longevity. These show a gradation in quality which is matched by their increasing depth in the bog and also reflects the different strata in the bog, thus describing an insightful peatland stratigraphy.

But Montague's landscape has historical as well as physical layers, and they must be unravelled to discover the landscape's value – and his own. Montague's landscape is a manuscript ("A Lost Tradition") that requires interpretation, but Montague is uncertain of his ability:

> like a blind man,
> Along the fingertips of instinct.

No one person can supply every perspective:

> The whole landscape a manuscript
> We had lost the skill to read,
> A part of our past disinherited.

Adopting the planter/native terminology, Montague is certainly native and it is specifically in native landscape that he feels comfortable. This landscape is warm and welcoming to Montague when, for example, he enters Tyrone from Belfast, or the Republic from Northern Ireland. In "Home Again-I", he leaves the dour bleakness of Belfast and rejoices on reaching Tyrone with its friendly and dominantly native people. Sometimes it seems that Montague wants to get back to pre-Plantation times, to some sort of exclusively native Irish history. Out walking one day, his Protestant companion repeatedly noted landmarks associated with illegal poitín distilling that the poet considers reflects negatively on natives. To counterbalance this, Montague contrives in his own remarks to focus on a tumulus on nearby Knockmany Hill which is not only pre-Plantation but also pre-Celtic. For him this copperfastens his native entitlement to this landscape ("The Errigal Road"). But then he mellows, seeing sectarian differences fading in the face of future environmental change, for example as creeping afforestation smothers existing landscape patterns.

"Border Sick Call" is a bleak portrait of survival and death, the wintry weather emphasising that the only real border is not between Northern Ireland and the Republic but between life and death. The poet and his doctor-brother shared an exhausting trek across snowy countryside to help medical patients. It is in this poem that Eiléan Ní Chuilleanáin finds echoes of "the noise of geological time".[6] In the poem, Montague asserts that his landscape holds its memory of the Ice Age through the presence of gravel and rock features such as eskers. But pardon me if I cup my ear and faintly hear the voice of that Armagh teacher!

Montague shares the Clogher valley with William Carleton (1794–1869), who also wrote about it. Its pastures and meadows are floored by Carboniferous rock, lying between Devonian uplands on the north and Slieve Beagh's Carboniferous plateau on the south.[7] The hills of Knockmany and Slievemore, cherished by both writers, are prominent drumlins and they both sit astride the same elevated ridge of Devonian sandstone, much younger than the metamorphic rocks of the Sperrins further north. But that Slieve Beagh hillside produced one newsworthy son also, although one of few words.

James Graham Fair (1831–1894) of Clogher became one of the Silver Kings of Nevada in the second half of the nineteenth century, at a time when silver was almost as valuable as gold. He had emigrated with his family to Illinois before setting off for California in the year of gold fever, 1849. His mechanical skills, combined with entrepreneurial flair and astute personality, ensured that he thrived in the goldfields. After moving to Comstock, Nevada, a major centre of silver mining, he quickly became a successful entrepreneur. In partnership with three other Irishmen – the Silver Kings – he developed the Big Bonanza silver mine, its grade reputedly ten times that of average Comstock ore. By the time Fair sold his stock in this mine in 1878 he had become wealthy and influential beyond all expectations. A tough and arrogant man who was not much loved, he nevertheless had employed in excess of 2,000 miners and there was a grudging admiration for his determination and achievements. He went on to serve six years without distinction in the US Senate and then – with both working partnerships and marriage terminated – he concentrated in his final years on consolidating and increasing his wealth. Perhaps a one-dimensional and unsatisfactory outcome for a family that departed the Slieve Beagh slopes with some optimism back in 1843.[8]

Tyrone seems to have two contrasting geological halves, the Sperrins to the north and Clogher valley to the south, and yet they are unified through their glacial landscape which shows a gradual transition from the smooth northern cover of boulder clay to the drumlins and moraines of the south. The green and peaceful Sperrins comprise a series of gentle ridges separated by quiet valleys. Drumlins and erratic boulders are both scarce here. The widespread pastures may pass over ridges into the adjoining valley but locally the crests have patches of forest, bog and craggy outcrop. The bedrock is Dalradian, just like Connemara but lacking the extrovert diversity of the latter's famous marble quarries and quartzite mountains. The Sperrins bedrock consists of schists that were deformed in various stages of collision during Iapetus Ocean closure. Those schists started life as marine sediments, varied mixtures of mud and sand, which may not seem glamorous but their hour would come later when hot circulating fluids would deposit attractive amounts of gold in them!

Gold was discovered at two locations in the Sperrins during the 1980s. Each deposit consists of a set of quartz veins in bedrock schist, with individual veins typically a few metres wide. One is at Curraghinalt on the slopes of the Glenelly valley east of Gortin town, which is currently being evaluated once more. The second, at Cavanacaw, occurs west of Omagh town in a tract of Dalradian rocks separated from the Sperrins. A small mine there supplies locally-sourced gold for jewellery manufacture.[9]

Of course, alluvial gold grains, derived from gold-bearing bedrock, were noted in the River Moyola as early as the mid-seventeenth century but it took a serious increase in gold prices to stimulate exploration. One man had successfully panned gold in the sediment of the Moyola River in the decades preceding the

1980s gold fever and he was a frail and gentle resident of Draperstown, Geordie Barnett (1876–1965).[10] Raised on a small farm, Geordie would in time neglect it in favour of devoting himself passionately to other pursuits, such as poetry, geology, archaeology and much more besides. His abiding love for the Sperrins never waned throughout the ninety years of his wonderful life and it is captured in ballads such as "Farewell to You, Gortin":[11]

> I have often roved around you or tramped along the gap,
> To see the woods at Beltrim or the bluebells of Lislap,
> Or climbed the heathery hillsides to the dew loughs
>   or the cairn,
> Or walked by Glenmacoffer for the gathering of
>   the ferns.

He lived on the eastern slopes of the Sperrins and he visited friends regularly further west at Gortin, whose country and company he really enjoyed. He describes them with the wistfulness of an emigrant ("The Land I Left Behind Me"):

> I'm lonesome since I left Tyrone,
> And crossed Glenelly valley,
> I would have liked by Garvagh's hills,
> Or Drumlea woods to dally.
> For they look down on Gortin town,
> By hills that oft remind me,
> That it is like a fairyland,
> The land I left behind me.

With little formal education, the unassuming Geordie was a reliable amateur geologist who never wandered far without hammer and hand lens. He made a particular study of the distribution of glacial erratics and the iron deposits at Slieve Gallion. Many geologists made early and frequent visits to Geordie's home during their field work and subsequently were warmly generous in their public acknowledgement of the assistance he provided. He himself had no difficulty in mixing geology and friendship, as when he enjoyed Christmas with Gortin friends while still managing to pan for gold ("The Girls of Gortin Town"):

> A week of rambles followed that, o'er roads and
>   mountains wild,
> And panning by the river too, part of the time beguiled,
> But soon I had to leave for home and cross the mountain
>   brown,
> And bid farewell to all my friends and the girls of Gortin
>   town.

Given the strong association of gold deposits with Dalradian rocks, it is fitting that a spectacular find of gold artefacts should have occurred in Dalradian terrain, along the Foyle Estuary of neighbouring County Derry. The hoard of magnificent gold objects was discovered during ploughing at Broighter and came into the possession of the British Museum. The Royal Irish Academy was not pleased at this and claimed the objects on behalf of the Crown on the basis that they were treasure trove, deliberately buried on dry land for safekeeping and later retrieval. The British Museum countered trenchantly that the area was actually submerged at the time, that the objects were cast overboard from a boat and that they were intended as votive offerings, never intended to be recovered. With no friendly resolution in sight, the two venerable institutions referred the matter to the courts, which decided in favour of the Academy. This must have been gratifying for Sir Edward Carson (1854–1935), counsel for the Academy, whose reputation had already been established in the public mind through his destruction of Oscar Wilde's reputation and career in a libel case. However, I wonder if in his later political life Lord Carson ever regretted his success, because the Academy's gracious response was to present the acquired hoard to the National Museum of Ireland in Dublin (of all places!), where it remains to this day.[12]

Oceans go through cycles of opening and then closing. The modern Atlantic Ocean, for example, is still in its opening phase. The closure of the precursor Iapetus Ocean has had a major impact in shaping Ireland as we know it today. But that ocean did also have a birth. Just as basalt magma heralded the start of the Atlantic so it was also a key component in the opening of the earlier ocean. It is still preserved in the Dalradian sequence, now metamorphosed to amphibolite schist, but only exposed on the north Mayo coast. However Tyrone does have strong evidence of that Iapetus Ocean floor, because a significant block is preserved as the Tyrone Plutonic Complex, dominated by rocks of basaltic composition. How about this for a description of Tyrone's basaltic legacy:

A special despatch from the explorers sent to Corkadorky by the Royal Myles na gCopaleen Institute of Archaeology states that large masses of diorite rock have been unearthed. The rocks look like adamellite and contain orthoclase, plagioclase felspar, micropegmanite starch, igneous hornblende, baking soda, gangrene-pale pyroxene, not to mention andesine strata tinged with accessory deposits such as zircan and apatite.

It's not too bad if we ignore the odd typographical error such as "felspar" (for feldspar), "micropegmanite" (for micropegmatite) and "zircan" (for zircon). There is some solid information here. But wait a minute, what place have "starch", "baking soda" and "gangrene" got in a rock that cooled from liquid magma? I am afraid there is more:

> *The Plain People of Ireland*: Begob appetite is right, you'd need a square meal and a pint of stout after that mouthful of chat. What book did you cog all them jawbreakers out of?
>
> *Myself*: The Encyclopaedia Britannica.
>
> *The Plain People of Ireland*: And a fine man he is when he's at home, God bless him.[13]

The author's words are not those of an amateur geologist but I do suspect they were written at the prompting of a professional. The author was Brian O'Nolan (1911–1966), son of Strabane and better known under the pseudonyms Myles na gCopaleen and

Flann O'Brien, while the prompter was J.A.G. McCluskey, Senior Geologist on the staff of the Geological Survey of Ireland. The link was the occasional social session the two enjoyed in company with others. Myles was not seeking to educate readers about Sperrins' magmatic history, however fascinating, but he was successful in entertaining them through the anarchic column he penned for *The Irish Times*.

I was pleased to see him commemorated in the town of his childhood, Strabane, where the sculptor captures a dishevelled assertiveness in his pose that seems entirely appropriate!

Notes

1. Quoted from "On First Looking into Chapman's Homer" by John Keats which appears on page 292 of John Hayward (Ed.) (1956) *The Penguin Book of English Verse*. Harmondsworth, Middlesex: Penguin Books.

2. John Montague (2012) *New Collected Poems*. Oldcastle, County Meath: Gallery Books. I have quoted from the following poems: "Bog Royal" (pages 145-6), "First Landscape, First Death" (pages 466-8), "A Lost Tradition" (pages 47-8) and "Process" (pages 141-2). In addition I have referred to the following poems: "Home Again-I" (pages 25-26), "Border Lake" (page 159), "The Errigal Road" (pages 286-288), "The Black Lake" (page 338), "Border Sick Call" (pages 363-376), "The Hill of Silence" (pages 342-345), "Between" (pages 389-390), "Slievemore" (pages 469-470) and "The Long Hangar" (pages 512-513).

3. For further discussion of Montague's treatment of landscape, see O'Grady, Thomas (2004) "'That first, best country': The literary landscape of Montague's Tyrone". In Redshaw, T.D. (Ed.) *Well Dreams: Essays on John Montague*. Omaha, Nebraska: Creighton University Press, pages 113-126.

4. Welch, Robert (1999) *The Structure of Process – John Montague's Poetry*. Coleraine: Cranagh Press.

5. Feehan, J. and O'Donovan, G. (1996) *The Bogs of Ireland*. Dublin: The Environmental Institute, University College Dublin.

6. Ní Chuilleanáin, Eiléan (2009) "Border Sick Call". In Fallon, Peter (Ed.) *Chosen Lights: Poets on Poems by John Montague in Honour of his 80th Birthday*. Oldcastle, County Meath: The Gallery Press, pages 122-4.

7. Further information on the geology of Tyrone is contained in W.I. Mitchell (Ed.) (2004) *The Geology of Northern Ireland: Our Natural Foundation*. Second edition. Belfast: Geological Survey of Northern Ireland.

8. The life of James G. Fair is described in Oscar Lewis (1967) *Silver Kings: The Lives and Times of Mackay, Fair, Flood and O'Brien, Lords of the Nevada Comstock Lode*. New York: Alfred A. Knopf.

9. More information on Curraghinalt prospect and Cavanacaw mine may be found at www.dalradian.com and www.galantas.com respectively.

10. E.E. Evans (1966) "George Barnett: An appreciation". *Ulster Journal of Archaeology*, third series, volume 29, pages 1-5.

11. Extracts from Geordie's poetry are taken from Graham Mawhinney (Compiler) (1992) *Geordie Barnett's Gortin: Poetic Tributes to Tyrone*. Draperstown, County Londonderry: Moyola Books. The poems used are as follows: "Farewell to You, Gortin" (page 6), "The Girls of Gortin Town" (page 11) and "The Land I Left Behind Me" (pages 14-15).

12. The story of the Broighter Hoard is told in Praeger, R.L. (1937) *The Way that I Went: An Irishman in Ireland*. Dublin: Hodges, Figgis & Co and London: Methuen & Co.

13. The quotations are from page 320 of Myles na Gopaleen (1968) *The Best of Myles*. London: Mac Gibbon & Kee.

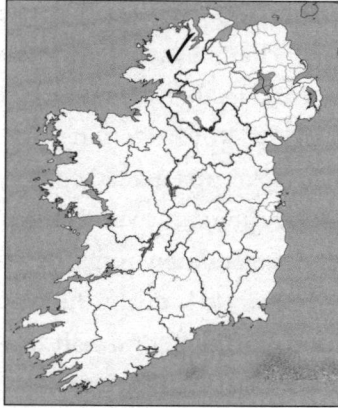

33

TRYING TO CAST OFF
THEM HILLS!
(Donegal)

*The past is consumed in the present and the present is
living only because it brings forth the future.*
– James Joyce[1]

F ew geologists are credited with having such a popular impact
as Sir Charles Lewis Giesecke (1761–1833), who is now reliably regarded as having contributed to the libretto of Mozart's *The
Magic Flute*. Born in Bavaria, he enjoyed a theatrical career, both
writing and performing, before switching his attention around
1800 to mineralogy, which had been a childhood interest. Now he
spent his time collecting minerals across Europe. He went on a
mission to Greenland and found himself stranded there, from 1806
to 1813, partly as a result of the Napoleonic Wars. Nevertheless he

made a significant contribution to our knowledge of its geology and mineral resources, which was acknowledged by the conferral of a Danish knighthood. He then became Professor of Mineralogy at the Museum of the Royal Dublin Society (RDS) until his unexpected death. Giesecke was a very competent and esteemed geologist whose work has generally stood the test of time and, for example, he discovered several new mineral species.[2]

Thirty years after Giesecke's death, his successor R. H. Scott published a curious book, the second half of which is a comprehensive catalogue of mineral localities from the county as documented by himself and earlier workers, including Giesecke. This makes clear the very thorough nature of Giesecke's work. But the first half of that book is equally fascinating because it gives an account of field investigations on the granites of Donegal.[3] Alas Scott produced no overall understanding of its granites and their origin and it would be many years before those granites received any further attention. This happened when Edward Hull, Director of the Geological Survey of Ireland, arrived with some colleagues to complete the first island-wide geological mapping. This task had been started on the Hook Peninsula in County Wexford over 40 years earlier and now Donegal was the final county to be mapped. Hull's initial conclusion, based on a comparative visit to the Scottish Highlands, was that Donegal possessed no granite at all but rather ancient gneisses similar to some in Scotland. However after more mature consideration, granite was once more considered to form the backbone of the mountainous county – and Donegal has clung onto granite ever since! Even so, the Survey work at that time led to no fundamental understanding of the nature of this granite.

It was left to an unlikely geologist to lead the research that would change our view not only of Donegal granites but of all granite! He had, as a youth, cut his geological teeth on fossilised shark's teeth and other fossils from the London Clay, the soft sedimentary layer beneath London city which accommodates an important element of its transport system. When W. S. Pitcher (1919–2004), affectionately known as Wally, accepted a job at Imperial College London he found himself among colleagues whose geological passion concerned magmatism and deformation in the Earth's deep crust. Professor H. H. Read, his departmental head, was a leading proponent in what became known as the Granite Controversy and it was inevitable that Wally would become absorbed in it also. This debate revolved around whether granite was transformed *in situ* from older rock, a process called granitisation, or was transported from depth and emplaced as a magma. Both hypotheses were running neck-and-neck when Wally, at Read's urging, packed his bags and headed for Donegal.

The wild and beautiful hills of Donegal would be Wally's intellectual home for the next 25 years. In his initial study of just one district, he ably demonstrated that what many considered an example of granitisation was actually a granite pluton. This drew international attention to both the Donegal granites and Pitcher's work there. Soon the magma argument prevailed and research focused on how space was actually created to accommodate large volumes of granite magma. So the genial Pitcher undertook a new challenge that would occupy another twenty years: To map the 3D geology of the extensive granite in the Peruvian Andes and how it related to the subduction of the Pacific Ocean beneath the South American plate. The resulting publications revealed many new insights and cemented his reputation as one of the global leaders in understanding granite.[4]

Donegal granite underlies much of the countryside and offshore islands to the northwest of a line from Glenties to Fanad. It formed during the final closure of Iapetus Ocean about 400 million years ago and was emplaced into Dalradian rocks that were already metamorphosed and deformed at an earlier stage in the ocean's closure. It turns out that the main control on granite development was a major fault zone extending through Donegal which tapped the lower crust and probably at times the mantle itself. Space was created by dilation parallel to this fault at the very time when magma was being generated and ascending along the fault. It solidified as granite rock at depths of 5 to 11kilometres below surface and we owe their present exposure to the huge amount of erosion that has subsequently taken place. Donegal granite comprises about eight separate plutons, most of which are now understood to be sheet-like in 3D form. It would be more accurate to say stacks of sheets, this description pointing to the operation of successive pulses of magma, maybe from different sources, over perhaps 20 million years. Some plutons with circular outcrop shapes, principally around Ardara, formed through a ballooning mechanism as the magma accumulated from a nearby fault zone, while space for the Rosses Pluton was created where the floor of the magma chamber foundered repeatedly to admit upward-surging pulses of magma.[5]

The Main Donegal Pluton underlies the rugged Derryveagh Mountains and the lower ground further to the northeast, including Barnes Gap which provides access from the east of the county to the scenic area around Horn Head. This latter district, underlain by Dalradian rocks, was the childhood countryside of the Donegal poet Moya Cannon (b. 1956). Here, for visitors, lay the wet wilds of Donegal. This is from a poem that I like to think got its title, "Barbari",[6] from the Venetian artist, Jacopo de' Barbari (c. 1460–c. 1516), in response to his bold use of colour. In Cannon's young years, departing migrants were cautioned that east of Barnes Gap they should consider every man a rogue. It is wonderful that, by implication, her Dalradian terrain alone would harbour some lofty ethical values!

Her home territory south of Horn Head may indeed be scenic but another of Cannon's poems ("The Foot of Muckish") reminds us that rural residents saw their landscape as essentially a workplace. For them, Muckish was not a beautiful pile of Dalradian quartzite, just a backdrop to a working bogland. Cannon now lives closer to the mountains of Connemara than of Donegal, but she just cannot shake off the latter ("Hills"): "My wild hills come stalking." These dark blue hills framed her horizon as a child. She enjoys them still and knows their colours – the red grass and the stark brightness and darkness of bog water. She avoids any vague impressionistic colour scheme in favour of bold colour.

"Loch" is an insightful ode to a mountain and how its slopes and corrie lake were shaped by Ice Age glaciation. Cannon is a Galway resident and she is describing Loch Mhám Ochóige, high up in the nearby Maumturk Mountains of Connemara. This "scraped bowl" of a corrie lake can be approached from above or below, but always with caution. She indulges her love of sunlight effects:

> the mountains are great shutters
> like the shutters in Dutch paintings
> which slant light onto a jug or a letter
> or a lady's yellow cloak.

So mountains come alive as bright sources of reflected light, places where the human spirit is refreshed. And the mention of Dutch paintings reinforces my hunch about Jacopo de' Barbari! This landscape becomes valuable only in its interactions with humans.

Moya Cannon muses about the value of some relatively constant alignment that would guide our passage through life ("Orientation"). But then she has already dismissed the notion of such constancy in the natural world itself:

> Crystals in cooling magma
> orient themselves to magnetic north
> as towards a constant
> although, over deep time,
> poles shift about like bedrock or stars.

This is of course upsetting for many people who mistakenly see both bedrock and stars as relatively permanent baselines. On the other hand, anyone who uses a compass for navigating will realise that the magnetic poles shift position gradually all the time. There are also sudden and dramatic changes in pole positions, when north and south poles spontaneously switch positions (the polarity reversals of an earlier chapter), and this has assisted in mapping ocean floor basalts and understanding oceanic evolution. So Cannon is alerting us that we should not seek permanency in those poles, no more than in our personal lives.

Talking of basalts, while ascending a volcano Cannon enters an old lava tube, a tunnel which remains where a solidified skin forms on a lava flow and the molten lava beneath drains away. Cannon finds that life is re-establishing itself, with bats, insects and plants being present ("In the Lava Pipe"). Resurfacing, she experiences the exhileration of sudden sunlight and this reminds her of the legend of Orpheus. He rescued his dead wife, Eurydice, from the underworld only to lose her as they emerged on surface when he could not resist a forbidden backward glance.

Cannon's territory is the entire western seaboard of Ireland, all the way from her native county to the karstic limestones of the Burren, County Clare. In the latter, Cannon forges empathy between limestone and humans ("Thirst in the Burren"). She finds no surface as kind to feet as its rain-scoured rock, yet the poet asserts no superior entitlement for humanity – both ferns and humans share a common thirst. In the later Burren poem, "The Fertile Rock", she watches as the ocean floods across the limestone foreshore, invading every crevice and spraying the salt-tolerant sea pinks. Once more, she is consciously sharing this landscape with all nature, without claiming anthropocentric precedence of any sort. Moya Cannon for me is a poet who exults in nature without seeking to exert a human-centred dominance. She is a poet of landscape who repeatedly sees its intrinsic importance yet recognises the value of human interaction with it. She is very conscious of a geological dimension to landscape, one that for her emphasises its constant change. And throughout she shares her fascination with light and shade and how they interact with the natural world.[7]

Back in the late 1880s, G. H. Kinahan (1829–1908), mercurial colleague of Edward Hull in the Geological Survey of Ireland, must have had his own struggle with light and shade as he sought to map the Rathmelton area in north Donegal, which would be the final sheet in the countrywide mapping that had started back in 1845. His map shows Dalradian rocks that once formed as sediments in a marine environment. The sands later formed quartzites that underpin prominent peaks like Slieve League and Muckish, the muds were transformed into slates and schists, often with elaborate folding, and the lime-rich sediment was metamorphosed into the white marble of which, for example, the delightful church at Dunlewey was constructed. These sediments all formed in a deepening sea as its underlying crust split and gradually pulled apart to give birth to Iapetus Ocean. The resulting sedimentary formations are remarkably extensive along the length of Dalradian outcrop, from Connemara to the Scottish Highlands, and the influence of the ocean is revealed by the presence of major dolerite sills. Deposition was also very persistent, ceasing only when the Iapetus Ocean was fully opened, and it may have lasted for as long as a third of a billion years!

This has caused some to question whether there are any significant "time gaps" in the sequence, just as we witnessed at Waterford railway station and elsewhere. The possibility of similar unconformities in the Dalradian is more difficult to diagnose given its highly deformed nature, but the contact of the Slieve Tooey Quartzite and the overlying Cranford Limestone has been proposed as one. The limestone in a relatively undeformed outcrop near Glenties has pebbles of the underlying quartzite which itself has deformation features not seen in the younger limestone – essentially a similar situation to Waterford. These are important observations which suggest that Dalradian sedimentation was not straightforward and could give us new insights into the opening of the Iapetus Ocean.[8]

Looking across the modern Atlantic Ocean, the Appalachian Trail is an amazing ribbon that extends unobtrusively for 3,500 kilometres along much of the Appalachian Mountains in the eastern United States. It snakes across hills and mountains, crosses valleys and traverses forests along the way, giving its four million users each year a unique adventure. They experience joy and pain, glare and shade, hope and despair, camaraderie and loneliness, warm sunshine and drenching rain, exhilaration and despondency, hot emotion and cool planning, renewal and exhaustion, and hopefully some fulfilment! Some are "thru' hikers", determined individuals who devote up to six months to completing the entire length of the trail. But no matter how far they have hiked, all will have experienced change – in the people they encounter, the fickle weather, unreliable gear, changing landscapes and their own shifting emotional and physical responses. Change is the only enduring constant!

The course of the Appalachian Trail is also distinguished by the fact that its bedrock was deformed and metamorphosed during the final closure of the Iapetus Ocean, when the Appalachian Orogen was created. This type of bedrock does not stop at the U.S. border but continues across maritime Canada to the Atlantic coast of Newfoundland and then traverses significant parts of northwest Europe and North Africa, where the orogen is called the Caledonian. Hikers in both the U.S. and elsewhere were keen to share the spirit of the Trail more widely and so it has evolved into the International Appalachian Trail (IAT), with the potential to traverse any region whose bedrock was part of the Appalachian Orogen. Its final course is still being determined and the link between Scotland and Ireland occurs in the shared kingdom of Dal Riada, after which the Dalradian rocks of both countries have been named. Starting in Antrim, Ireland's segment of IAT follows pre-existing trails, mainly parts of the Ulster Way, until it reaches Donegal and the Slieve League coastline. The majestic sea cliffs of Slieve League at 600 metres are among the most imposing in this part of Europe.

It is here that the IAT, on its eastward course from the U.S., makes landfall in Europe.[9]

Slieve League is composed of quartzite which originated as sand grains in shallow continental seas before Iapetus Ocean opened. That ocean closed and the Atlantic fully opened before the glacial events occurred that sculpted the mountain's present profile. Those events in the past 70,000 years had a profound impact on Slieve League's landscape. A narrow ridge, or arête, has been created between two major corries here and it is called One Man's Pass to reflect its perilous reputation for hikers. Intending climbers should follow the advertised safe routes to the top. Gazing out from that summit we are witnesses to one of Europe's great seascapes, ever changing as currents and tide agitate the seawater. Seabirds swoop and feed, fishermen earn their living, ships ferry people on great adventures. All the time those same underlying processes of change are happening on land and to land, but perhaps not so perceptibly. That ever-changing pattern may seem melodic rather than chaotic, depending upon our response: The Earth is inherently unstable and its processes never stand still. James Joyce expressed the idea eloquently:

The past is consumed in the present and the present is living only because it brings forth the future.[1]

Notes

1. From page 286 of James Joyce (1916) *A Portrait of the Artist as a Young Man*. London: Penguin Popular Classics (1996).

2. A. Whittaker (2007) "The travels and travails of Sir Charles Lewis Giesecke", In P.N. Wyse Jackson (Ed.) *Four Centuries of Geological Travel: The Search for Knowledge on Foot, Bicycle, Sledge and Camel*. Geological Society, London, Special Publications, number 287, pages 149-160.

3. R.H. Scott (1863) *Granites of Donegal: On the Granitic Rocks of Donegal, and the Minerals Therewith Associated*. Dublin: University Press.

4. Donald Hutton (2004) "Obituary of Professor Wallace Pitcher". *The Independent*, Friday 17 September 2004.

5. W. S. Pitcher and D. H. W Hutton (2003) *A Master Class Guide to the Granites of Donegal*. Dublin: Geological Survey of Ireland.

6. Extracts from Moya Cannon's poetry were taken from the following two collections: Moya Cannon (2007) *Carrying the Songs*. Manchester: Carcarnet Press. I quoted from "Orientation" (page 46) and "Hills" (page 66). I referred to "Barbari" (page 33), "Thirst in the Burren" (page 57), "The Foot of Muckish" (page 67) and "Mountain" (page 100). Moya Cannon (2011) *Hands*. Manchester: Carcanet Press. I quoted from "Loch" (page 36) and referred to "The Fertile Rock" (page 26) and "In the Lava Pipe" (pages 53-54).

7. Eamonn Wall (2011) "Carrying the Songs: The Poetry of Moya Cannon". In Eamonn Wall *Writing the Irish West: Ecologies and Traditions*. Notre Dame, Indiana: University of Notre Dame Press, pages 157-176.

8. For information on unconformities in the Dalradian see Hutton, D. H. W. and Alsop, G. I. (2004) "Evidence for a major Neoproterozoic orogenic unconformity within the Dalradian Supergroup of NW Ireland". *Journal of the Geological Society of London,* volume 161, pages 629-640.

9. For more information on the Appalachian Trail and IAT-Ireland, see www. gsi.ie/NR/rdonlyres/82C717C4-1D43-4ED7-BD1B-946ED1A57DD9/0/ IATSlieveLeagueLandfall.pdf (accessed 26/9/2014).

Index

Index

Index

Index

Index

Index

Index

Index